Official

Microsoft

FrontPage 2000

Book

W. Brett Polonsky

PUBLISHED BY
Microsoft Press
A Division of Microsoft Corporation
One Microsoft Way
Redmond, Washington 98052-6399

Library of Congress Cataloging-in-Publication Data
Polonsky, W. Brett, 1965-
    Official Microsoft FrontPage 2000 Book / W. Brett Polonsky, Kerry
  A. Lehto.
        p. cm.
    ISBN 1-57231-992-5
    1. Microsoft FrontPage.   2. Web sites--Design.   3. Web publishing.
  I. Lehto, Kerry A., 1966-   . II. Title.
  TK5105.8885.M53P65   1999
  005.7'2--dc21   98-52137
                                                          CIP

Printed and bound in the United States of America.

5 6 7 8 9   QWT 4 3 2 1

Distributed in Canada by Penguin Books Canada Limited.

A CIP catalogue record for this book is available from the British Library.

Microsoft Press books are available through booksellers and distributors worldwide. For further information about international editions, contact your local Microsoft Corporation office or contact Microsoft Press International directly at fax (425) 936-7329. Visit our Web site at mspress.microsoft.com.

Acquisitions Editor: Susanne M. Forderer
Project Editor: Saul Candib
Manuscript and Technical Editing: Helios Productions

For Gage and Emma
The two reasons I do any of this.
And for the other special people in
my life, you know who you are.
Thank you.

Contents at a Glance

Table of Contents

PART I

The Beginning Stages

PART II

Creating and Managing Your Site

PART III

Building Your Pages

PART IV

Finishing Touches

Foreword

Since you're reading this book—or you picked it up off the shelf at the bookstore—you probably need to build a Web site. You're a small business owner who needs to create a presence on the Internet. Or a department manager who requires an internal Web site for your group on your corporate intranet. Or an aficionado of the film *Buckaroo Banzai* who wants to share with the world your extensive collection of trivia about the Lectroids from Planet Ten.

In any case, you need to get your Web site up quickly, and it needs to look professional. You're busy, and the Web site you need to build is one of a dozen urgent tasks on your plate, not your life's ambition. If I'm describing you, FrontPage is exactly the right solution, and you have picked up exactly the right book.

When we first released FrontPage 1.0 back in October 1995, the slogan on the box said, "Professional Web Site Publishing Without Programming." A lot has changed in the world since then. The Internet is now a phenomenon, not a backwater. A Web site is now a necessity, not a hobby. Web addresses like **www.acme.com** adorn advertisements where 800 numbers used to appear. But the purpose of FrontPage today is exactly the same as it was then: enable non-technical people to create professional-quality Web sites, very quickly.

When Microsoft acquired our company, Vermeer Technologies, in January 1996, our Vermeer FrontPage 1.0 product was so new, and our 35-person company was so small, we had sold a total of only 289 copies. On April 8, 1996, almost exactly 2 years after the founding of Vermeer, we moved from Cambridge, Massachusetts to Redmond, and we felt as though we had strapped on rocket boosters. The newly renamed Microsoft FrontPage 1.1 was released to manufacturing just 16 days after our Redmond arrival. It sold 150,000 copies in 4 months, and in August 1996 it was the 3rd-best selling software package in retail stores across the country, outselling even Microsoft Office itself. Less than 7 months after finishing FrontPage 1.1, we completed FrontPage 97, the first Microsoft product to ship simultaneously in 6 languages. (In fact, the Japanese version of FrontPage 97 hit store shelves 3 weeks before the English version.) Microsoft FrontPage 98, released in November 1997, packed in more new features and ease-of-use improvements than any previous FrontPage release and became a runaway best-seller. And this latest release, Microsoft FrontPage 2000, is the easiest and most powerful version yet, available worldwide in 15 languages, and the first to be included as part of a high-end edition of Microsoft Office.

One of the key advantages of FrontPage is its completeness. It is not just a "what-you-see-is-what-you-get" Web page editor. It is a tool for building a whole Web site. You can start with a wizard to create your basic Web site. You can see the tree structure of your site, and when you use your mouse to change the structure, FrontPage will automatically recreate your Web site's navigation bars. You can automatically check all the internal and external hyperlinks. You can apply any of 60 professionally-designed graphical "themes" to your entire Web site and then change the theme tomorrow with a few mouse clicks. You can create an image map just by drawing geometric shapes on any image in a page. Insert your own image, or choose from the extensive clip-art library, and then resize, crop, fade, bevel, or thumbnail that image right in the page. You can draw tables with your mouse, use frames, change page colors, add "rollover" buttons, add a search feature, insert a page counter, or cause text to spiral, all by choosing menu items and clicking toolbar buttons.

An important goal of every release of FrontPage is to take the best of the latest Web technologies and make them accessible to everyone. With FrontPage 2000, it's easy to add advanced database access, cross-browser Dynamic HTML, Java applets, JavaScript features, Cascading Style Sheets 2.0 positioning, and Active Server Pages technology. You can use check-in and check-out for collaborative version control, with flexible access control over any portion of your Web site. And for customized solutions, FrontPage 2000 is fully extensible with custom menu items and built-in Visual Basic for Applications 6.0.

When it comes time to publish your Web site onto the Internet, just click on the "Publish" button in FrontPage. There's no need to learn about FTP programs, Web server configuration files, or UNIX access control commands. As the FrontPage team likes to say: FrontPage targets the lower 90%

of the market. In other words, it's designed for you, the busy non-technical professional.

W. Brett Polonsky, the author of this book, is a man on a mission. I remember when I first met Brett. It was February 5, 1996, and I had just demonstrated FrontPage 1.0 to an in-house crowd of Microsoft folks in the Kodiak Room on the Redmond campus. Brett was in the audience, because he was one of those 289 people who had purchased FrontPage before the Vermeer acquisition. In a consulting role, he was helping a group at Microsoft create an early intranet Web site, and he was already championing the use of FrontPage to his colleagues. Brett, and his original book co-author, Kerry Lehto, approached me immediately after the demo.

Brett and Kerry told me they were going to write a book about FrontPage 1.1. "But the new version of FrontPage doesn't exist yet," I told them. "No problem," they said, "we'll start writing the book from the preliminary product specifications." "Who will buy the book," I asked, "there are so few FrontPage customers." "Don't worry," they said, "FrontPage 1.1 will be a big success, and the book will sell." "Who would be willing to publish the book?" I queried, "there are no books currently available for FrontPage." "Microsoft Press," they said, "but they don't know it yet. We'll convince them."

And Microsoft Press was convinced. *Introducing Microsoft FrontPage*, by Lehto and Polonsky, was the first FrontPage book on the market and was instantly a hit. Barnes & Noble stores even created an end-aisle display for it. Kerry has since moved on to other projects, but Brett has continued to carry the torch with the renamed *Official FrontPage 2000 Book*. Through four editions, it is has been the largest selling FrontPage book, it is by far the best overall book for the broadest spectrum of users, and it is an obsession for Brett.

Brett cheerfully works with extremely early Beta versions of new FrontPage releases, tactfully overlooking any "instabilities" that he encounters in the Beta code. He doggedly researches each feature, and produces compelling examples. By the time he delivers his manuscript to Microsoft Press, he's more expert on the breadth of features in a new FrontPage release than most of the FrontPage software engineers themselves. And with almost three years of best-selling FrontPage books behind him, he's certainly the most adept at teaching FrontPage of anyone I know. Brett runs a successful Web site design business, yet with his years of expertise, he still prefers to create Web pages using FrontPage rather than type the raw HTML by hand.

Most of all, Brett enjoys his work, and his enthusiasm shows on every page of this book. I found it to be thoroughly accessible, informative, and fun, and I believe you will, too.

This book exemplifies the attitude of most Web-site creators: Half the fun is getting there. Enjoy yourself, and may you have great effectiveness and success.

Randy Forgaard
Co-founder of Vermeer Technologies, Inc.
February 1999

Introduction

Welcome to FrontPage

The Internet, the World Wide Web, intranets, extranets—all of these things have become as common as the telephone, for businesses as well as for the home enthusiast. The vast array of technologies that have taken hold alongside them have become a part of our everyday lives and will continue to change the way we live and work. Intranets, which use Internet technologies within a business or across an enterprise, once the latest trend, have spawned a new one. The newest type of "net" has businesses sharing information by linking intranets together to form the new "buzz," extranets. One can only guess what will come next.

Similar to other booms the computing world has witnessed, thousands of companies have formed to search for a piece of the Internet pie. Scores of good Internet-related products are available, but most of us don't have the time or the expertise required to sort through them, learn their pros and cons, and put them to use, whether at work or at home.

Microsoft FrontPage 2000 makes it easy for you to establish a presence on the World Wide Web or create a Web site for your organization's intranet. Designed to fit seamlessly into the Microsoft Office suite of applications, FrontPage is the first easy-to-use Internet product that allows you to develop an entire Web site and connect it to many kinds of servers. If you want to set up a Web site but you're not a programming whiz, don't worry—FrontPage can do the programming for you. But FrontPage is also robust enough for amateur and professional developers who do want to toy with the HTML code.

Talk About Easy!

The Official Microsoft FrontPage 2000 Book is your in-depth, one-stop shop for learning the ins and outs of FrontPage. You'll learn how to develop and maintain a Web site, develop high-quality Web pages, and how to get those new sites up on the World Wide Web. You'll also learn how to incorporate material from Microsoft Office files into your site, and link to, from, and within those files. You'll learn about some exciting new additions in FrontPage 2000, such as exact 2D pixel positioning, which lets you place content in a specific position on a page. Also, an improved CSS (cascading style sheet) interface, and CSS templates, make using a style sheet as easy as it gets. And with the new FrontPage Report View, you can keep tabs on the various aspects of your Web sites. For example, you can easily see how many files are in your site, or how many hyperlinks you have, and even if any of them are broken.

Because some of you like to lift the hood and tinker with the controls, this book also includes information about more advanced topics, such as Secure Sockets Layer (SSL) security, using the Database Results Wizard to display information from a database, editing the source code of your Web pages with improved HTML support, and the FrontPage Server Extensions.

A Look at the Book

Part 1, "The Beginning Stages," introduces you to FrontPage; talks about the birth of the Internet, the World Wide Web, and intranets; and explains how FrontPage fits into all three scenes. You'll learn some great tips on producing sites for the Web and for your organization's intranet, and you'll learn about the exciting new ways in which FrontPage works in conjunction with Microsoft Office.

Part 2, "Creating and Managing Your Site," tells you everything you need to know about creating and administering Web sites. With FrontPage, you can view your site in different ways—including the exciting Navigation view, which lets you create a site map and translate it to navigation on your pages. In Part 2 you'll also learn how to use the FrontPage templates and wizards. FrontPage has designed dozens of new Web, page and frames templates—just pick one and you're on your way.

Part 3, "Building Your Pages," looks into the FrontPage Page view, which you'll use to create and edit your Web pages. Here, you'll find in-depth instructions for creating terrific-looking Web pages that can include video, audio, marquees, colored text, tables, frames, character formatting, font styles, and much more. You'll find Page view as easy to use as a word processor. Part 3 also contains some hearty content on Web site graphics, how FrontPage uses them, and ways to make them appear faster in a browser. A detailed look at the FrontPage components and forms is also presented in this part.

Part 4, "The Finishing Touches," introduces you to the many advanced features of FrontPage, such as cascading stylesheets, dynamic HTML, the Database Results Wizard, ActiveX, Visual Basic, and JavaScript, as well as some accessibility tips. The final chapter talks about using servers with FrontPage. Here, you'll learn about the FrontPage Server Extensions, which extend a server's capability to take advantage of features available in FrontPage. These extensions are available for a wide variety of servers that use platforms such as Microsoft Windows 95 and 98, Microsoft Windows NT, and various flavors of UNIX.

Tips and Notes

The book also includes Tips and Notes that provide more details about the subject at hand. They show you ways to save time, such as clicking a toolbar button or using a keyboard shortcut instead of using a menu command. Just as there's more than one way to get from Cairo to Cooperstown, Tips offer alternative ways to carry out tasks, and they give you additional information on a topic. Notes give you a little something extra to think about or caution you against performing actions that can lead to trouble.

Who Should Read This Book?

The Official Microsoft FrontPage 2000 Book is designed for both beginning and advanced FrontPage users. Just as FrontPage is designed for nonprogrammers, so is this book. It's ideal for those who want to learn how to use FrontPage to create a World Wide Web site or an intranet site.

This book picks up where the product's online help leaves off; within these pages, you'll find in-depth descriptions and scenarios about possible uses of FrontPage that draw on my experience in Web site creation, design, and management. I hope this book will help you fill in the holes and answer your questions as you make your FrontPage sites "sights to see."

PART

The
Beginning
Stages

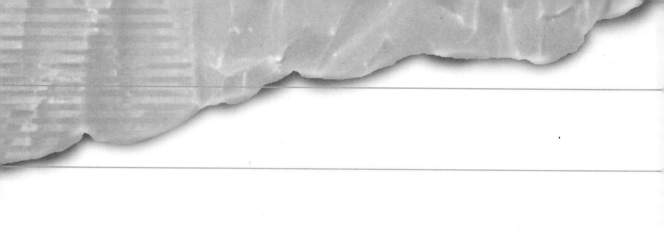

CHAPTER 1

FrontPage and the Internet

It's Here, It's Now

There's no escaping the Internet; it's become almost as essential as the fax machine. Businesses large and small are using it to tap information sources worldwide, communicate by e-mail, and post World Wide Web sites; millions of individuals "surf" the Web from their homes and offices. The sites filling today's Internet differ considerably from those populating it just a year ago. Many of today's larger sites allow you to display the information that you want to see, in the way that you want to see it. Web sites have become increasingly interactive, from enabling visitors to use secure transactions to buy and sell products to incorporating personalization and customization features. It might be hard to believe, but it's safer today to use your credit card on a secure Internet site than it is to hand it to a waiter at a restaurant.

This chapter provides some background on the Internet, the World Wide Web, and intranets. It describes how Microsoft FrontPage 2000 fits into this scene, explains how easily it integrates with Microsoft Office 2000, and shows how you might fit into the latest wave of this technology.

5

The Net, the Web: What's the Difference?

The Internet is older than you might think—it's been around for almost thirty years. When you consider that the first electrical computer was built just over half a century ago, you realize that the Internet is quite the veteran in the computing world. It started out in the late 1960s as a U.S. government communications network (called ARPAnet), and was used mainly by the government, universities, and other research institutions until the mid-1980s, when it expanded and took on the name Internet.

So how does it work?

Computers operating together within a group constitute a *network*. The Internet is one huge network of computers that consists of thousands of smaller networks all over the world. You might think of a computer as a leaf on a tree: many similar leaves comprise the branches, and you could think of each of these branches as a network of leaves. All these networks together form the entire tree, in the same way that all the computer networks connected together form the Internet. The diagram in Figure 1-1 illustrates the basic organizational makeup of the Internet.

The computers on the Internet share a common language, and that language is stated in *protocols*—sets of agreed-upon rules governing how the computers interact. The standard protocols used for exchanging data on the Internet are the Transmission Control Protocol and the Internet Protocol; the combination of the two is known as *TCP/IP*. This combination of protocols organizes information into tidy little packages before shipping it across the network. Each package contains a portion of the information being sent, along with a description of what the information is, where it's coming from, and where it's heading. Sending data across the Internet is like disassembling a jigsaw puzzle in one room and reassembling it in another room. To put it together again quickly, you have to identify the pieces in relation to each other and put them back together in sequence.

How about the Web?

In the late 1980s, when the Internet was growing gradually by adding a few major networks here and there, a scientist named Tim Berners-Lee began seeking a better way for his colleagues at the European Laboratory for Particle Physics (known by its French acronym, CERN) to communicate by computer. At the time, the only information that could be transmitted across the Internet was simple text on computer screens. Berners-Lee and his associates created an interface to link information from various sources. The eventual result was the definition of the *URL, HTTP,* and *HTML* specifications on which the World Wide Web is based. Today, Web technology allows users to create a formatted page of information that they can then "link" to other pages of information and access across a network.

PART

6

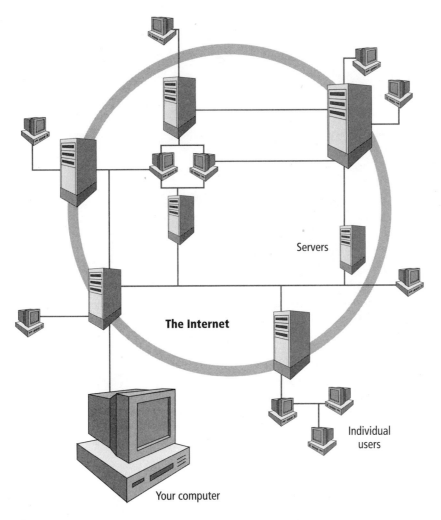

The Internet

Servers

Individual
users

Your computer

Figure 1-1

An example of a typical Internet showing servers and users working together.

In simple terms, the *Web* is a collection of information that is accessible through the use of *Web browsers*. The first significant Web browser was Mosaic, developed by the National Center for Supercomputing Applications (NCSA) at the University of Illinois at Urbana-Champaign. The market now offers more than two dozen Web browsers, and that number continues to grow. Currently, Netscape Navigator and Microsoft Internet Explorer (see Figure 1-2) hold the lion's share of the Web-browser market.

A Web browser consists of a window that displays Web pages and, typically, also includes toolbars and menu commands that let users explore pages and sites and adjust the browser's settings. Because of the proliferation of

Web browsers and the variety of ways you can configure them to display information, a Web page viewed in one browser could, in theory, look significantly different in another browser. However, this problem has lessened as Netscape and Microsoft have come to dominate the browser market, because their browsers display pages similarly.

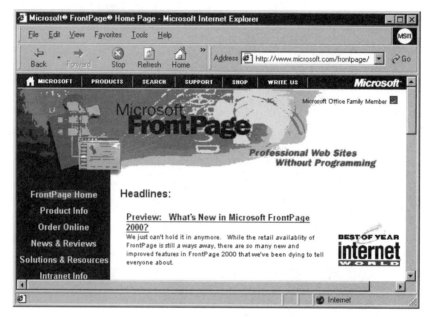

Figure 1-2

A Web page from the FrontPage area of Microsoft's World Wide Web site, as viewed in Internet Explorer 4.0.

In addition to text, Web pages can include graphics, sounds, animation, and other special effects. Individual pages can be linked to other pages to provide access to additional information. All this information is transmitted across the physical medium by means of the protocols of the Internet. That's why many people think of the Web as being synonymous with the Internet.

The Web has grown at an incredible rate. Thousands of people have their own Web sites, and numerous businesses have put their names up in Web lights. (The term *home page* is often used to refer to a Web site; actually, a home page is just the opening page of a Web site—its default page—

and it usually has links to other pages. All these pages together make up the Web *site*.) The Internet and the Web have dramatically changed people's business habits in the last few years. Have you noticed that it's now standard to include your e-mail and Web addresses on your business card?

When you develop a Web site, you want to streamline its pages so that visitors can download it quickly. But at the same time, you want it to have a good, professional-looking design and you also want to be able to update it frequently. FrontPage makes all these requirements, and more, possible—even easy! The next chapter gives you some pointers on how to create a successful Web site.

Where do intranets fit in?

Now that you know what the Internet and the World Wide Web are, you might be wondering what an *intranet* is. The key to understanding these terms is in the prefixes: *inter* (between or among) and *intra* (within). The Internet connects computers from a variety of different organizations; an intranet (sometimes called an *internal Web*) connects computers networked within a single organization. The term *intranet* also implies that the network supports Web technology. So basically, an intranet is just like the Internet, except that an intranet's content is accessible only to the organization's users and not to users across the world-wide Internet. Intranets can also be linked to the Internet, but they don't have to be.

Large corporations are already realizing the potential of intranets, and smaller businesses are not far behind. Intranets offer an effective and efficient way to communicate within an organization. In the coming years, intranets should do for businesses what e-mail has done in the past few years—make communication easier.

Frequently, the networked computers on an intranet are at one location, such as a single office; sometimes they can span several departments within an organization. An intranet can encompass remote locations as well. Suppose Cascade Coffee Roasters has branches in Washington, Wyoming, and Winnipeg, and all the company's computers are networked together. The company can set up an intranet so that its employees can communicate and share information by using their computers. Sounds like a typical network, right? Well, it's an intranet because it's a network that supports TCP/IP and because employees can use a Web browser to access information on its servers. Figure 1-3 shows a possible setup for a company's intranet.

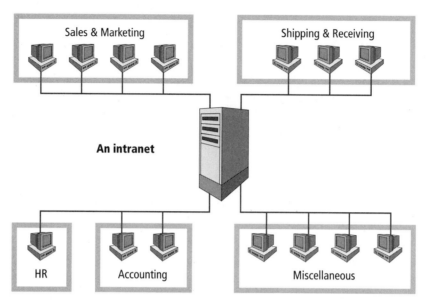

Figure 1-3

An example of a typical Intranet showing the relationships between various departments in a company and the Web server they share.

So what's an extranet then?

You may have heard the term *extranet* floating around lately. An extranet is basically an intranet that makes some of its areas available to people outside the company. Suppose that the Cascade Coffee Roasters intranet site contained information on the amount of Hawaiian beans in stock. By entering a password and user name, the Hawaiian supplier could access that area of the intranet. This way Cascade Coffee Roasters could share certain internal information without making the entire contents of their intranet visible to outsiders.

Some typical uses for an extranet might be to:

● Share specific trade information with other companies

● Communicate with suppliers and vendors

● Share company information with specific customers

Today, many large corporations are making plans to connect their intranets with other companies' intranets in order to create a shared extranet.

FrontPage in the Spotlight

Web site developers have a "cast of thousands" when it comes to choosing a *Web authoring tool,* and competition between products is driving up the quality of these tools. The choices include HTML editors that require HTML mastery; graphical Web-authoring applications that require some HTML expertise; and the star performer, FrontPage, which requires little or no HTML knowledge. FrontPage has become the premier Web-authoring tool by offering a powerful product that makes developing professional-looking Web sites extraordinarily easy.

The perfect partnership: FrontPage and Microsoft Office

The popular Microsoft Office suite of applications includes Microsoft Word, Excel, PowerPoint, and (in some editions) Access. The Premium edition of Office 2000 also includes FrontPage. The content creation capabilities of Office combined with the Web site management and Web page creation features of FrontPage provide an ideal way to create Web sites. Here are some ways in which the two make a seamless partnership:

- FrontPage takes advantage of the Office Web controls for analysis and reporting.

- In the FrontPage Folders, Navigation, and Hyperlinks views, Office documents have the same icons as they have in Windows Explorer.

- FrontPage's capability for verifying and repairing links extends to any Office documents within your site that contain links.

- FrontPage shares the Office themes and clip art.

- You can easily copy material from Office files onto your FrontPage Web pages. For example, when you copy part or all of an Excel spreadsheet onto a page in Page view, either by dragging or by using the Clipboard, FrontPage automatically converts it to an HTML table.

- You can drag Office documents from the Windows Explorer to FrontPage, and those documents will be imported automatically into your site.

Ready for launch!

When you build or update your Web site, you can open Office files in their native application from within FrontPage; that way, you don't have to concern yourself with opening the Office application separately. When you double-click an icon of a document created in Word, Excel, or PowerPoint, FrontPage automatically launches the appropriate application so that you can edit the document in its native environment. Of course, you need to have the application installed on the machine you're working on.

- **Office interface**. FrontPage 2000 shares the interface features of Office. Toolbar buttons, menu commands, dialog boxes, and keyboard shortcuts are designed to be instantly recognizable by Office users.

11

CHAPTER 1

- **Office thesaurus.** Just in case you're at a loss for words, FrontPage includes the thesaurus used in Office.

- **Office spelling checker.** FrontPage allows you to check the spelling of text on the current page or check the spelling of the text on selected pages or on the entire site, in each case by using the same spelling checker and dictionary used in Office.

None of us has ever won a national spelling contest. (If you have, you can leave the room.) But have you ever noticed the number of misspellings on Web pages? They can be pretty danged funny, but they're also sad when you consider that the information on the Web is presented for all the world to see. A misspelling in a site on an intranet can be even more embarrassing. Suppose you misspell your boss's name or title in a corporate bio. That could get you fired—or worse, you could end up having to sit in the corner all day in a time-out.

FrontPage could save you a little embarrassment if you use the dictionary and suggestion routines available in Word, but no spelling checker can substitute for good spelling knowledge. Of course, if you're going to rely on a spelling checker, you might as well use the best!

Coming Up

Now that you have a better idea of how FrontPage fits into the Internet and intranet scenes and how it works together with Microsoft Office, it's time to plan your first Web site. You'll learn how to do this in Chapter 2, and you'll also learn how to make your Web sites appealing and useable.

CHAPTER 2

The Web Site Development Process

Planning the Information Flow

Surf on the World Wide Web today and you'll find some very good sites—
ones that you can load quickly and are pleasing to the eye, organize information into well-defined areas, are easy to navigate, and are well written. These
sites simply invite you to come in, take off your shoes, stay awhile, have some
fun, and learn something new.

If you find yourself hanging around a site without realizing it, you've
probably found a site that's been well planned and designed. Take a step
back and try to see the big picture here. Can you see the structure, the
organization? Does the information flow easily? Understanding how information flows through a site is the first step in creating a functional, easy-
to-use site. If you understand the principles of information flow and
implement them in your site, you're already miles ahead of most other Web
site developers.

Many site developers don't take the time to understand how their information flows; they're only concerned with putting words and pictures on
a page. Although many sites proudly boast that they receive more hits

15

(connections) than their competitors do, the number of visitors isn't a good indicator of how good a site is. How long a visitor stays at a site is a much better indicator. If visitors to your site remain there long enough to explore its structure and the variety of its content, you know you've done the job right. Those leisurely visits mean that users can find what they need, get around, and get back without having to think too much about how they've done it. Usable sites are those that inspire such visits, and building such a site should be one of your primary planning goals.

To create an effective Web site, you need to visualize the flow of information and the various paths that a user can take through the site. In other words, you need to see your site from the user's point of view. Planning a site can involve a substantial amount of work, but it certainly doesn't have to be all work—if you have fun in the planning stages, you'll probably end up with a better site.

When you use Microsoft FrontPage 2000, you don't have to be a Webmaster to create a site that visitors will return to time and time again. The kind of site you create and the kinds of information you include depend on your target audience. This chapter discusses how to target sites to an Internet audience or to an intranet audience within your business or organization.

Guidelines for a Good Site

The best Web sites are ones that look appealing, get the message across succinctly, and don't make users wait too long for information to appear on their screens. The following are some guidelines for creating a successful site:

- **Have a clear purpose.** What are your goals? Just to get on the Web? If so, you're like many others, and you shouldn't be surprised if your site ends up like most others. Make your goals as specific as possible. Perhaps you want your site to show off your company's products. That's all fine and dandy, but consider your strategies. How do you want to position your products in the Web market? Asking these deeper-level questions helps you define your goal more clearly. Unless you have a well-defined goal, your site is doomed to a trip to the Internet graveyard.

- **Always keep your audience in mind.** Who are the primary and secondary audiences for your site? How old are they? What do they do for a living? How much time do they have available to look at your site? How fast (or slow) is their connection to the Internet? For every piece of information, every graphic, and every content decision you make, ask yourself, "How will the audience react to this?"

- **Use items that visitors can download quickly.** The number one reason that people leave a site quickly—or don't visit a site at all—is that it takes too long for the information to appear on their screens. Large graphic files cause users to twiddle their thumbs, and it's all too easy for them to click a Stop button in their browser to stop loading your page. For more ideas on how to streamline graphic size, see Chapter 8.

- **Make your site visually appealing.** You've undoubtedly seen some plain, boring sites on the Web. What makes them plain? Perhaps it's a lack of color or a lack of variation in text and heading sizes. You've probably seen some cluttered and chaotic sites as well—sites that use too many fonts in too many sizes or colors, for example. As you build your site, remember that a well-composed page brings you one step closer to a well-done site.

- **Don't try to put everything on one page.** Be careful not to clutter your pages with too much information. Naturally, writers like to write and graphic designers love to create cool images. As the developer of the site, it's up to you to create that delicate harmony between these two very different groups of people. A good rule of thumb is to create a page that lets a typical user see the most important items that you've included—all without having to scroll through more than two screens.

  Try to strike that balance between text and art: think about who's going to be reading those pages. Think about how difficult it can be to read a lot of text on a computer screen, and write the content for your pages accordingly. Try adding white space by increasing the page margins or by using tables creatively. (To learn more about using tables, see Chapter 6.) Think about your graphics in terms of the value they add to the page. Are they serving a purpose, or do they just look good? But remember that good-looking graphics sometimes serve the purpose by themselves. All Web site developers are striving to create pages that look good, contain useful information, and allow users to explore the site easily.

TIP

We often think our sites are right on target for our intended audiences, but it's easy to miss the mark. To avoid this, be humble and try to have your site plan and content reviewed by as many people as possible, and especially by potential members of your audience. This step is critical, but site developers often overlook it.

CHAPTER 2

● **Organize your content in intelligent ways.** Maybe you've heard the saying that "content is king." It's true. How many times have you visited a site and thought, "There's nothing here"? Perhaps some good content is buried deep within the site, but the only visitors who will "dig it up" are those who come across it by chance. If you have some information that you feel your visitors must see, don't bury it in hidden pages. Make your important information as obvious and easy to find as possible.

Don't forget that your site will likely be more than one level deep. Organize secondary material into groups of related information. For example, suppose you're setting up an online catalog for a music store. Would you list your jazz CDs and rock CDs in the same section? Of course not. Admittedly, it's a glaringly simple example; but if you examine all your information to see whether you've categorized it appropriately, you'll end up with a site that's much better organized.

● **Include appropriate buttons for exploring the site.** Most site developers use linked buttons, usually graphical ones, to represent the various areas within the site. Developers usually put these *navigation* buttons on all pages within a site and group them together on each page. Keeping them together and in the same place on every page makes them easier to discover and more useful. Users can simply click a navigation button to move to another section of the site, and when they get there, they know they'll find the navigation buttons in the same area of the page. Consistency breeds familiarity, and familiarity creates repeat visits.

Here are some things to keep in mind when you create navigation buttons:

● Include a button that takes users back to the home page. If your visitors are buried five levels deep into a site, they should, in the event that they want to start over, be able to click a button to return to the first page. If they're stuck using the Back button in their browser, chances are that they'll get frustrated and leave your site. In other words, don't rely on the user's browser to do the navigation for you; be sure to design it into the site yourself.

- Be prepared for visitors who have turned off graphics in their browsers. It's a good idea to create a linked text-only version of your navigation in addition to the linked graphical button version on each page in your site. That way, users can pick the version they want to use to explore your site. Most of the time, you'll see a text version right next to the graphical buttons or aligned along the bottom of each page.

The bottom line is this: make it easy for visitors to move through your site. When you design a site, ask yourself whether you'd logically want to move between certain points. Answer that question, and you're bound to come up with good ways to make your visitors happy little surfers.

- **Take advantage of the Navigation view in FrontPage.** Navigation view can prove particularly helpful if you have a difficult time visualizing information. Start with your home page and work down. This visual representation can help you "see" your content, organize it more clearly, and avoid having to reorganize it as you build your site. It also helps you to see your site's structure more clearly, and it can lead to new ideas for improving the site's structure and flow. For more information on the Navigation view, see Chapter 3.

- **Test your site thoroughly.** Your Web audience can use a number of different browsers, each of which might present your site quite differently. Test your site using as many different browsers as possible, on different platforms (such as Windows 95 or 98, Windows 2000, UNIX, and Macintosh), and at different modem speeds. Wise owls test every page and every link in their sites using several different browsers and modem speeds. You can easily monitor the status of your hyperlinks, as well as many other areas of your site, in Reports view. See Chapter 3 for more information on those features.

Another great way to test your site is to choose the Preview In Browser command from the File menu while you're in Page view. The Preview In Browser feature lets you preview your page using any browser installed on your machine. It also lets you preview the page at different window sizes. If you normally run your monitor at a screen resolution of 1024 by 768 pixels, for example, you can find out how your Web page will look at a window size of 640 by 480 pixels. For more information about previewing sites, see Chapter 7.

TIP

Another way to treat your audience kindly is to provide a searching mechanism so that visitors can find information in your site quickly. Using the FrontPage Search Form Component, you can add a complete search engine to your site in just a few seconds. To find out how, see Chapter 9.

Planning an Intranet Site

If you're in charge of developing an intranet site for a business or another organization, you have no small task ahead of you. You have many of the same things to think about as you do when you develop a public site for the World Wide Web, with a few interesting exceptions. Because you usually know the exact audience for the site, you have the luxury of being more focused and specific. You should have a good idea about such points as what types of computers members of the organization use, how fast those computers are, which browser the members use most often, and how members access the site (by modem or by direct connection). Knowing these details can greatly affect how you develop the site. Up-front planning is as important for developing successful intranet sites as it is for developing World Wide Web sites.

Depending on the size of your company, the site can be large and can involve many people in charge of different sections. FrontPage makes managing intranets easy; see Chapter 5 for details.

Does your organization need an intranet? Traditionally, you see companies using the old-fashioned printed method for generating internal information such as corporate policies, training information, phone listings, and company news. After the information is printed, it has to be distributed, often across geographical regions. Every time information is updated or changed, the company needs to reprint and redistribute it. Generating, maintaining, and distributing information in this manner is not only costly for the company, but it also wastes resources.

When you have an intranet in place, you can easily and quickly update company information, and you can make it available to everyone (or to those who have the correct access rights). Different departments can be responsible for maintaining specific areas or pages of the site and for keeping the company abreast of changes as they occur. This process is seamless and painless.

Questions to Ask

When you create an intranet site, pay attention to the same issues of design, organization, and navigation that you address when you build a site for the World Wide Web. In addition, if you can address the following intranet-specific issues up front, you can save yourself a great deal of trouble.

- **Audience.** What members of the company or organization will have access to the site? What kinds of information will the site include? Will all of the information in the site be accessible to everyone?

- **Work in progress.** Who will update the site? Who will be in charge of which sections and which tasks? Spell this out as clearly as possible before you create the site because, as you go along, you'll probably discover more tasks that someone needs to perform regularly. Using the FrontPage Tasks view, explained in detail in Chapter 3, you'll find it easy to assign and manage tasks.

- **Keeping it under control.** How will you keep the site from getting out of control? The key to controlling the size of a site is in controlling who can add material to it. If everyone in your company can add pages, change information, add links, and so on, your site will quickly seem like a runaway freight train bound for the bottom of Whiskey Gulch.

Perhaps your business or organization already has a network in place, but the processes for routing files and viewing others' documents and presentations are cumbersome—you have to connect to a network location, move the files to your computer or open them on another computer, launch the appropriate application to help you view and manipulate the files, and so on. The data may be available, but it's presented poorly; for example, when you're looking at a network location, all you see is a list of files. And unless you know where to look for a specific file, it can be difficult to find a file on a network, especially if you don't know the exact file name.

Intranets allow users to share information in a visual form. Suppose you want to find out your company's sales information for the previous quarter and a Microsoft Excel file contains that information. In a typical network setting, you have to find the appropriate file, open it, and then view the information in Excel on your own computer.

Using an intranet site enables company personnel to access information without having to memorize a network location. All they have to do is find the company sales information page on the intranet and then click a

21

link to open the file from the network. Alternatively, that information could appear directly on a page in the site. If users can't find the sales information page easily (which indicates a bad design), they can find it in a few seconds by using a Web search engine.

Security

You can use network security features to protect many of the files used on your intranet. After all, these files are stored on the network itself. If you want only certain personnel to be able to change information in files used on an intranet, for example, you can restrict access at the network level.

Content

A company or organization can harness the power of an intranet in many ways:

- **Make documents and other corporate information widely available.** Companies can use an intranet site to house policy manuals, training manuals, company schedules, product data, and the like. This can save tremendous amounts of time, effort, and money.

  Suppose Sophia works in the lingerie department at a department store and she needs specifics on what kind of perfume the store sells so that she can propose a bundling of lingerie and perfume for a holiday promotion. Instead of calling the head of the perfume department (who would pass the request to an assistant, who would then direct Sophia to a file on the network containing pricing, availability, and sales information), Sophia can simply go to the appropriate intranet site and access that information herself.

- **Update your employees on company news.** An intranet site is an ideal forum for a news bulletin about your company. If you want to provide employees with information about the annual picnic, you can put it in one place for all to see. An intranet site also is an ideal place for gathering your company's press releases for employees to read.

- **Use the intranet site for in-house promotions.** Even though the primary purpose of an intranet site is to streamline information flow within a company or organization, that doesn't mean it can't be fun to use.

- **Connect your intranet site to the Internet.** By using security measures such as firewalls and proxy servers (discussed in Chapter 5), you can link your intranet site to the Internet and still keep the intranet secure. You can provide links to your competitors' Web sites (to keep your employees up to date on their activities) and to other useful and timely information your employees might need. If information about your company appears on others' Web sites, you can link to those locations so that your company's personnel can see what all the hoopla is about.

Coming Up

Now that you have some ideas about what you can do with a Web site, it's time to learn the specifics concerning how to use FrontPage to create your site. Chapter 3 starts you out on that journey.

CHAPTER 2

PART II

Creating and Managing Your Site

Inside Microsoft FrontPage 2000

Your Site, From See to Shining See

Okay, you've been designing Web sites for a while now, and you're pretty good at it—but you know all too well that it can be a managerial nightmare, with dozens of HTML pages linked every which way, and little buttons and graphics here and there. You have to deal with writers and graphic designers, not to mention your boss, and every one of them is looking to you for answers. Somewhere, in the midst of all this mayhem, you still need to map out your site. You know that you need the time and place to be able to visualize your site. How many times have you tried to diagram your site on paper, drawing links this way and that? And, of course, you have to be able to get your boss, or your client, to "see" what you're trying to do.

As for you beginning Web site developers, you may be wondering whether you haven't gotten in over your heads with all this Web stuff. When you put your ideas down on paper and chart out a few pages, the process seems pretty straightforward, right? But once you begin drawing links between all your pages, you might feel like you're climbing Mt. Everest with a day pack, one bandage, and a bag of BBQ chips.

If you want to use a single program to organize your site, you've come to the right place, because that's what FrontPage lets you do. FrontPage gives you many different ways to view your site, allowing you to view and ma-nipulate it as a whole. There's no need to worry about making separate, manual changes to these views; FrontPage updates each view as you make changes to your site, so that you can see the changes instantly in any view. This instant-update feature greatly simplifies site creation and maintenance, and it will no doubt save you hours of time for every site you work on. If you work with particularly large sites, it might save your sanity as well.

You can maintain consistency, maintain links, and perform operations across the entire site. For example, just as you don't want to check the spelling in a word-processing document one paragraph at a time, you don't want to check the spelling in a Web one page at a time either. FrontPage allows you to check the spelling in an entire site. FrontPage pioneered the notion of treating a Web as a single unit, and its various views are the means by which you manipulate this new Web type. FrontPage calls this single unit a "Web."

Starting FrontPage

When you launch FrontPage for the first time, you'll see the main window, which contains everything that you need to create and manage your Webs. This window is your one-stop "Web workshop," as Figure 3-1 shows.

When FrontPage opens, it doesn't display a Web in the window. That's the case each time you start the application unless you tell it differently.

To have FrontPage automatically open the last Web you worked on, choose Options from the Tools menu, and then on the General tab in the Options dia-log box, check Open Last Web Automatically When FrontPage Starts.

● **Open an Existing FrontPage Web or Page.** If you've already created sites in FrontPage, you can easily open any site or page. From the File menu, choose Recent Files to see a list of the last few pages you've worked on. Or choose Recent Webs from the File menu to see a list of the most recent sites you've opened.

You can also choose Open from the File menu to display the Open File dialog box. From here you can browse to find any files on your computer or, by clicking the Search the Web icon, find a file on the Internet. You can also choose Open Web from the File menu to bring up the Open Web dialog box. Like the Open File dialog box, Open Web lets you browse to find any Webs on your computer.

PART

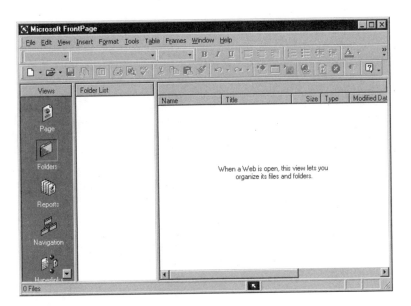

Figure 3-1

The FrontPage main window, with no site open.

- **Create a New Web**. You can also create a new FrontPage Web. To create a new site, choose New from the File menu and then choose Web from the submenu. The New dialog box appears, as shown in Figure 3-2 on the next page. From there, you can select one of the Web types that FrontPage offers as well as the location for the new site. The next section details this process.

Creating a Web from Scratch

When you launch FrontPage, you'll see the FrontPage main window, with no site open. If you're already in FrontPage, just use FrontPage's menu commands to create or open your sites. The site's framework can consist of simply a name and a preconstructed page or two that you can work on later. FrontPage saves this framework in the location of your choice, usually the computer where you're building the site.

The New dialog box lists several wizard and template choices. One of the easiest ways to create a site is to use one of these templates or wizards, which can eliminate many preliminary design hassles. Chapter 4 explains in detail how to use templates and wizards.

CHAPTER

3

In the New dialog box, you must perform two steps to create a new Web.

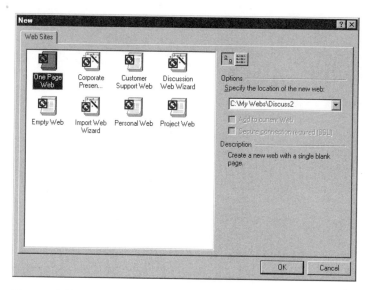

Figure 3-2

The New dialog box.

1. Choose the type of FrontPage Web that you want to create. You can choose to use a FrontPage wizard or Web template. Your choices are as follows:

   One Page Web. Choose this option if you want to create a site that consists of one blank page. When you choose this option, FrontPage creates a one-page site and the appropriate folders. Then you can begin to build the rest of your site.

   Corporate Presence Wizard. This wizard is an excellent place to start if you're creating a business site. It asks you a series of questions and offers numerous kinds of pages you can use to highlight your business. For more information on the Corporate Presence Wizard, see Chapter 4.

   Customer Support Web. This template helps you set up a customer support site for your business.

   Discussion Web Wizard. This wizard helps you create a discussion group that has threads, a table of contents, and full-text searching. For more information on the Discussion Web Wizard, see Chapter 4.

   Empty Web. This template creates a new site with nothing in it.

PART

Import Web Wizard. If you have a non-FrontPage site or individual Web files that you want to import to FrontPage, you can import them by using the Import Web Wizard. You'll find a complete description of the Import Web Wizard in Chapter 4.

Personal Web. This template lets you create a personal Web that you can use to display information such as employee data, biographical information, your interests, and more.

Project Web. This template lets you create a new site to help you manage a project. It includes a list of participants, project status, project schedule, and more.

2. Name your new Web and, if necessary, change its location. It's always a good idea to change the default name FrontPage gives the new Web to one that's specific to your Web. When you click OK, FrontPage creates your Web, using the new name, in the location you specify. FrontPage, by default, uses a local location. Alternatively, you can choose one of the locations listed in the drop-down menu of the Specify The Location Of The New Web text box, by clicking the down arrow to the right. Or you can type a new location directly in the text box.

But wait—what if the location you want isn't listed? Again, there's no need to worry: All you have to do is type the name of the desired location in the list box. For example, if the current location is C:\MyWebs\corp4 on your local computer, and you want FrontPage to create your new site in the corp5 folder, which isn't in the list, just edit the text field to read C:\MyWebs\corp5, and FrontPage creates the Web appropriately.

If you want to add your new site to an existing FrontPage Web, make sure that the existing Web is open before you begin the process, and then activate the Add To Current Web option.

If you're creating the site in a secure location, and that location supports SSL (Secure Sockets Layer), select the Secure Connection Required (SSL) check box. For more information on SSL, see Chapter 5.

When you've finished making your selections, click OK. FrontPage then sets up your new site. This might take a few minutes, depending on the speed of your computer and on the type of site you've chosen to create. FrontPage creates a folder for the site in the location you've designated. It gives the folder the same name that you gave your site. If you use a template to create your site, FrontPage adds files to this folder for each of the pages in the template. If you use a wizard, you'll see a series of screens on which you can customize your site before the pages are created by FrontPage. For more information on using wizards, see Chapter 4.

When the process is complete, FrontPage displays the site in the main window.

Opening an Existing Site

You can open any Web in FrontPage, regardless of the Web authoring application with which it was created. You can also open a FrontPage Web (or any of its component files) from a browser such as Internet Explorer.

Opening Sites or Files Authored in FrontPage

If you've already created a site in FrontPage and you want to open it in Windows Explorer, or if you want to open a single file, here's how to do it:

Open an existing Web. Choose Open Web from the File menu to display the Open Web dialog box. The default location FrontPage uses to create a site is C:\MyWebs, so this is a good place to start if you're not sure where the site is located. If the site you want to open is not listed, you can browse to find its location. Figure 3-3 shows the Open Web dialog box.

Select the folder of the site you want to open and click OK. FrontPage will open the site in the main window.

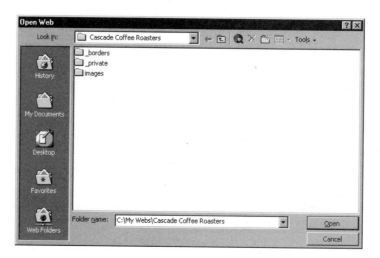

Figure 3-3
The Open Web dialog box.

Open a file in a Web. Choose Open from the File menu to display the Open File dialog box. All the files currently in the Web are listed, as well as the Web's folder structure. Figure 3-4 shows the Open File dialog box.

Choose the file you want to open and then click OK. The file opens in the FrontPage Page view, ready for you to work on it.

Figure 3-4
The Open File dialog box.

To open a Web or a file quickly, you can click the Open button on the Standard toolbar (the same Open button that you find in many Windows 98–based applications) and then choose either Open or Open Web from the submenu. Alternatively, you can choose a site or a file from the recently opened Webs or the recently opened files listed at the bottom of the File menu.

Opening Sites Authored in Other Applications

If you want to open a site authored in another application, the best-case scenario is when the site is on a Web server where the appropriate FrontPage Server Extensions are installed. The Server Extensions gather the additional information that FrontPage needs and make the site's content available for editing. So, if the right FrontPage Server Extensions are installed, you might not have to change a site's format in order to work with it.

To open such a site, follow the procedure outlined in the previous section, "Opening Sites or Files Authored in FrontPage." For more information on the FrontPage Server Extensions, see Chapter 11.

If, however, you want to open a site from a server that does not have the FrontPage Server Extensions installed, doing so is still pretty easy. You use the Import Web Wizard, which is described in Chapter 4.

Using the FrontPage Views

When you think of a Web, do you see it spatially (as a bunch of interconnected pages) or do you think of it linearly (as a bunch of collected pages in a row)? Either way is fine, of course—it all depends on your point of view. FrontPage has adopted the popular Outlook-style user interface and gives you six different ways to view and manipulate your site. Perhaps the single most powerful feature of FrontPage is that it enables you to view your site in these different ways, as Figure 3-5 shows.

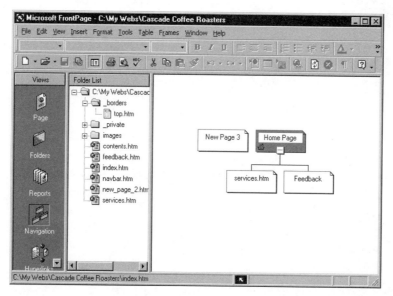

Figure 3-5
A typical site in FrontPage, shown in Navigation view.

Unique icons representing each view are listed vertically at the left side of the window under the Views heading.

The next several sections present each of the views in turn, to show you the unique ways in which they enable you to look at and create a FrontPage Web. We then show you some of the features that are common throughout all of the views.

Page View

Page view is where you actually add content to pages in your site. Page view is where all the HTML happens, as well as where your creative vision is put to the test. Part 3, "Building Your Pages," describes this view in detail.

Folders View

If you use Windows 95 or Windows 98, you should find Folders view easy to understand. Folders view is similar to that of the Windows Explorer. It presents the folder structure of your Web, wherever its location. It also presents the contents of those folders for you, so you don't need to be concerned with keeping track of your site's files.

To look at a site in Folders view, click the Folders icon on the Views toolbar or choose Folders from the View menu.

TIP If you want to remove the Views menu in order to give yourself more room to work, click the Views Bar command on the View menu to remove the check mark. Conversely, when the Views menu is hidden, you can show it again by choosing Views Bar from the View menu.

For a look at Folders view, see Figure 3-6, on the next page. The figure shows a site called Corp, which was created with the Corporate Presence Wizard. For instructions on creating a site, see "Creating a Site from Scratch," earlier in this chapter.

Folders view divides the screen into two vertical windows to the right of the Views bar. The left pane shows the folder structure of the site. The top-level folder contains files and subfolders. When FrontPage builds Webs, it uses specific folders according to the type of site you want to create. A Web created with the Project Web template, for example, might have different subfolders than a Web created with the Corporate Presence Wizard.

CHAPTER

3

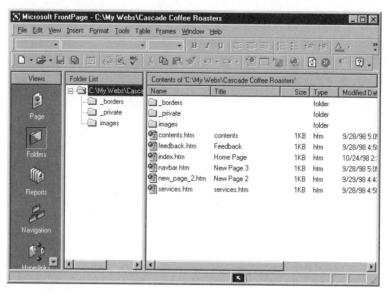

Figure 3-6

Folders view.

In the preceding graphic, notice that C:\MyWebs\corp is highlighted: it's the local location for the site, C being the hard drive, and corp being the folder in which the site is located. All of the site's files are collected in the subfolders below this top-level location. The number of folders for a given site is not static, however; you can create your own folders to organize your files. To learn how, see the next section, "Creating Your Own Folders."

The right pane of the window in Folders view contains a list of the contents of the folder that is selected in the left pane. You might recognize this as the same convention used in Windows Explorer. The folders and files listed in the right pane are accompanied by descriptive information, such as name, title, size, type, date last modified, identity of the person who modified them, and any comments about the file.

Figure 3-7 shows the contents of the images subfolder for the *corp* Web.

To sort the list of files based on a column in Folders view, click the column heading. FrontPage sorts files in ascending alphabetical order, except when you sort according to the Modified Date column; in such cases, FrontPage sorts files in chronological order beginning with the most recently modified file.

In your FrontPage journeys, you're likely to see a number of different icons in the right pane in Folders view, appearing beside the names of the files and folders. One icon is the yellow folder icon itself; that one's easy to figure out. Another icon that you often see looks like a painting; it denotes image files, such as JPEG and GIF files. A third icon looks like a page with lines on it; that one indicates HTML files, and you can expect to see these quite often. You might also see a familiar icon that resembles a mini-version of an icon from your favorite Microsoft Office program. When you import any Office file into a site, FrontPage uses the same icons that you're used to seeing in Office to represent the native file. For more information, see "Importing a File to a Site," later in this chapter.

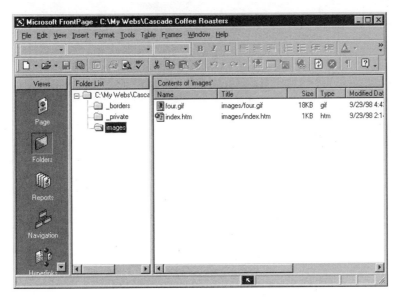

Figure 3-7

Folders view showing the contents of the Images folder.

Creating your own folders

Suppose you're a Webmaster in charge of maintaining a site on your company's intranet and the site includes numerous Office files from various contributors. One way to organize those files is to collect them in a folder structure called Office. Then the Office folder might include a Word folder in which you can store Word files. Here's how to add a new folder:

1.   Open a Web in Folders view, and then in the left pane select the folder in which you want the new folder to go.

2. Choose New from the File menu, and then choose Folder from the New submenu. A new folder appears in each pane of Folders view. The new folder is highlighted, ready for you to give it a name.

3. Name the new folder *Office,* and then press Enter.

4. Select the Office folder in the left pane.

5. Repeat steps 2 and 3, naming the new folder *Word.* Figure 3-8 shows what the folder structure should look like.

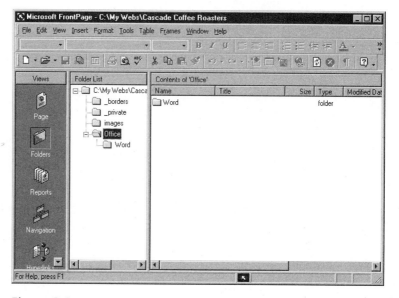

Figure 3-8

Folders view showing the Office folder and Word subfolder.

To add a new folder in Folders view quickly, right-click in either the right or left pane and choose New Folder from the pop-up menu.

Now, when your co-workers send you their Word files for the site, you have a logical place to store them. Better yet, perhaps you can train them to import the files themselves! To learn how to import those files, see "Importing a File into a Site," later in this chapter.

PART

Moving or Copying Files
Using the Drag-and-Drop Technique

As you work in the various views, you may want to use the drag-and-drop technique to move files from one place to another. For example, you could be working in Navigation view, adding a new page to your site, and you want to locate the page in a certain folder. You could drag the file from Navigation view to Folders view, in the exact folder you want. This is just another way you can use the views together to create your sites. Implementing the drag-and-drop technique is simple:

1. Select a file (or a group of files).

2. To move the file, press and hold the left mouse button (using the right mouse button gives you the option to either copy a file or move it). Drag the selection onto one of the icons on the Views bar. The corresponding view becomes the active view, visible in the right pane.

3. While still holding the mouse button, move the mouse back over to the right pane, and then release the mouse button. The selection has been moved successfully to the location you've chosen.

You perform the drag-and-drop technique the same way in Folders, Navigation, and Hyperlinks views, but the technique can produce different results depending on which view you use it in. So we discuss the drag-and-drop technique separately for each view that uses it.

Other drag-and-drop techniques in Folders view

Folders view uses the drag-and-drop techniques to help you work with the various views. For example you can drag a single file (or a selection of files) onto the Navigation icon in the Views bar to switch to Navigation view. Then, you can attach the file or files to a parent page. For more information on the Navigation view and parent pages, see "Navigation View" later in this chapter. You can also drag a single file onto the Task icon in the Views bar to oepn Tasks view, and then drop the file into the Tasks window. The New Task dialog box opens, where you can create and assign a new task based on the file you moved. For more information on the Tasks view, see "Tasks View" later in this chapter.

Here are some other good uses for Folders view:

- **Finding all files of a specific file type (such as Office files) in a folder.** Group the list by type of file by clicking the Type column, and then look for the specific file type.

- **Renaming a file.** Rename a file in exactly the same manner as you would in Windows Explorer. Right-click a file and select Rename from the pop-up menu. You can then rename the file, and FrontPage automatically updates any links to that file.

- **Modifying the folder structure.** Rearrange the folder structure of your Web by dragging files from one folder to another, just as you would in Windows Explorer. FrontPage automatically reconfigures the links.

You can also change column widths in Folders view. Place your mouse in the column heading area, near a border between the columns. When the cursor changes to a crosshair that has left- and right-facing arrows, click and drag to adjust the width.

Reports View

As you begin to develop larger and larger sites, you'll find that the sites can contain dozens of pages, hundreds of hyperlinks (internal and external), and plenty of pictures, as well as many other site "worries." The ability to organize all the vital statistics of your site in one location would be invaluable. Well, this is your lucky day; FrontPage has created a Reports view that lets you do that, plus a lot more. You can also use the Reports toolbar as a means of accessing reports.

To see your site in Reports View, you can choose the Reports icon from the Views menu. Or, to view by the various Reports, select the view of your choice by choosing Reports from the View menu and making your selection from the submenu. As you can see in Figure 3-9, there are many different ways to filter your reports.

Because you can view and manage your site in many different ways, the Reports view shows you your site in many different ways.

- **Site Summary**. This report gives you a quick overview of the most important areas of your site so that you can react quickly to any potential problems. If you need to know how many hyperlinks are in your site and how many of them are broken or unverified, a quick glance at the Site Summary report shows you all of that and more. Figure 3-10 shows the depth of information available in a site summary report.

PART
II

40

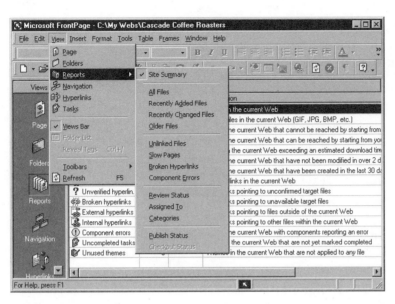

Figure 3-9
Reports view showing submenus.

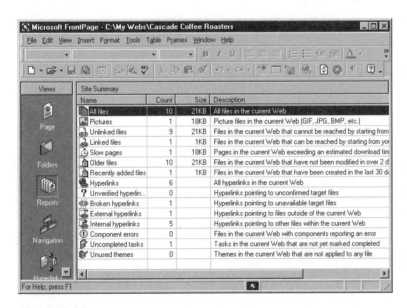

Figure 3-10
Site Summary report view.

● **All Files.** If you've ever wanted to see a complete list of every-thing in your site but were afraid to ask for one, fear no more. That's exactly what you get when you select the All Files report.

To sort any of the reports based on a column, click the column heading. Files are sorted in ascending alphabetical order, except when you sort according to the Modified Date column; in such cases, FrontPage sorts files in chronological order beginning with the most recently modified file. (A second click on the headings reverses the sort order.)

● **Recently Added Files.** To see a list of the most recently added files, select the Recently Added Files report. FrontPage lists the files from top to bottom, placing the most recent ones at the top.

● **Recently Changed Files.** If you're curious about which files have been changed recently, select the Recently Changed Files report, and you'll be enlightened.

● **Older Files.** To see a list of files that are older than a certain number of days, select the Older Files report.

● **Unlinked Files.** Usually, your site might contain a few files that don't link to anything. These files could be images or pages that contain form results. To see a list of unlinked files, select the Unlinked Files report.

● **Slow Pages.** When you create your pages, it's always good to know how long it will take to download them at a certain con-nection speed. The Slow Pages report tells you how many sec-onds it will take to download a page at a specified modem speed. You can define these variables in the Options dialog box, as de-scribed in the next section, "Reports View Options."

● **Broken Hyperlinks.** If you're buzzing around, creating pages that contain links to here and there, it's only a matter of time before you create a link that doesn't work. If you want to see for your-self, use the Broken Hyperlinks report. A link to a page that you haven't created yet also appears as broken on the Broken Hyperlinks report. Once you know where the broken hyperlinks are, you can easily go and fix them.

Once you've verified the hyperlinks in your site, you'll more than likely need to do some link editing. To fix a broken link, right-click that link in the Broken Hyperlinks report and then choose

Edit Hyperlink from the pop-up menu to open the Edit Hyperlink dialog box, shown in Figure 3-11. Following are the options in the dialog box.

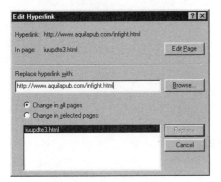

Figure 3-11

The Edit Hyperlink dialog box.

- **Hyperlink.** The first item listed in the dialog box shows the link's current destination.

- **In Page.** The second item listed in the dialog box shows the page containing the link.

- **Edit Page.** To move to the page that contains the link, click Edit Page. The page opens in Page view, and the link is selected, allowing you to edit or remove it. (For information on editing a link in the Editor, see Chapter 7.)

- **Replace Hyperlink With.** Change the URL in the Replace Hyperlink With text box or click the Browse button to search for the new address.

- **Change In All Pages.** If you want the new link that you just replaced to be changed on every page in your site that contains the old link, click the Change In All Places option button. FrontPage searches the entire site and changes the old link to the new one you just made. It's a good idea to let FrontPage do this for you.

- **Change In Selected Pages.** If you want FrontPage to change the new link only in certain pages where it appears, select Change In Selected Pages and then choose the pages from the list.

CHAPTER

3

After you make your choices in the Edit Hyperlink dialog box, click the Replace button. FrontPage goes through your site and makes the appropriate changes. If you don't have time to fix the link right away, or if you need some time to find a correct address, you can add the task to the Tasks view by right-clicking the link and then choosing Add Task from the pop-up menu. For more information on the Tasks view, see "Tasks View," later in this chapter.

- **Component Errors.** One of the reasons FrontPage is so cool is that all the custom components come prepackaged. These components eliminate a great deal of HTML coding that most of us mortals don't want to have to mess with. If there are errors in any of the components that appear in your site, they show up here on the Component Errors report. Many components require that you save the page to a Web server in order for it to work. If you're just starting to build your site and you haven't posted it to a Web server yet, you'll see these components appear as errors in the report. Don't worry, though; this report simply helps you keep track of your components and whether or not you've posted the pages containing them yet.

- **Review Status.** Another great way to organize and view the files in your site is to develop a review process. For instance, you can specify that the products page, Prod01.htm, requires review by the manager Dick. Flagging a file this way lets everyone know that the page can't be worked on until Dick has seen it. To assign a review status, click the space in the Review Status column next to the file you want to change; the column field changes to a drop-down menu. You can choose any of the reviews listed or simply enter a name for a new one. Figure 3-12 shows the Review Status window.

- **Assigned To.** If many people are working on different files in your site and you want to keep track of who's supposed to work on what, add their names in the Assigned To field. To create an Assigned To entry, click the space in the Assigned To column next to the file you want to change; the column field changes to a drop-down menu. You can choose any of the names listed or simply enter a new one.

You can add names in the Assigned To field in either the Review Status report or the Assigned To report.

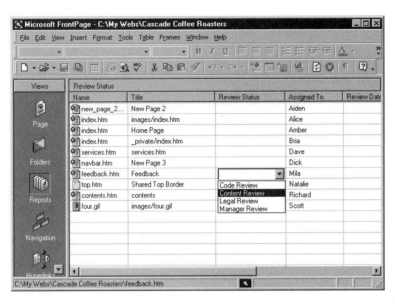

Figure 3-12
Review Status window listing reviews.

- **Categories.** As you build your sites, you might want to define categories to organize individual content items. For example, maybe you have some pages that are still in the development stage. You can assign these pages to the Ideas category, and then you can easily sort the files to see all the Ideas pages. You can select one of the categories supplied, or you can create your own. Use the Properties dialog box to define these parameters, as the "File Properties" section in Chapter 7 explains.

- **Publish Status.** There are times when you might want to publish only certain files to your Web server. By using the Publish Status report, you can define whether a file is ready for publishing or not. To mark a file Publish or Don't Publish, click the field in the Publish column next to the file you want to change; the column field changes to a drop-down menu. You can choose either Publish or Don't Publish. If you choose Don't Publish, the file will not be published when the rest of the Web is published.

- **Checkout Status.** If you're using a source control program such as Microsoft Visual Source Safe (VSS) with your site, you can use this report to check the status of any content that is currently checked in or out.

45

Reports view options

Now you may be thinking, "Hey, if I view a report, for example, the Recent Files report, and I want it to show only files that are less than ten days old, how can I do that?" Again, you're in luck. The developers of FrontPage have thought of everything. To see all your Reports View options, choose Options from the Tools menu and then click the Reports View tab. You'll see the Options dialog box, as shown in Figure 3-13.

Use this dialog box to specify options for the Recent files, Older files, and Slow Pages reports. You can also specify the minimum connection speed you assume your site visitors will use. And if you hate all those pesky little lines that show up in the Reports views, it's easy to turn them off here, too. Enter the information that you want to change and click OK. FrontPage automatically updates existing reports to reflect your changes.

Figure 3-13

The Reports View tab of the Options dialog box.

Navigation View

You can map out your Web in many different ways. You can buy a few packs of sticky notes and plaster them all over the walls. You can use a few hundred 3- x 5-inch cards and try to keep them organized, or you can doodle little sketches all over the place. The makers of FrontPage, however, decided to save you some time and trouble—not to mention a few trees. To that end, they included a way of mapping out your site structure directly within FrontPage. It's called Navigation view: it enables you to design your structure visually, and it even lets you print out a map of that structure. You can also use the structure you build in Navigation view to create navigation bars on a page in your site. For more information on navigation bars, see "Using Navigation Bars" in Chapter 7.

PART

To see your site in Navigation view, select Navigation from the Views bar or choose Navigation from the View menu.

Figure 3-14 shows a typical site, with the Folder List displayed in Navigation view.

As you can see, Navigation view presents pages visually as a rectangular box; the title of the page is in the middle. Navigation view divides the screen into two vertical panes. The right portion is a workspace in which you can design your structure, and the left portion is a simple folders view. The folders view corresponds with the contents of the Folders view, described earlier in the "Folders View" section of this chapter. These two "folder" views always match; if you move items around in the folders pane of Navigation view, the same items are moved in the Folders view.

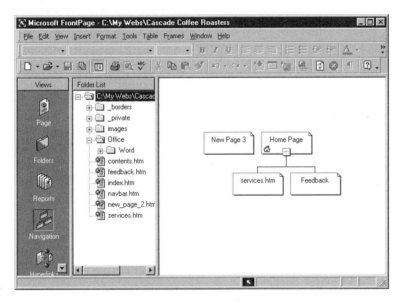

Figure 3-14
Folder List in Navigation view.

If you need more room to work on your navigation structure, click the Folder List command on the View menu to remove the check mark. This removes the folder list from view. You can also remove the Views Bar by removing the check mark from the Views Bar command on the View menu.

CHAPTER 3

Editing the page title

You can use several different methods to edit the title of a page easily in Navigation view:

● Right-click the page and then choose Rename from the pop-up menu.

● Click the page once to select it, and then click the title. The title becomes highlighted and you can enter the new name.

● Click the page once and then press the F2 button on your keyboard.

Changing the title of a page changes only its "friendly name," the title that appears in the header of most browsers; it has no effect on the page's URL. For example, the name of your home page is usually something like *Default.html* or *Index.html*, but the friendly name is usually something like the name of the company or the name of a department.

After you finish changing the page name, you can click anywhere on the background or press Enter on your keyboard to save the change. If you accidentally double-click a page, don't worry; you'll just end up opening the page in Page view. For more information on working with pages, see Chapters 6 and 7.

Parents, children, and peers

When designing the structure of your site, you usually build from the top down—in another words, you create your pages at different levels. This structure forms the hierarchy of your site and helps define the priorities of the content on the site. Most of the time, you place the more important information higher in the hierarchy to make it easier to find. You usually include related or supporting information on lower-level pages, making them accessible by means of links from higher-level pages. Knowing that your site's hierarchy and link structure can get rather confusing, the developers of FrontPage have incorporated a naming system that defines the relationships between pages.

● **Parent pages.** Parents are pages that have child pages linked below them.

● **Child pages.** Child pages live directly below a parent and usually are linked to the parent page by a graphic or text hyperlink or by a navigation bar.

● **Peer pages.** Peers are pages that share a common parent.

You might think of your pages as people—stay with me here—you can see that pages can be parents, peers, and children all at the same time, just as people can.

Figure 3-15 shows a typical site structure, where Home is the parent to Services and News, Services and News are peers to each other, and Services 2 is a child page of Services; in the same way, Services is a parent to Services 2. You might be asking yourself, "What is that Feedback page doing in the list, then?" Well, the Feedback page is a global, or *top-level*, page. A top-level page is one that visitors can access from every page in the site that contains a navigation bar link to it. Because FrontPage creates the navigation bars based on the hierarchy designed in Navigation view, and because the top-level page is parallel to the Home page, it's not subject to the hierarchy. Top-level pages appear to the left or right of the home page in Navigation view. For more information on navigation bars, see "Using Navigation Bars" in Chapter 7.

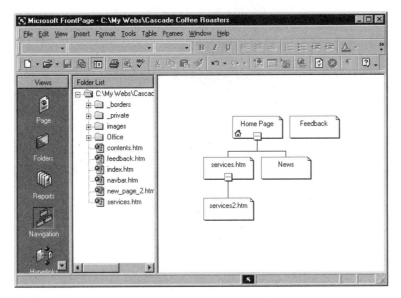

Figure 3-15

A basic navigation structure in Navigation view.

You can easily add a new top-level page by right-clicking anywhere on the background of the structure pane and then choosing New Top Page from the pop-up menu. You can also access the FrontPage Web Settings dialog box by choosing Web Settings from the pop-up menu.

CHAPTER 3

As you can see in Figure 3-16, FrontPage indicates pages that are linked together by including a line between them. This convention gives you an easy visual depiction of the site's hierarchy. If a page is a parent, you can collapse the child pages (including any of its lower-level child pages) by clicking the minus sign. In turn, you can expand the structure by clicking the plus sign, one parent at a time, to see the respective child pages. Being able to collapse and expand the site's structure is very useful when you have a large site composed of many different levels.

Changing the structure

You can use the drag-and-drop method to move your pages around, creating your structure as you go. Elsewhere in FrontPage, you use the drag-and-drop technique to move files between views (see "Using the FrontPage Views" earlier in this chapter). But within Navigation view, you can move files within the same pane or between both panes. You can drag a file from the left pane over to the structure pane, and you can move pages around within the structure pane.

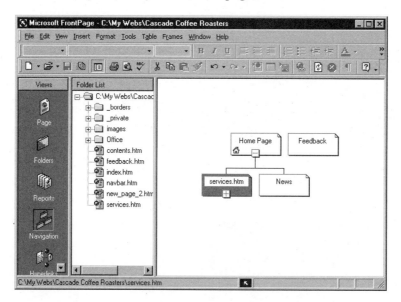

Figure 3-16

Navigation view showing a collapsed structure.

Here's how to bring a page into the structure pane from the folder pane:

1. Click and hold the left mouse button on the file that you want to move from the left pane.

2. Drag the file over into the structure pane. As you move the mouse around the upper pane, still holding down that button, you can see a dotted outline of the page you're moving.

3. Move the outline near another page in the structure view, and a dotted line appears connecting the pages, as shown in Figure 3-17.

4. When you have the page positioned where you want it, release the mouse button to drop the page into place.

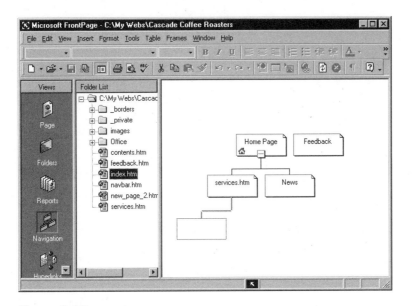

Figure 3-17
A new page outlined in Navigation view.

You can now see the page in the structure pane, its title visible, each page connected by a blue line. Don't worry; you have complete design control. You can move the pages in the structure pane around—and around—until you get them just the way you like. That's the heart of Navigation view; the whole idea is to give you a view in which you can build the flow of information that forms the foundation of your site.

To add new pages to your site, see "Adding a New Page to a Site," later in this chapter.

NOTE

Changing the structure in Navigation view works only when you use Navigation bars. Any changes made in Navigation view affect only pages that contain Navigation bars. For information on adding Navigation bars, see "Navigation Bars" in Chapter 7. If you import a site, you have to place Navigation bars on the pages of the imported site before you use Navigation view.

If you build a large site, you'll notice that when many pages are expanded in Navigation view, some of the pages move beyond the view that your monitor affords. You can use the scroll bars to move around, or you can use a simple sleight-of-hand to move the view anywhere you like. To pull off the latter feat, just click and hold anywhere on the background, and continue holding the mouse button until your mouse pointer changes into a hand. Then, as long as you continue to hold down the mouse button, the view moves around the window whenever you move the mouse.

If you've built a site that consists of many pages, you may be asking yourself, "With all these pages, what if I can't find my way home?" or "Where's my home page?" There's no need to click your ruby slippers; your home page is always located either at the top of the view or at the upper left corner of the view. It's also easy to spot, because it's the one that has the little house icon in its lower left corner.

Deleting a page from your structure

Deleting a page from the structure pane in Navigation view is easy. You can use any of the delete options described in "Deleting Files," later in this chapter. When you attempt to delete a page from the site structure, FrontPage asks if you want to remove the page from Navigation view only, or to delete the page completely from the Web. Choose wisely.

Adjusting your view

After you begin building your site, its structure can get rather lengthy. Unless you have one of those cool 21-inch monitors, finding your way around can get complicated. FrontPage gives you a few ways to change and improve your view. You can access these options by right-clicking in the structure pane and selecting an option.

- **Zoom.** By using Zoom, you can adjust the size, in percentages, at which the navigational structure appears in the window. You can also select Size To Fit from the Zoom option. Using Size To Fit automatically resizes the structure so that it's as big as possible, while all pages remain visible in the structure pane.

- **Rotate.** Some people like to view the site structure from top to bottom, while others prefer to view it from left to right. The Rotate command enables users to toggle between both views.

- **Expand All.** In Navigation view, hidden or collapsed child pages are indicated by the plus sign. If you want to see the entire structure of a site and you don't want to click every plus sign, you can use the Expand All command. Choosing Expand All opens all hidden or collapsed child pages, exposing the entire structure of your Web. If your structure is already completely expanded, or if it contains no plus signs, Expand All has no effect on the view.

● **View Subtree Only.** You must select a page in the structure pane in order for View Subtree Only to be available. When you choose View Subtree Only, the entire structure collapses, leaving only the selected page viewable. You can also right-click an individual page in the structure pane and choose View Subtree Only from the pop-up menu.

The Navigation dialog box

By choosing Toolbars from the View menu and Navigation from the resulting pop-up menu, you open the Navigation dialog box. From within the Navigation dialog box, you can easily perform many tasks in Navigation view.

● **Zoom.** You can change the Zoom of the site structure by clicking the Zoom drop-down list and selecting the percentage of zoom that you like.

● **Portrait and Landscape.** This button toggles between presenting your site structure in a portrait (vertical) format or in a landscape (horizontal) format.

● **External Link.** You must select a page in the site structure before you can choose an external link. Selecting the External Link button brings up the Select Hyperlink dialog box. Use the Select Hyperlink dialog box to select a page to link to. Once you select a page and click OK, the new link is added to the navigation structure as a new page.

● **Include In Navigation Bars.** You must select a page in the site structure before you can use this button. The Include In Navigation Bars button toggles between including the selected page in the Navigation Bars and excluding the page from the Navigation Bars.

● **View Subtree Only.** This button functions as a toggle, just like the Include In Navigation Bars button.

Applying the changes

So you've been playing around in Navigation view for a while, and you have the structure just the way you want it—it's perfect, a work of art—and now you want to save it. Well, FrontPage automatically saves the structure in the Navigation view as you go, but if you want your navigation bars to recognize the new structure, you have to update your changes. For more information on navigation bars, see "Using Navigation Bars" in Chapter 7.

CHAPTER

3

To apply the changes you've made to the site structure, right-click in the structure pane and choose Apply Changes from the pop-up menu. FrontPage might take a minute or two to complete this task, depending on the size of your structure.

Printing your site map

People often need to see and feel something in order to understand it, and a site structure can be a hard thing to explain. Having a printed copy of the site structure can be handy, not only to share with your boss, but also to share with other members of the Web development team, the client, your significant other, and so on. You never know, it may even be suitable for framing.

FrontPage prints the site structure exactly as it appears in Navigation view, even if you can't see it all on your monitor, so be sure to expand the view to show all the levels you want to print. To save room when printing, FrontPage prints only the plus signs, to indicate unseen portions of the structure; it does not print the minus signs.

If you want to scc in advance how the structure will look when it's printed, choose Print Preview from the File menu. The Print Preview window gives you a few options. For more information on Print Preview, see "Print Preview" in Chapter 6.

When you have arranged the structure to your satisfaction, you can print it by choosing Print from the File menu or by pressing Ctrl+P. Either option opens the standard Print dialog box.

Adding a Navigation view to an old site

If you upgrade from an earlier version of FrontPage or import a site from another program, and if you want to take advantage of Navigation view to build your site's structure or to use Navigation bars, you're in luck. FrontPage automatically places a Home Page in the top pane, ready for you to begin the building process. From this point on, Navigation view works the way it does with any other site.

Hyperlinks View

Hyperlinks view is the graphical representation of the links within a segment of your Web. To see your site in Hyperlinks view, choose Hyperlinks view from the View menu. Another quick way to see your site in Hyperlinks view is to click the Hyperlink icon on the Views bar.

Figure 3-18 shows how a site looks in Hyperlinks view. Hyperlinks view divides the screen into two panes; the left pane presents an outline of your site in a folder view, and the right pane shows the files of your site as large icons, linked together by a series of lines. The file names appear directly beneath the icons. Links are shown in a left-to-right fashion, links to the page appearing to the page's left and links from the page to other pages and elements appearing to the page's right.

In Figure 3-18, the plus sign indicates that you can expand the view; therefore, more links either are coming to or going from the page. Clicking the plus sign expands the view. After you expand a view, the plus sign changes to a minus sign, indicating that you can collapse the view.

If you let your mouse pointer hover over an icon, a pop-up ScreenTip appears, indicating the file name and other information.

Many different icons appear in both panes of Hyperlinks view. For example, envelope icons that are adjacent to a *mailto:* protocol indicate links that send e-mail, that is, links on pages that allow users to send e-mail directly from the page. For example, you might include such a link on your pages to give your users a convenient way to provide you (the Webmaster) with feedback. Icons of paintings indicate image files, and globe icons indicate links to the World Wide Web. As in Folders view, you also see icons for Office files when they're part of your site.

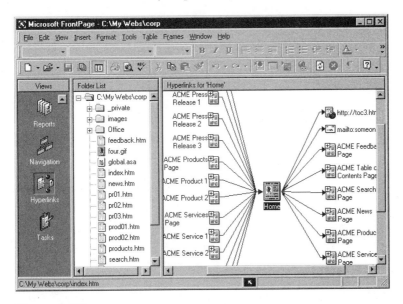

Figure 3-18
Hyperlinks view.

Just as in Folders view, clicking an item in the left pane causes the information in the right pane to change. In Hyperlinks view, when you click something in the left pane, that item appears centered in the right pane, along with any of its links to other files or addresses. Clicking the plus and minus signs expands and contracts the outline, respectively.

Hyperlinks view is especially useful for determining just how many links come to and go from each page, as well as for seeing what other pages within your Web link to your page. Suppose you posted a new page on your intranet a week ago, and now you want to know how many others in your organization have linked to your page. You can simply look at your page in Hyperlinks view to find out.

Hyperlinks view also comes in handy if you need to verify that you've included all the links that you think you have on a particular page. Suppose you promised several departments in your organization that you'd link to their home page from your "For More Information" page and those links are embedded in the paragraphs on your page. Well, you can view all the links on your page in one place—Hyperlinks view—and check that against your list, instead of having to look at the page in an editor, find the links, and then check them against a master list.

Another way that Hyperlinks view can prove useful is in finding all pages that point to a particular page. Also, by expanding the links (clicking the plus signs), you can find various paths through your site. This is useful, for example, in figuring out how many mouse clicks it takes to get from one particular page to another.

Modifying the view

The size of the Hyperlinks view window and the size of your monitor dictate how much of your site appears in Hyperlinks view. As you expand the site, you might notice that more and more links drop out of view on your screen. You can view the off-the-screen material in one of two ways. You can either use the scroll bars at the bottom and side of the window or click any open area, keep the mouse button depressed until the pointer changes to a hand, and then, while continuing to hold the mouse button, drag the material wherever you want it.

There's also a way to center any item on your screen in Hyperlinks view: right-click the item and choose Move To Center from the pop-up menu. You'll also notice that because Hyperlinks view is a representation of links, it can seem to go on forever. If you think spatially, you'll see that if page A is linked to page B, which is linked to page C, which is linked back to page A, then you're already going around in circles. And that's only one example. It's best to use Hyperlinks view for viewing small portions of your site. You can get a good overall view of your site by collapsing everything; when you need to see specifics, it's time to expand those icons.

Tasks View

It's said that Albert Einstein chose not to memorize his phone number because he believed that memorizing such details took up too much space in his brain and too much energy. He preferred to reserve his brainpower and energy for his creative endeavors, and he would simply write down any details that he could look up later.

Don't you wish you could do that with the many small details about your site so you wouldn't have to remember them all? If you have to write down a long list of tasks, however, keeping track of them is difficult. Luckily, FrontPage supplies a better solution: Tasks view.

Tasks view is a list of tasks that need to be completed for a given site. It not only records all those nagging details, but also allows you the luxury of not having to organize them. It lists each task, describes it, prioritizes it, indicates who's assigned to complete it, and more, freeing you up to take care of other details. In addition, Tasks view is completely customizable, allowing you to change and rearrange the tasks to your heart's content.

To show Tasks view for your site, choose Tasks from the View menu or click the Tasks icon on the Views bar. Figure 3-19 shows the Tasks view window containing a list of tasks ready to be completed.

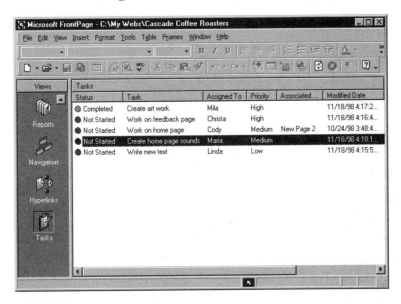

Figure 3-19

Tasks view.

The leftmost column, the Status column, lists the status of a task. The second column, the Task column, describes the tasks. The next column, the Assigned To column, lists who's responsible for completing each task. The Priority column notes whether the task has a priority of high, medium, or low. The Associated With column indicates the page or file that requires editing for completion of the task. The Modified Date column lists the date on which the task was last modified. And, finally, the rightmost column, the Description column, provides a description of each task.

The following items describe the features of the Tasks view.

- **Showing history.** If you want to see a list of all of the tasks ever assigned in the Web, including those marked as completed, view the Task History. Right-click in the Tasks view pane and choose Task History from the pop-up menu. When you select Task History, FrontPage adds all of these tasks to the list, along with the date on which the task was marked as completed. When Task History is not selected, the Tasks view shows only tasks that still remain to be completed.

- **Sorting the columns.** Sorting the columns can be useful for large lists, and it's easy to do—you simply click a column heading. Suppose you want to find out how many tasks are assigned to you. Just click the Assigned To column heading and then find your name in the column; FrontPage groups all of the tasks assigned to you. In Tasks view, as in the other views, sorted tasks are in ascending alphabetic order unless you want to sort by date—from most recent to oldest.

  You can also adjust column widths by first moving your mouse pointer between the column headings until the pointer changes to a crosshair that has left and right arrows, and then clicking and dragging. This method lets you expand a column to see detailed descriptions that are too long to fit otherwise.

- **Completing a task on the spot.** This is one of the most helpful features of Tasks view. If you see a task in the list that's assigned to you or someone else and you want to complete the task right then and there, you can do so. Suppose you want to complete the "rework graphic" task shown in Figure 3-19. All you need to do is select the task, right-click, and then choose Edit Task from the pop-up menu. The page opens for the task that you need to complete. Even better, the page opens to the very spot described in the task, so you don't have to search for it. If a task is not associated with a particular page, the Edit Task button is unavailable. When you save the page containing the unfinished task, FrontPage asks you whether you want to mark the task as completed in Tasks view. Make sure you're really finished before you mark the task as completed—once you do so, you can't undo that action.

- **Assigning Tasks.** If you want to change the person who's assigned to perform a certain task, click in the Assigned To column in the field next to the task you want to assign. Select a name from the drop-down list or enter a new name.

- **Changing the details for a task.** You can reassign a task, change the priority of a task, and change the description of a task in the Task Details dialog box. You can access the Task Details dialog box by right-clicking a selected task and then choosing Edit Task from the pop-up menu. Alternatively, when a task is selected, you can choose Open from the Edit menu. Either way, the Task Details dialog box opens, as shown in Figure 3-20.

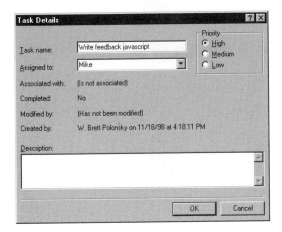

Figure 3-20

The Task Details dialog box.

To change the task name, to assign the task to a different person, or to change the description of the task, simply replace the existing text. To change the priority, select the appropriate option button. You can also enter descriptive notes in the text field at the bottom of the dialog box. You'll notice that not all details can be changed—only those mentioned here. For tasks created by you or other users, you also can change the task name. If you want to start the task right now, click Start Task to go to the page that contains the task. Or, when you finish entering the new information, click OK to return to Tasks view.

- **Marking a task as completed or deleting a task**. If you want to mark a task as completed, or if you want to delete a task altogether, right-click the task and choose either Mark As Completed or Delete from the pop-up menu. After a task has been marked completed, its status changes, and the colored ball that indicates the status changes to green in Task view. The Delete option is useful when you no longer want a task to appear in the Tasks view history.

● **Adding a task.** If you don't need to link a task to a particular page, click the New Task button on the menu bar while in the Tasks view or right-click in the Tasks view pane and then choose New Task from the pop-up menu. If you want to link a new task to a page in your site, start in one of the other views (for example, the Reports view), right-click the page, and then choose Add Task from the pop-up menu. With either method, the New Task dialog box opens, as shown in Figure 3-21.

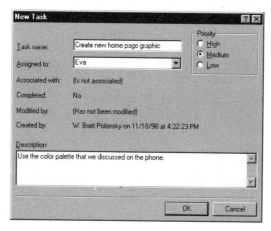

Figure 3-21
The New Task dialog box.

Enter the task name in the Task Name text box and assign it to someone in the Assign To text box. Mark the priority as High, Medium, or Low in the Priority section of the dialog box. Finally, add a description of the task in the text box at the bottom and then click OK. Be sure to use a short but specific description, because the column widths in Tasks view are often rather narrow.

Managing tasks using Tasks view
Tasks view can be a powerful management tool. It enables you to assign or reassign tasks, observe what work has been completed in a site, and

determine what work still needs to be done. You can perform the following team management tasks using Tasks view:

- **Evenly distributing the workload.** If someone on your team has a great deal more work to perform on a site than others do, you can distribute the workload more evenly by reassigning some of that person's tasks.

- **Seeing whether a task is completed.** R.U. Awake, your team's resident procrastinator, often takes a long time to get things done. To check on R.U.'s progress, you can look at Tasks view and sort the Task column to find a task. If the task doesn't appear in the list, R.U. gets a reprieve; if it's still there, it's time for R.U. to write on the whiteboard 50 times, "I will get my Tasks view tasks done on time."

- **Determining the state of your site.** You can determine a site's condition in many ways by using Tasks view. One way is to simply look at the number of tasks to be completed. Another way is to sort the tasks by priority: if you see many high- and medium-priority tasks remaining, you have more work to do. Conversely, you have less work to do if most of the remaining tasks are low-priority tasks.

- **Determining what pages or files need the most work.** Sorting on the Linked To column can give you an indication of which pages and files in your site need the most work. If you have many tasks associated with a few pages, you can assign more resources to those areas.

What Do the Views Have in Common?

You can customize some of the features that are common to the Folders, Reports, Navigation, and Hyperlinks views. These are the views that contain file names and lists. Here's the rundown:

Adjusting the column widths

You can change column widths. Place your mouse in the column heading area, near a border between the columns. When the cursor changes to a crosshair that has left- and right-facing arrows, click and drag to adjust the width.

Opening files from a view

Folders, Reports, Navigation, and Hyperlinks views aren't just a compilation of pages and links; they're also avenues for opening their associated files in Page view or in whatever application you want to work in to manipulate

CHAPTER 3

those files. For example, to manipulate a Graphics Interchange Format (GIF) file that appears in a view, you can launch the application and edit the file with a few clicks of the mouse.

You can open files from any view in which you see the file name listed. To open a file, right-click the title or the icon, and then choose Open from the pop-up menu. If the file is an HTML file, the page opens, ready for you to edit. If you choose the Open With command, you can open the page using any other editor. After you choose Open With, you see a list of editors in the Open With Editor dialog box; you can select an editor and click OK.

But what if you want a different editor (other than the default one) to open when you choose the Open command for a particular type of file? Or what if your editor doesn't show up at all in the Open With Editor dialog box? You can change the editor type by choosing Options from the Tools menu and then clicking the Configure Editors tab. (See "Configuring Editors," later in this chapter.)

You can also double-click a file in one of these views to open it. The file opens in its associated editor.

Viewing file properties

To view properties for a file, select the file and then choose Properties from the File menu. The Summary tab in the Properties dialog box provides information such as when the file was created, who created it, when it was modified, and who modified it. It also includes a text box in which you can add comments to the file.

You can access the properties for an item by right-clicking the item and then choosing Properties from the pop-up menu.

On the General tab, you'll find general information about the file, such as its name, title, type, size, and location. The location can be a file location or a *URL*. A URL (*Uniform Resource Locator*) indicates the address of a *resource* (a file) on a network and the method by which you can access it. URLs can use various protocols; the most common one on the World Wide Web today is *HTTP* (*HyperText Transport Protocol*). The terms *URL* and *HTTP address* refer to the same thing.

PART

Refreshing a view

To update the views in FrontPage, choose Refresh from the View menu. Choosing the command refreshes all views for the current site. If more than one person is working on a site at any time, refreshing the site allows you to see all of the changes.

Changing the size of a view

A split bar separates the panes in the Folder, Navigation, and Hyperlinks views. To move the bar and change the amount of the window devoted to each of the views, place your cursor directly over the bar until it changes to a double-line cursor that has left- and right-facing arrows. Then click and drag the bar.

One-Button Publishing

If you want to move your site to another server, FrontPage makes it easy. For example, suppose you've been building your site locally and you want to move the site to a high-volume server that powers your intranet, or to a Web server connected to the Internet. You can use the Publish Web button on the File menu to copy an open site to a server. It's an easy task—one that you can do at the click of a button. Here's how to do it:

1. Open the site you want to copy and select the Publish Web button from the toolbar. The Publish FrontPage Web dialog box appears, as shown in Figure 3-22.

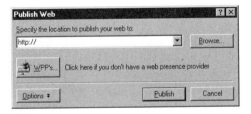

Figure 3-22
The Publish Web dialog box.

2. Select a location from the drop-down list or enter the name of the Web server directly. You can also enter a path name if you want to place the site on a hard disk or LAN. If you don't know the location, or if it's not listed in the drop-down list, you can use the

Browse button to select a new location. If you want to communicate with your site using Secure Sockets Layer (SSL) security, check the Connect Using SSL check box.

3. If you want to publish only changes to the Web, select the Options button and then check the Publish Changed Pages Only check box. This is a good idea, because you'll save time publishing only the pages you need.

4. Click OK. FrontPage locates the server and publishes the Web as directed.

You also can use these methods to publish to Web servers that don't have the FrontPage Server Extensions installed. In these cases, FrontPage publishes your site to the destination server using the *FTP (File Transfer Protocol)* protocol. (It does ask you for information, such as the FTP server name, user name, password, and destination folder.) You also can save sites to online services such as America Online, CompuServe, and others. Check with your Internet service provider for instructions on how to publish to their servers.

Site Management Odds and Ends

So far in this chapter, you've learned that you can use FrontPage to create, open, and publish sites, to view them in several different ways, and even to change the way they look using Themes. FrontPage also sports a host of other functions that you can use in your everyday site management.

Closing a Site

Because FrontPage can display only one site at a time, it closes the current site whenever you open another site or create a new one.

Deleting a Site

To delete the site that's currently open, choose Delete Web from the File menu. You'll see the Confirm Delete dialog box, asking you if you really want to do this. You also have the option to remove only the FrontPage information, preserving all of the other files and folders, or to delete the Web entirely.

Be sure to delete sites by using the Delete Web command, not by manually removing their files from a server. If you remove the files manually, FrontPage might not recognize that they've been deleted.

Consider this before you delete: once you delete a site, even if you've removed it properly by using the Delete Web command, you can't recover it—not even from the Recycle Bin in Windows Explorer, or from any directory that FrontPage might have created for the site.

Deleting Files

You can delete files by selecting them in Folders view, certain Reports views, Navigation view, or Hyperlinks view and then choosing Delete from the Edit menu, or by right-clicking the file and choosing Delete. FrontPage asks you to confirm the deletion before it carries out the action.

If you're building your site one page at a time, perhaps not taking advantage of one of the Web wizards, be sure to add and delete pages individually. If you do use a Web wizard, be careful when deleting pages: you don't want to delete any links or pages that are referenced in other areas that the wizard created.

Adding a New Page to a Site

You can add a new page to a site from within the Page, Folders, and Navigation views. You can add a new page to your site in a few different ways:

- Choose New from the File menu and then choose Page from the New submenu.

- Click the New Page button on the toolbar.

- Right-click in the file list portion of the window and choose New Page from the pop-up menu.

- Use the Copy and Paste buttons, respectively, on the FrontPage toolbar.

When you create your new page, FrontPage adds it to the Web as a *Newpage.htm*. It's a good idea to rename the page right away, so you don't end up with *Newpage2.htm*, *Newpage3.htm*, and so on each time you add a page.

Importing a File to a Site

An application's ability to incorporate documents created in earlier versions of the program or in competing programs is one way of determining its value: "utility" versus "futility." You shouldn't have to lose the work you've already done in another Web authoring application if you're moving over to FrontPage. If you've already created pages or files (for example, RTF or HTML files) that you'd like to include in your current site, FrontPage allows you to do so easily.

CHAPTER 3

You can import Word documents, Excel spreadsheets, and more to your sites—FrontPage allows you to import non-Microsoft files to your site, as well. An intranet site can consist of dozens, hundreds, or even thousands of documents. If you're in charge of getting those documents into the site, you'll be relieved to know that you can import all of those files at once if you want to.

You can import files to a site using one of two methods: by choosing a menu command or by dragging files into FrontPage from elsewhere on your computer. Here's how to use the menu command:

1. Choose Import from the File menu. The Import dialog box appears, as shown in Figure 3-23.

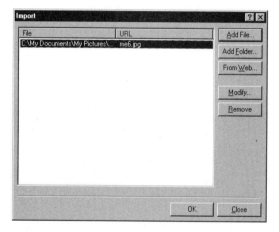

Figure 3-23
The Import dialog box for importing a file to a FrontPage Web.

2. Click the Add File button. The Add File To Import List dialog box opens, and in it you specify the file or files you want to import. Locate the folder that contains the file by using the folder controls at the top of the dialog box. Be sure to select the type of files to be listed by using the Files Of Type drop-down list. (If you're not sure of the type of file you're looking for, select All Files from the drop-down list.)

3. Select the file or files that you want to import. You select files here in the same way that you do in Windows Explorer. To select a group of contiguous files, click the first file in the group, press the Shift key, and then click the last file in the group. To select multiple noncontiguous files, press the Ctrl key while clicking the

files you want to select. To remove a file from a selection, press the Ctrl key while clicking the file.

4. Click Open to close the Add File To Import List dialog box and add the files to a list in the Import File To FrontPage Web dialog box.

5. If you need to add more files to the list, repeat steps 2, 3, and 4. To remove files from the list before you add them to your site, select them and click the Remove button.

6. If you want to change the URL of any file, select the file in the Import File To FrontPage Web dialog box and then click Edit URL. This button comes in handy when you want to save a file separately from the other items in the site; you enter the new URL (pointing the file to the folder of your choice) in the Edit URL dialog box that appears, and then click OK.

7. Click OK to add the files to your site.

FrontPage closes the Import File To FrontPage Web dialog box after it finishes importing the files. The imported files are not linked to any pages in the site.

You can add image files to your site by using the Import command. As described later in Chapter 8, you can do this in several different ways, but if you know you're going to use specific files in your site, the Import command allows you to add them all at once.

You can also add files from a Web by clicking From Web in the Import File To FrontPage Web dialog box. This launches the Import Web Wizard, which guides you through the steps involved in importing a Web. For more information on the Import Web Wizard, see Chapter 4.

Dragging a file into a site

There will be times when you want to import just a file or two to your site, in which case the use of the Import command is simply too time-consuming. For those times, FrontPage supports dragging those files, which works similarly to dragging files onto a view, described in the sidebar "Moving or Copying Files Using the Drag-and-Drop Technique"earlier in this chapter. The only difference is that you drag a file from a location outside your Web into your Web.

Changing Site Settings

Nightmare on Web Street, scene one: you've just completed a site for your company that includes the company's phone and fax numbers on nearly every one of its 169 pages. After you come up for air, you read in the morning

CHAPTER 3

paper that your area code is about to change. After you wonder where the heck you've been for the past six months, you face the dismal prospect of editing every one of those 169 pages. You could use a utility program to search for the old area code and replace it with the new one, and there are other ways to get the job done. But how about a one-step automated process?

TIP

You also can use FrontPage's Find and Replace commands to change information on all of the pages in your site that don't use parameters and configuration variables. For more information, see Chapter 7.

FrontPage uses placeholders, also called *parameters* or *configuration variables*, so that it can track where this information is used in the current site. The templates and wizards in FrontPage add some parameters automatically. You can define your own and insert them using the FrontPage Substitution Component, discussed in Chapter 9. By using the Web Settings command on the Tools menu, you can update the information wherever it occurs in your site. You also can access the FrontPage Web Settings dialog box in any view by right-clicking in the view pane and choosing Web Settings from the pop-up menu. Choose the command to open the FrontPage Web Settings dialog box, which has six tabs (see Figure 3-24).

Figure 3-24
The Web Settings dialog box.

Parameters tab

If you constructed your site with a template or wizard that contained pa-rameters for later authors to fill in, or if you've defined your own param-eters, those show up here.

You can add parameters by clicking the Add button. The Add Name And Value dialog box appears, prompting you for the name and value of the parameter (whatever information you want to enter). Click OK to exit the dialog box and add the new parameter to your list.

To change the parameter information, such as in the area-code scenario described above, select the parameter you want to change, click Modify, and then enter the new information in the Modify Name And Value dialog box that appears. Click OK to save the information and exit the dialog box. FrontPage then automatically updates the parameter in all pages of your site on which that parameter appears.

Clicking Remove removes the selected parameter from the list and au-tomatically adjusts pages that contain that parameter

Configuration tab

To change the name and title of your site, click the Configuration tab in the FrontPage Web Settings dialog box, replace the information, and then click OK.

TIP

It's important to give your site a name that you can recognize easily among a list of sites. Each time you open a site to work on it, you select the site from a list. If you create numerous sites on your server, that list can get long and confusing. You can save yourself future headaches by giving your site an intuitive and dis-tinctive name at the outset.

Advanced tab

The Advanced tab of the FrontPage Web Settings dialog box allows you to set or modify advanced settings, including the following:

● You can configure how FrontPage supports *image maps* in the Image Maps section. Image maps are graphic images that contain one or more invisible hyperlinks on various regions of the image. From the Style drop-down list, select the server type for the im-ages, and then set an optional prefix if the Prefix text box is enabled. The default setting, FrontPage, allows you to use image maps no matter what Web server you use, as long as you have the FrontPage Server Extensions installed. Check the Generate Client-Side Image Maps check box if you want FrontPage to generate image maps from the client and not from the server.

It's a good idea to check this check box. FrontPage generates client-side image maps in such a way that if a browser doesn't support client-side image maps, it simply ignores the client-side image map information in the HTML file. Therefore, checking this check box can cause no harm, and in fact, often gives you gains in speed—see Chapter 8 for more details.

● In the Default Scripting Languages section, you can specify the scripting languages for the Client and the Server. The options available are VBScript and JavaScript. To learn more about using scripting languages in FrontPage, see Chapter 10.

If you use the Form Field Validation feature, described in Chapter 9, FrontPage automatically generates JavaScript or VBScript right on the page to perform the validation. This setting allows you to select which language to use. If you use JavaScript, it works with both Internet Explorer and Netscape Navigator. If you choose VBScript, it works only with Internet Explorer.

● In the Options section, check the Show Documents In Hidden Directories check box to display documents in hidden folders. Hidden folders are preceded by an underscore (_). By default, you can't view pages and files in hidden folders in FrontPage. This feature allows you to act as a moderator for a discussion group; individual messages in a discussion are kept in a hidden folder.

Language tab

The Language tab allows you to set the default language, the Server Message, and the Default Page Encoding for your site. The Server Message setting is used by the FrontPage Server Extensions so that when error messages need to be returned to the browser, the specified language is used. The Default Page Encoding setting specifies the default character set for new pages.

Even if the FrontPage user interface isn't available for a particular language, you can still create sites for essentially any language, using the extensive list of HTML encodings available from this dialog box.

Navigation tab

If you're using Navigation Bars in your site, you can customize the labels on the navigation bars here. Just enter the new text in the appropriate fields and click OK. For more information on Navigation Bars, see Chapter 7.

Database tab

On the Database tab in the FrontPage Web settings dialog box, you can Add, Modify, Remove, and Verify any database associated with your Web. You can view the status of the database as well as its name. For more information on using databases in FrontPage, see Chapter 10.

Configuring Editors

Have you ever opened a file from Windows Explorer? If you have, you know that the file opens in an application in which it can be viewed and edited. FrontPage offers the same feature. When you double-click a file in your Web such as a GIF or JPEG file or any Office file, FrontPage opens the file in the application specified in Windows Explorer.

If you want to invoke an editor that's different from the one currently specified in Windows Explorer, here's how. Begin by choosing Options from the Tools menu. The Options dialog box appears (see Figure 3-25). Click the Configure Editors tab.

Figure 3-25
The Configure Editors tab of the Options dialog box.

The list box on the tab has two columns, one for the extension of the file type to edit and the other for the application that's used to edit the file. As you can see, the dialog box includes default settings for some common file types and their editors.

To add a file type, click the Add button. The Add Editor Association dialog box opens. Add the extension that identifies the file type in the File Type text box, and enter the name you want to use for the editor in the Editor Name text box. Then enter the name and location of the executable file (the

CHAPTER 3

one that launches the application) in the Command text box. If you don't know its exact location, click the Browse button to search your folders for the executable file. When you finish, click OK.

To modify settings for an existing entry, select the entry and then click the Modify button. This takes you to the Modify Editor Association dialog box, where you can change the editor name and the command that executes the editor.

You can also remove an entry in the list by clicking the entry and clicking Remove.

FrontPage allows you to designate only one editor application per file type. If you don't specify an editor for a particular file type, FrontPage uses the default Windows editor for that file type.

TIP

FrontPage doesn't ask you to confirm the removal of an entry on the Configure Editors tab when you click Remove. If you remove an entry by mistake, you must reenter it by clicking Add.

Recalculating Hyperlinks

Recalculating hyperlinks updates, or refreshes, your site. If you've made significant changes to your site, such as removing entire pages, it's wise to go through the recalculating hyperlinks operation. This is especially true if you've added, deleted, or modified documents in your site without using FrontPage. All you need to do is choose Recalculate Hyperlinks from the Tools menu. FrontPage warns you that the process might take a long time and asks you if you want to proceed. You can recalculate hyperlinks in any view.

When you use this command, FrontPage performs the following tasks:

● It updates the display for the current site in the Explorer views.

● It updates your list of links for the current site. If you delete material from your site, it's a good idea to use the Recalculate Hyperlinks command to ensure that the latest changes are recognized.

● It updates the text index that's created by a FrontPage Search Component. When you implement searching on a page using this FrontPage component, FrontPage creates a text index for the component to use. When you add a page or save a modified page in your site, entries are added to the text index, but no entries are deleted. Thus, if you delete material from a page and then save the modified page, the text index still contains entries for the deleted material. Whenever you delete material, including entire

PART

II

pages, from your site, you need to use the Recalculate Hyperlinks command to update the text index. For more information on the FrontPage Search Component, see Chapter 9.

Coming Up

As you can see, you can use FrontPage not only to view a Web, but also to build and manage it. The next chapter describes how to use two additional key parts of FrontPage—templates and wizards.

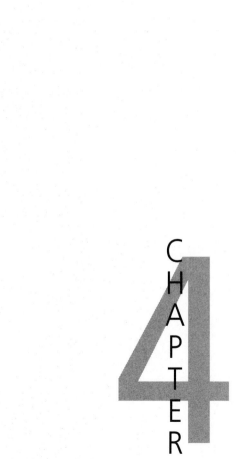

CHAPTER 4

Templates
and Wizards

Life in the Fast Lane

Imagine what an announcer would say if Microsoft FrontPage 2000 were ever featured in a late-night infomercial: "Tired of staying up night after night memorizing thousands of HTML commands? Tired of taking hours and hours to create that one final page that'll make your Web shine?" In a fictitious world, you'd also be really excited about the prospect of losing five pounds and getting great abs while sitting there creating Web sites. But we're here to tell you that, with its templates and wizards, FrontPage can actually save you so much time that you might even be able to take your family on that three-week cross-country trip to Wally World that you've been dreaming about for the past fifteen years.

Everyone's looking for a shortcut, and FrontPage gives you a huge one—you don't have to know a lick of HTML to create professional-looking Webs. FrontPage also provides a couple of other pretty cool shortcuts in its templates and wizards. A *template,* as you might know, is a "shell" that you use as the basis for a new document. A *wizard* is an interactive software module of one or more screens that asks you questions, offers you choices, and then generates a customized document as a result. Using both templates and wizards, you can produce a document that will serve as a framework for your finished product—a framework that you can modify if you like and use as a container for your content.

This chapter explores FrontPage's templates and wizards. It shows you how to work with them, and it gives you plenty of examples along the way. You'll find that using templates and wizards is a terrific way to get started on your Web and that they're sensational time-savers as well.

Templates

Templates are examples of Webs or pages that FrontPage provides to fill a particular need. Like wizards, they give you a framework or solid starting point for a Web or a page; when you choose a template, you get an exact copy of the template itself, containing dummy text that you replace with your own copy. Wizards, however, offer you interactive, real-time choices to help you create a customized Web or page.

Web Templates

Most of the Web templates in FrontPage are based on small Webs; they have few items that need customizing. You can, however, enhance these pages by adding images, text, links, and other items while you're in FrontPage's Page view. You can also add your own pages to Webs you create using Web templates.

You can access the Web templates in FrontPage by choosing New from the File menu and then choosing Web from the submenu that appears. In the New dialog box (see Figure 4-1), you can select one of the following Web templates to use as the basis for your Web or page:

- **One Page Web.** If you want to start with the most basic of Webs, this is the template for you. The One Page Web template does just what you'd expect—it creates a Web that contains only a single page, which has no content.

- **Customer Support Web**. This template creates a place where your customers can go to report bugs, to find solutions to previously reported problems, and to suggest improvements for your products and services. This is an ideal Web for software companies, but it's applicable to many other kinds of businesses, too.

- **Empty Web**. When you want to create an entire Web from scratch, you can use this template. It creates an empty Web that contains no pages. You do all the rest by adding content in FrontPage.

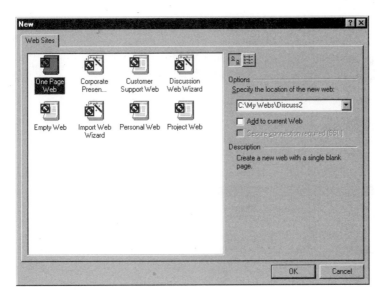

Figure 4-1

The Web Sites tab of the New dialog box showing Web templates.

- **Personal Web**. If you're creating a Web where you want to high-light your personal interests, along with some pictures and links, try out the Personal Web template.

- **Project Web**. Use this template to create a Web that serves as a central informational forum for a project. This template creates a home page, a page that lists members of the project team, a sched-ule page, a status page, a search page, various forms and discus-sion pages, and a page that links to all public discussions about the project.

The other Web templates listed in the New dialog box are Web wiz-ards. I talk more about the Web wizards in "Web Wizards," later in this chapter.

Page Templates

FrontPage offers you a wide variety of page templates, ranging from a bare-bones Normal page to a fairly complex Three-Column Staggered page. Adding pages to an existing Web with a page template is a fast and easy way to customize a Web.

Using page templates

In order to use a page template, you must be in Page view. (For more information on Page view, see Chapter 6.) The process is simple:

1. Select Page view by clicking the Page icon on the View menu.

2. Choose New from the File menu and then choose Page from the submenu.

3. In the New dialog box that appears, select a template from the General tab (see Figure 4-2), and then click OK.

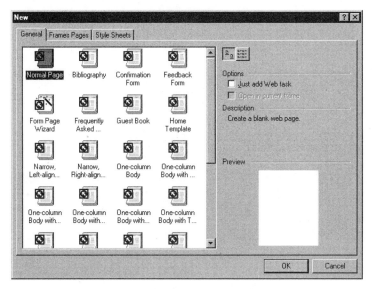

Figure 4-2
The General tab of the New dialog box, Page option.

NOTE

The list of Page templates also includes the Form Page Wizard; for more information on this wizard, see "The Form Page Wizard" later in this chapter. The New dialog box also contains a Frames Pages tab and a Style Sheets tab. For more information on creating frames pages, see the next section, "Making Frames"; for more information on style sheets, see Chapter 10.

You can choose from a wide variety of page templates to create new pages in your Web. The templates are listed in the window on the left side of the New dialog box; a description and preview of each appears on the right side of the dialog box. You can view the templates as a list or as large icons by clicking the appropriate button, located above the description. If you have a frameset currently open (frames and framesets are discussed later in this chapter) and you want your new page to open the current frame, select the Open In Current Frame check box. If you want to add the new page to the Tasks view so that it can be worked on later, select the Just Add Web Task check box.

You'll find that the templates have many varied uses and that some of them are designed to be used together in the same Web. Take a look through the templates; if you know your options, you'll be better prepared to create the Web you want.

When you finally decide on a template, FrontPage creates a page using the template you select and then presents it in Page view for you to work on.

Whenever you create a new page from a page template, it includes dummy text, or "lorem ipsum ..." (sometimes called *Greek text*) to show where your text can go, and placeholder text, like "Place Main Title Here," that you replace with your own text. The example shown in Figure 4-3, created with the Two-Column Staggered Body page template, shows both dummy text and placeholder text.

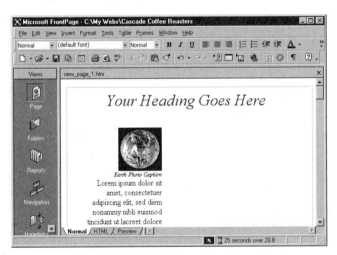

Figure 4-3
Page view showing the Two-Column Staggered Body page template.

Making Frames

Frames enable you to divide a browser page into rectangular regions, each of which displays its own page. You can place one or more frames on a page. The collection of the "frames" pages, and the information needed to present them correctly in the browser, is referred to as a *frameset,* which is actually a separate page that the viewer never sees. This means that you can create a page on which different regions have different content. Changing the content of one region doesn't necessarily change the content of another, but if you want, links in one frame can cause the page displayed in another frame to change.

Here's a classic example of the use of frames: Imagine a Web page divided vertically into two regions, each of which is a frame. The left frame is occupied by a Contents page, containing a complete list of links to all pages in the Web. The content of the frame on the right side of the screen changes depending on what link you click in the table of contents on the left side. If you click a link to an Issues page in the Contents frame, the Issues page appears on the right side; if you click the Results link, the Results page appears, and so on. Figure 4-4 depicts such a scenario.

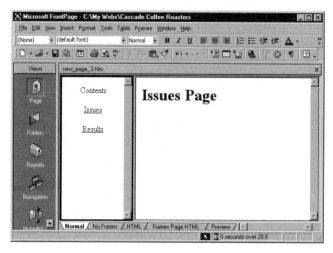

Figure 4-4

A page divided into frames. Click a link in the Contents on the left side, and that page appears on the right side.

Frames have become very popular with Web designers, some of whom have gotten a little carried away, dividing their pages into five, six, or even more frames. Because the use of so many frames can make a Web really slow to appear (not to mention annoying), FrontPage gives you ten frame templates, each containing no more than four frames in the frameset.

Using frame templates

You create a frames page by using a frame template in Page view. The process goes like this:

1. Select Page view by clicking the Page icon on the View menu.

2. Choose New from the File menu and then choose Page from the submenu.

3. In the New dialog box that appears, select a template from the Frames Pages tab (see Figure 4-5), and then click OK.

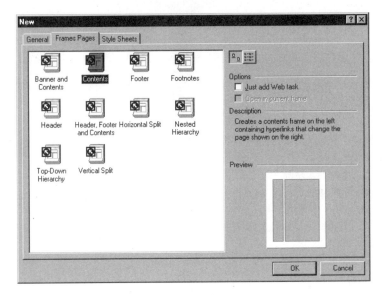

Figure 4-5

The Frames Pages tab of the New dialog box, Page option.

In the New dialog box, you can preview how your frameset will look when it's built. After you decide on a frameset, FrontPage builds the necessary pages. For more information on working with frames, see Chapter 6.

Custom Templates

Because everyone has a different style, and because you might have specific needs that the predefined templates don't address, FrontPage allows you to create and save your own page templates. (To find out how to create custom Web templates, see the next section, "Custom Web Templates.")

Perhaps you want to create several similar pages that don't look much like any of the existing FrontPage templates. If you create your own template to use when generating these pages, you can minimize the number of changes you need to make to each. Of course, you can always open a FrontPage page template, alter it to suit your needs, and then use that as a new template.

CHAPTER 4

For example, using a custom page template is a great way to stream-line the gathering of employee information at a company. You can create a specific form that has places for each kind of information you need from your employees and then save that form as a template. You can then distribute that template within your organization for all to use.

Creating and saving a custom page template requires only a few steps:

1. Start with the Normal Page template and insert the content that you want to appear in your new template, for example, custom logos, navigation buttons, and so forth.

2. Choose the Save As command from the File menu. You'll see the Save As dialog box. In the Save As Type drop-down list, select FrontPage Template.

3. Give your template a file name, such as *formtemplate*.

4. Click OK in the Save As dialog box, and you'll see the Save As Template dialog box, shown in Figure 4-6, containing the file name you entered in step 3.

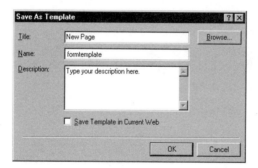

Figure 4-6

The Save As Template dialog box.

5. Change any information that you want, and add a description of the template in the Description text box. If you want to save the current template in place of another template, click Browse and find the template that you want to replace.

6. Click OK in the Save As Template dialog box. FrontPage warns you that it's saving this new template in a folder on your Web. Click Yes; FrontPage then saves the page as a template and returns you to Page view.

Once you've saved the template, that template (including the description you entered) appears in the New dialog box whenever you create a new

PART

page, along with all the page templates and wizards included with FrontPage. If you want to save your template to a different location, include a path name in the Title field of the Save As Template dialog box.

Custom Web Templates

You can use the FrontPage Developer's Kit to create both custom Web templates and custom Web and page wizards. For information on how to obtain this free kit, see the FrontPage area of Microsoft's Web site at www.microsoft.com/frontpage/.

Wizards

How long do you suppose it would take to create, from scratch, a Web for your business that includes all of the following?

- A home page that has places for an introduction, mission statement, company profile, and contact information

- A What's New page that contains links for press releases, articles, reviews, and information about your Web

- Numerous products and services pages, each having room for a description of the product or service, images, pricing information, and more

- A Table of Contents page that indexes your Web and that is updated automatically as your Web structure changes

- A feedback form that asks users for specific information, such as their name, title, address, phone number, fax number, and e-mail address

Using HTML to create a Web that includes all of this would take quite a long time. For many, it would be akin to putting an automobile together piece by piece—it's easy to see where the big pieces go, but incorporating the smaller pieces and getting them all to work together smoothly is difficult. Would you believe that when you use FrontPage, creating a Web like the one just described can take less than five minutes? You can do it all by using the Corporate Presence Web Wizard (one of several wizards included with FrontPage) and then customizing the Web with a couple of dozen clicks of the mouse and a little typing here and there. When you're done, you have a set of linked pages complete with elements that are ready for you to customize further.

FrontPage offers two Web wizards that create the framework for entire Webs, plus an additional Web wizard that allows you to import non-FrontPage Webs. FrontPage also includes one page wizard, the Form Page wizard, which creates a form page that you can use to collect information

CHAPTER 4

from Web visitors and then save that information back to a page on your Web or to a text file on the server.

Web Wizards

The two Web wizards that create brand new FrontPage Webs for you are the Corporate Presence Web Wizard and the Discussion Web Wizard. The Corporate Presence Web Wizard creates the framework for a Web that includes the items described in the previous section. The Discussion Web Wizard produces a Web in which users can participate in discussions on various topics. Let's examine the Corporate Presence Web Wizard first and then the Discussion Web Wizard.

Keep in mind that you can easily change a Web-wizard-produced Web later if you want to. You can add to the pages, delete items or pages, and modify the pages in any other way you like.

Corporate Presence Web Wizard

Using the Corporate Presence Web Wizard, you can create a Web to showcase your business without having to do much up-front work. Let's step through the process of using this wizard, as someone might when designing a Web for the fictitious Snake River Winery:

1. In any view, choose New from the File menu, and then choose Web from the submenu. In the New dialog box that appears, select Corporate Presence Wizard.

2. Give your new Web a name and location (for the purposes of this example, use SRW for Snake River Winery), verify the location, and then click OK. FrontPage warns you that there is no folder called SRW, and it asks you if you want to create one; click Yes. FrontPage begins to build the Web's folder structure at the location you specified in the New dialog box. For more information on changing the location, see Chapter 3.

3. Now you'll see the opening screen of the Corporate Presence Web Wizard (see Figure 4-7). It contains a brief description of the wizard and informs you that you need to answer a few questions about how you want your Web to appear. Several buttons appear at the bottom of the screen:

    ● **Cancel.** Clicking Cancel stops the wizard and takes you back to the Explorer. Because some of the material for the Web has already been created, you are asked whether to delete the Web.

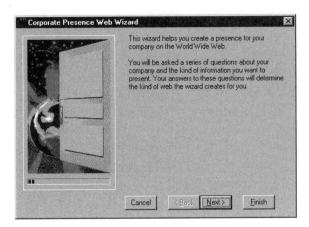

Figure 4-7

The opening screen of the Corporate Presence Web Wizard.

- **Back.** When the Back button is available, you can click it to return to the previous screen or screens and change any information you have already entered.

- **Next.** Clicking Next takes you to the next screen in the wizard.

- **Finish.** The Finish button ends the wizard process at whatever point you click it. You can stop using the wizard at any time before the final wizard screen. When you click Finish, FrontPage immediately begins to populate the Web with all the information you've supplied up to that point.

  Click Next to proceed.

4. The screen shown in Figure 4-7 gives you several options for pages to include in your Web. Notice that the Back button is now available.

   The Snake River Winery is building a sophisticated Web and intends to include all of the available types of pages (see Figure 4-8, on the next page). The Web starts with a required home page, the contents of which you can customize in the next step of the wizard.

   - **What's New page**. For users who return to the Web many times, this page can provide information on recent updates to the Web. Perhaps a new Merlot is being offered in the fall, or maybe there's a special group rate for tours of the winery in July. The What's New page can link to these items in your Web.

CHAPTER 4

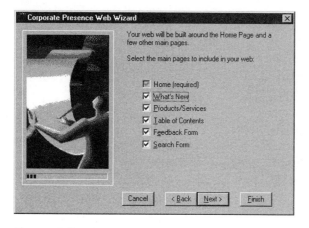

Figure 4-8

*The main page options screen for the Corporate Presence
Web Wizard.*

● **Products/Services page**. Simply because the winery sells
   products, and especially because the products have mass
   appeal, the Products/Services page is a wise addition to the
   Web. Here the winery can highlight all its wines and other
   products; this also might be a good place to tell people how
   to order.

● **Table of Contents page**. Those who want to see an overview of what the winery's Web has to offer can go to this
   page, which links to all other pages in the Web. It's wise to
   include some sort of overview page in your Web. These
   pages can help prevent users from getting lost in your Web.

● **Feedback Form**. The winery management wants to know
   what users think of the products offered in the Web and what
   they think of the Web itself. Visitors to the site can use the
   Feedback Form to submit comments to the winery.

● **Search Form**. The winery considers a search form an at-
   tractive feature for its Web. It allows users to search the Web
   for any word that might appear on its pages. Enabling the
   search form is easy: just select the Search Form check box
   in the wizard. FrontPage automatically compiles a word list
   that the search form uses when someone searches the Web.

   For each page that you decide to include in your Web, the
   wizard presents you with a subsequent screen that you can use

to further customize the page. The wizard shows no screens for pages you don't select in this screen.

Click Next when you're ready to move on.

5. A screen appears that presents several options for the format of your home page (see Figure 4-9). Your choices include creating spaces for an introduction, mission statement, company profile, and contact information for your company. You're not asked to supply the exact information (such as the text of your mission statement) at this time; you enter that later in Page view. The wizard simply creates a space for you to fill with the actual content at your leisure.

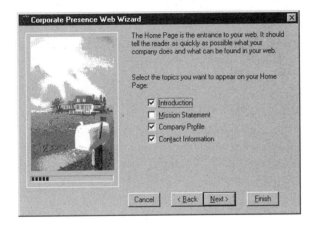

Figure 4-9

The home page topics screen for the Corporate Presence Web Wizard.

The folks at the Snake River Winery want their Web to look professional, so at the very least, they'll include the introduction, company profile, and contact information. Including the contact information is vital; potential wholesalers or individual customers who view the Web might want to find out more about purchasing products.

Select the check boxes for the topics you want to include, and then click Next.

6. Options for the What's New page appear in the next screen, shown in Figure 4-10, on the next page. Select any of the three check boxes if you want to include that type of information on the page. FrontPage creates subsections for any items that you want to include on the What's New page.

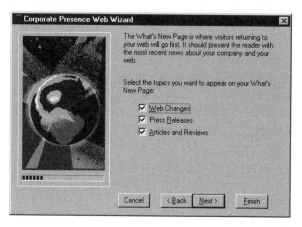

Figure 4-10

The What's New page topics screen for the Corporate Presence Web Wizard.

If a contact phone number changes at the Snake River Winery, the winery can alert its Web visitors to the new number on the What's New page in the Web Changes section. You easily can add any other breaking news about the company to this page later on.

The What's New page is also a great place to put information about the industry, such as a list of upcoming trade shows, positive information about stock trends, or other business news. It's great to have a place in your Web where visitors can expect new, timely content. Such information can lure customers back to your pages, where they'll be exposed to your products again and again. You can use the Press Releases section and the Articles And Reviews section for this purpose.

Select the kind of information you want to include on your page to start with, and click Next.

7. The next screen provides options for the Products/Services page (see Figure 4-11). Enter the values for the number of products and services you want to feature on this page; FrontPage allows you to enter between 0 and 5 for each. The wizard creates sections on the page for the number of products and services you enter in this screen.

The Snake River Winery plans to highlight its three best wines in the Web, so enter *3* in the Products box. The winery also prides itself on providing top-flight customer service, so enter *1* in the Services box to provide a section to highlight that aspect of the company.

Click Next to move to the next screen.

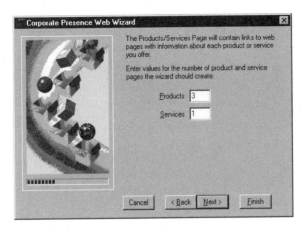

Figure 4-11

*The Products/Services page options screen for the Corporate
Presence Web Wizard.*

8. In this screen (see Figure 4-12, below) you specify how you want
   to customize any product or service pages you have in your Web.
   The wizard shown in the figure gives you choices for providing
   placeholders for product images, pricing information, and information request forms on the Products pages, and for providing
   capabilities lists, reference accounts, and information request
   forms on Services pages.

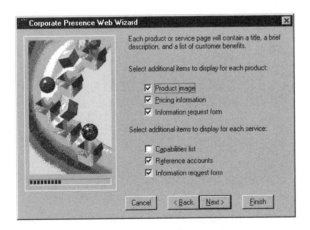

Figure 4-12

*The Products/Services item placeholders screen for the Corporate
Presence Web Wizard.*

Select the options you want to include on those pages, and then click Next.

You can tab through the content options in the wizard screens instead of using your mouse. To check or clear a check box, use the spacebar.

9. The next screen provides options for the Feedback Form, shown in Figure 4-13, where you specify the information you want to receive from your audience. Think carefully about this, keeping in mind the kind of audience you expect to view your pages. If the audience doesn't have plenty of time to fill out every item, seeing many items at once might overwhelm them. Even though it takes only seconds to fill out a feedback form, Web surfers tend to click out of a page if it looks like too much work.

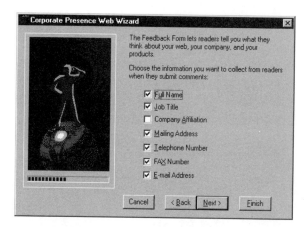

Figure 4-13

The Feedback Form options screen for the Corporate Presence Web Wizard.

Select the options you want for the Feedback Form, and then click Next.

10. The next screen, shown in Figure 4-14, features a neat option: it allows you to specify how to store the feedback you receive from your visitors. If you plan to manipulate the information using a database or spreadsheet application (such as Microsoft Access or Microsoft Excel), select the first option; FrontPage then stores

PART
II

the information in tab-delimited format. If you don't plan to use such an application, select the second option to have FrontPage store the information in Web page format.

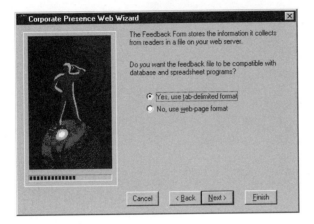

Figure 4-14
The feedback storage options screen for the Corporate Presence Web Wizard.

The Snake River Winery is not a large company, but management does expect its Web to receive heavy traffic. It's easier and reduces company workload to manipulate feedback information in Access and Excel, so management wants to save the feedback information in tab-delimited format. So, select the Yes, Use Tab-Delimited Format option.

Make your choice, and then click Next to continue.

11. Here you see a screen that presents options for customizing the Table of Contents (TOC) page, shown in Figure 4-15, on the next page. You can select options to update the TOC automatically each time a page is edited, to show pages not linked to the pages that appear in the TOC, and to use bullets for top-level pages.

If you anticipate that your Web will be small or that it won't be updated often, it's a good idea to select the Keep Page List Up-To-Date Automatically check box. If you anticipate that your Web will be large or that it will grow significantly, however, you should not select this check box, because updating the page list can be time-consuming in these cases. You can update the TOC manually later on, so don't be overly concerned about this option.

Select the options you want to customize your TOC page, and click Next.

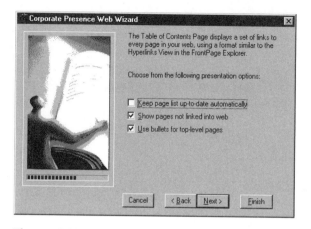

Figure 4-15

The Table of Contents options screen for the Corporate Presence Web Wizard.

12. The next screen you see deals with the items that you want to appear at the top and bottom of every page in your Web (see Figure 4-16) . You can include your company's logo, a page title, and links to your main Web pages at the top. Other items you might choose to include are links to your main Web pages at the bottom, along with your Webmaster's e-mail address, a copyright notice, and the date on which the page was last modified (which FrontPage automatically supplies).

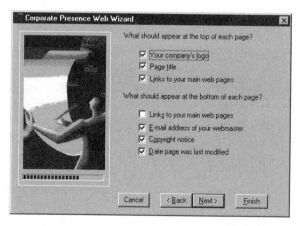

Figure 4-16

The options screen for top and bottom of page in the Corporate Presence Web Wizard.

Again, these options control whether or not FrontPage leaves room for the item, not the actual content of each item. You can select all of the options you want, even if you plan to use different items on different pages.

The Winery Web will sport a different logo for the pages in each section, so select the Your Company's Logo check box to include a space for the logo. Later, you can manually insert a different logo at the beginning of each page.

FrontPage doesn't check the contents of each space, so you can be flexible in how you use these options. If the winery wants to include the e-mail address of someone other than the Webmaster on the pages, for example, you should select the E-mail Address Of Your Webmaster check box to leave the space open. You can change the e-mail address later on.

Select the options you want, and then click Next.

13. The next screen gives you the option of showing an Under Construction icon on all unfinished pages of your Web, shown below in Figure 4-17.

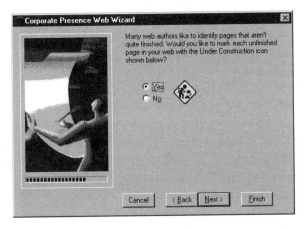

Figure 4-17
Corporate Presence Web Wizard, Under Construction options screen.

Select Yes and then click Next.

14. The next two screens, shown in Figures 4-18 and 4-19 (on the next page), ask for your company information, such as the company's full name, one-word name, address, phone number, and fax number; the e-mail address of the Webmaster; and a general-information e-mail address. These options are huge potential time

savers, because you enter the information just once, and FrontPage inserts the information in the placeholders already in your Web. For example, in an earlier screen of the wizard (refer back to Figure 4-15), if you requested that FrontPage display your Webmaster's e-mail address at the bottom of every page, all you need to do is type the address here, and FrontPage inserts that address in every page.

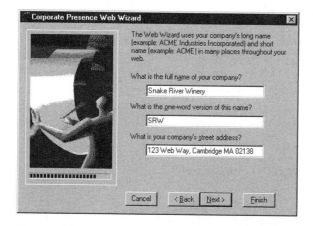

Figure 4-18

The first screen for company information in the Corporate Presence Web Wizard.

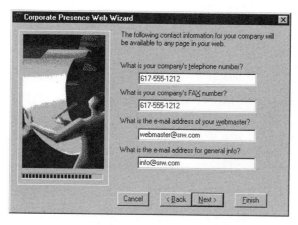

Figure 4-19

The second screen for company information in the Corporate Presence Web Wizard.

If you need to make changes to this information later on, you need to change it in only one place. (You can change these settings later on by choosing the Web Settings command on the Tools menu.)

The Snake River Winery wants to start with all of this information on its pages, even though it might decide later not to include some of it.

Enter this information in both screens, and click Next to move on.

15. In the next screen, you can control the "look and feel" of your Web using the FrontPage Web Themes, as shown in Figure 4-20.

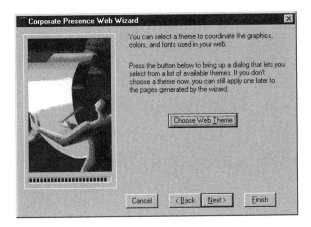

Figure 4-20

Options for choosing Web Themes in the Corporate Presence Web Wizard.

If you want to use one of the FrontPage Web Themes, click Choose Web Theme. The Choose Theme dialog box opens, as shown in Figure 4-21, on the next page. (For more information on the Themes, see Chapter 7.)

Scroll through the list of themes and decide which one best fits your Web. Snake River Winery wants the Web to have a rugged look, so we'll use the Expedition theme and select Vivid Colors, Active Graphics, Background Image, and Apply Theme Using CSS.

After you choose a theme, click OK.

CHAPTER 4

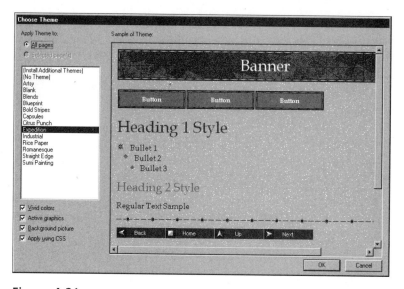

Figure 4-21

The Choose Theme dialog box.

16. Now you're back in the Corporate Presence Web Wizard, right where you left off.

The final screen, shown in Figure 4-22, tells you that FrontPage has gathered all the information it needs to create your Corporate Presence Web. It includes a Show Tasks View After Web Is Uploaded check box. Tasks view is a list of tasks that need to be completed in your Web. FrontPage adds several tasks to the list after it creates this Web; among them are the tasks of customizing various pages by adding specific text and other files and of replacing images. Chapter 3 explains Tasks view in greater detail.

Click Finish, and FrontPage fills in the Corporate Presence Web, in the location you specified, using the information you supplied, and then it saves the Web. FrontPage then opens in Tasks view, because we've directed it to do so. From this point on, you can fill in the fine details of your Web and personalize it to suit your needs.

That's all there is to creating the structure for a Web using the Corporate Presence Web Wizard—a bunch of tiny steps, all of which add up to enormous time savings.

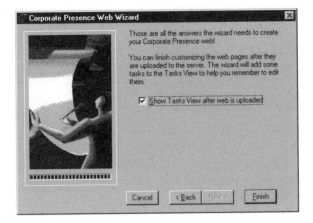

Figure 4-22
Options for displaying Tasks view in the Corporate Presence Web Wizard.

Discussion Web Wizard

The Discussion Web Wizard creates a threaded discussion group about a topic of your choice. Site designers often add a discussion group to an existing Web; such groups can be useful Web components. Each user can contribute thoughts and associate them with a particular ongoing conversation (*thread*). Each separate entry from a user is referred to as an *article*. The user also has the ability to search for existing articles. The wizard asks you to decide the following:

- What kinds of pages you want to include
- The title of the discussion
- Some input fields to separate topics of discussion
- Whether the discussion will take place in a protected Web (meaning that only registered users can participate)
- How the table of contents should sort the posted articles
- Whether the Table of Contents page should be the Web's home page
- The information you want reported about each article found in a search of past discussions
- The colors for the background and text
- Whether you want to create the Web using frames

As always, you can change the Web as needed and add or delete features to these pages later on.

97

Administering a Discussion Group.

You can administer a discussion group in FrontPage quite easily. If you're in charge of administering such a group, here are a few things you can do:

- **Edit articles**. Each page that a user completes and sends to the discussion group is called an article. FrontPage saves articles as HTML files in a hidden folder, typically named _disc1_. To see a list of articles, you need to tell FrontPage to show files in hidden directories. You can do this by choosing Web Settings from the Tools menu, clicking the Advanced tab, and then checking the Show Documents In Hidden Directories check box. When you click OK, a dialog box appears asking you if you want to refresh the Web now. If you click Yes, the hidden pages will appear.

  You edit an article by first finding it in the discussion folder and then double-clicking it. The article appears in Page view, where you can delete text—such as objectionable language. You can then save the modified article and users will be able to view the edited article.

- **Delete old articles.** If you can see the files in hidden folders, you can sort the files and delete messages that are no longer needed. In Folder view, sort the list of files in the discussion Web by date, and then delete any files that you don't need by selecting them and pressing the Delete key.

  You can limit access to your Web by allowing only registered users to access the site. In the Discussion Web Wizard, a screen gives you the option to have all discussions take place in a protected Web, which means that only registered users of the discussion Web can access the articles. If you opt to use the protected Web, FrontPage gives you some simple directions for steps to complete on a registration page after you complete the wizard and create the Web.

Import Web Wizard

If you have other Web sites that you'd like to turn into FrontPage Webs, you can use the Import Web Wizard to do so. This wizard imports a folder of files from your hard disk or LAN and creates a new FrontPage Web from them. The folder doesn't necessarily have to be a complete Web site; any folder of files that you want to use to create a FrontPage Web will do.

Here are the sweet-and-simple directions for importing sites using the Import Web Wizard:

1. Choose New from the File menu, and then choose Web from the submenu.

2. In the New dialog box, select the Import Web Wizard, specify a name and location for the new Web, and then click OK. FrontPage warns you that the name and location don't exist and then automatically creates the folder. The Import Web Wizard dialog box appears (see Figure 4-23).

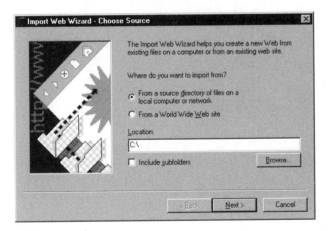

Figure 4-23
The opening screen of The Import Web Wizard - Choose Source dialog box.

NOTE

You can also access the Import Web Wizard by selecting Import from the File menu and then choosing From Web in the resulting Import File To FrontPage Web dialog box.

3. In the Import Web Wizard - Choose Source screen (shown above), choose whether you want to import from a local computer or network, or from a World Wide Web site.

If you select the first option, you must locate the folder of files you want to import. Click Browse, select the folder in the Browse For Folder dialog box, and click OK. If the folder includes subfolders of files you want to import as well, select the Include Subfolders check box in the Import Web Wizard - Choose Source screen.

If you choose the second option, From a World Wide Web site, you must enter a Web location, and if the server requires SSL, select that check box. These options are shown in Figure 4-24.

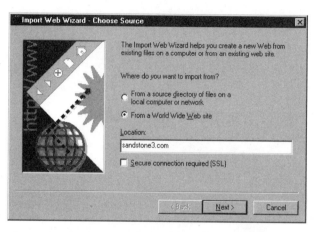

Figure 4-24

The Import Web Wizard - Choose Source dialog box, showing Web site as the source.

Click Next to continue.

4. If you chose to import from a local computer or network, you see the Import Web Wizard - Edit File List dialog box, shown in Figure 4-25, which contains a list of all the files (including files in subfolders) within the folder you selected. You can specify which files to import at this stage. If you plan to create a new Web and you're importing an older Web as part of it, for example, you might not want to include certain files if you don't plan to use them.

To omit a file from the list of files to be imported to your new Web, select the file and click Exclude. If you remove some items from the list and want to start over with the original list, click Refresh, and the original list will appear again.

When you're satisfied that you want to include all the items in the list in your new FrontPage Web, click Next.

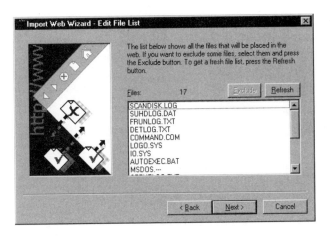

Figure 4-25

The Import Web Wizard - Edit File List dialog box.

5. If you chose to import from the World Wide Web, click Next, and then you see the Import Web Wizard - Choose Download Amount dialog box, shown in Figure 4-26. Here you set limits for levels and file sizes, and you have the option to limit the import to text and image files, as well.

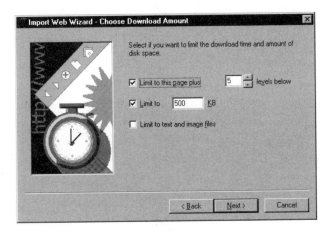

Figure 4-26

The Import Web Wizard - Choose Download Amount dialog box.

Select the options you require and then click Next.

6. You see the Import Web Wizard - Edit File List screen (See Figure 4-25), which contains a list of all the files, including files in subfolders, within the folder you selected. You can specify which files to import at this stage. For example, if you plan to create a new Web and you're importing an older site as part of it, you might not want to include certain files if you don't plan to use them. Select the options that you require, and then click Next.

7. Now you've reached the Import Web Wizard - Finish screen, the last screen of the wizard. Click Finish to have FrontPage create the new Web. If you want to change some information you've entered in the wizard previously, click Back until you reach the screen that contains the information that you want to modify. Change the information and then click Next until you reach this final wizard screen once again.

That's all it takes for FrontPage to import a folder of files and create a new Web from them. FrontPage preserves the old folder structure that you've imported and adds its own folders to the Web, such as the _private and images folders for storing private and image files, respectively.

Form Page Wizard

The Form Page Wizard creates a form that you can use to gather input from users and save the results to a Web page or text file on the Web server. This form can be useful in situations in which you need to gather contact information, account information, product information, and so on, from your visitors. You can place the resulting page in your Web and link it to other pages.

Using the Form Page Wizard

To add a page to your Web using the Form Page Wizard, do the following:

1. Select the Page icon from the view menu in FrontPage.

2. Choose New from the File menu and choose Page from the submenu. Select the General tab in the New dialog box that appears.

3. From the list of page templates, select the Form Page Wizard. Note that when you select a template or a wizard, a description of the item appears in the upper right portion of the New dialog box. After you select the wizard, click OK.

4. Move through the screens of the wizard and answer the questions that FrontPage asks you. Using these wizards is the same as using the Corporate Presence Wizard, described earlier in this chapter, but the questions are, of course, different. For example, FrontPage asks you to name the page instead of a Web.

PART
II

5. When you reach the final screen, click Finish; FrontPage creates the page and displays it in Page view. You can then edit the page, adding text and/or images, linking it to other pages, and so on.

Custom Wizards

Anyone can create custom Web wizards and page wizards for FrontPage using Microsoft Visual Basic or Microsoft Visual C++. You can learn how by consulting the FrontPage Developer's Kit. Look in the FrontPage area of Microsoft's Web site at **www.microsoft.com/frontpage/** for information on obtaining this free kit.

FrontPage templates and wizards can free up some extra time for you to get more things done in your life. Maybe they'll even free up enough time that you can put up one of your favorite signs on your office door: "Gone to the Monster Truck Races…GO BIGFOOT!!!"

Coming Up

Speaking of freeing up time, FrontPage also helps you to implement security, manage tasks, update content, do testing, and go live with your Web. Chapter 5 looks at these topics.

CHAPTER 4

Managing
Your
Web Site

FrontPage Makes It Easy

You've worked hard to plan and design your Web, and you've started putting it together. You've begun to turn all those ideas into actual pages, and now—"Whoa there, varmint! How am I ever going to get all this done? Who's going to make sure it's kept up-to-date? How can I be sure it works perfectly before it goes online? And how can I be sure that my office mate, G.T. Trustnomore, who makes more than I do with half the talent, doesn't get into my Web and mess it up?"

Dozens of questions like these can go through your mind at all stages of developing your Web, especially if your company or organization has a large Web-site development team. But even one-person development teams have to consider numerous Web-site issues. Before those worries running through your head turn into a monster headache, read on to find out how Microsoft FrontPage 2000 simplifies things.

Whenever you think of Web site administration, be happy that you're using FrontPage. FrontPage handles most of your administrative tasks—you can see what work needs to be done in your Web, assign those tasks as necessary, deal with *proxy servers* (also known as *firewalls)*, and much more. This chapter explains how FrontPage helps you deal with all these issues, beginning with security.

Security

In the Old West, security came in the form of a weathered tough guy and his trusty six-shooter. Today, with information traveling over the airwaves and through phone lines at the speed of light, security is trickier—especially when some twelve-year-old hacker from Missouri keeps finding ways to break through even the most complicated security measures. So, when it comes to protecting your Web, you'll be glad to know that FrontPage makes that twelve-year-old kid shake in his boots with fear—well, almost.

Making Use of SSL

Secure Sockets Layer (SSL) is a protocol that allows for secure communication between a server and a client. SSL doesn't prevent access to the communicated data, but it does encrypt the data. In order for SSL to work properly, both the server and the client must support SSL. Both FrontPage and Microsoft Internet Explorer support SSL, as does Netscape Navigator. FrontPage also allows the creation of links that start with **https://** instead of **http://**. Links that start with **https://** indicate a secure link using SSL.

Before you go any further, you'll want to know whether the server you're communicating with supports SSL. There are a couple of ways to find out:

● Check with the person administering the server. It's possible for the administrator to disable SSL support, so it's always a good idea to check first.

● If you're running Microsoft Internet Information Server or Netscape's Commerce, FastTrack, or Enterprise server, you're probably fine. But it can't hurt to check with the server's administrator in these cases, too.

When you have an SSL-enabled Web server and when you enable SSL in FrontPage, all communications between the FrontPage client and the server are secure. This means that the information is encrypted as it travels between FrontPage and the Web server, wherever they're located. This security comes in handy in several situations.

● If you're on the road and you need to make changes to a Web that's on a server back home, you can open the Web, make your changes, and save the changes back to the server.

PART
II

- If your business or organization has more than one office but only one Web server, someone at a remote office can make changes to the Web.

- If your corporate or personal Web lies on an Internet service provider's *staging* server (a server that houses in-production Web sites), and you access that server to make changes to your Web using FrontPage, the information is encrypted as you send it. This prevents a hacker from looking at the information before you go live with the Web.

Server Permissions

Web servers often have built-in permission mechanisms that allow you to restrict access by using a password/user name scheme, an IP address mask, or a combination of the two. (Note: Microsoft Internet Information Server and the Windows NT/2000 Workstation Peer Web Services restrict access using standard Windows NT/2000 security, and they don't support access restriction by means of IP address masks.)

An *IP address,* which is a standard way of identifying a computer that is connected to a network, contains four numbers separated by periods; each number is less than 256. An example is 150.200.45.65. An *IP address mask* uses a combination of actual values and asterisks (also known as *wild cards)* to create a model of an acceptable IP address. Masks are used to determine whether a computer has access to a location on the Internet, such as a FrontPage Web. An example of an IP address mask that would permit connections to the IP address above is 150.200.*.*. Computers that have IP addresses beginning with 150.200 would be given access to a FrontPage Web, and computers whose IP addresses do not begin with those numbers would be denied access. If an IP mask is in place, all users must be working on a computer that has access to the location, and they also must have the correct permissions to access the FrontPage Web. By default, all computers are given permission to access FrontPage Webs.

For more information on server permissions, consult your server's documentation.

Proxy Servers

A *proxy server*, also called a firewall, protects a network from uninvited outside access. For example, communication can be inbound—communicating from the outside through the proxy server to your internal server—or it can be outbound—communicating from your server through a proxy to another server on the outside. Communication related to the Web site is permitted only through the proxy, so uninvited guests are barred from your

CHAPTER 5

system.

If your local network uses a proxy server, you must specify that server in order to communicate with it. To specify a proxy server for your machine or to specify any server that can be used without going through the firewall, follow this procedure:

1. Choose Options from the Tools menu and then click the General tab in the Options dialog box, if necessary (see Figure 5-1).

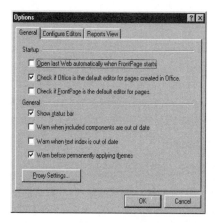

Figure 5-1

The General tab of the Options dialog box.

2. Click the Proxy Settings button. This brings up the Internet Properties dialog box with the Connections tab selected.

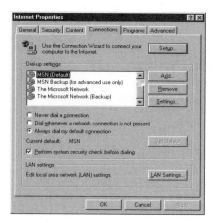

Figure 5-2

The Connections tab of the Internet Properties dialog box.

PART

3. Click the LAN Settings button. This brings up the Local Area Network (LAN) Settings dialog box.

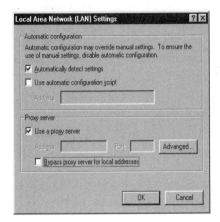

Figure 5-3
The Local Area Network (LAN) Settings dialog box.

4. Select the Use A Proxy Server check box in the Local Area Network dialog box, and then click the Advanced button to bring up the Proxy Settings dialog box.

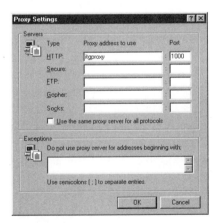

Figure 5-4
The Proxy Settings dialog box.

5. In the HTTP Proxy text box, enter the name of the proxy server and the port, for example, *itgproxy:1000.* You can get the name and port from your network administrator.

You can also create proxy settings for Secure, FTP, Gopher, and Socks protocols. If you want to use the same proxy server for all protocols, select the Use The Same Proxy Server For All Protocols check box. If you want to list exceptions to the proxy settings, add them in the Exceptions section of the Proxy Settings dialog box.

6. After you update the information in the Proxy Settings dialog box, click OK in all dialog boxes to accept your changes.

The proxy server information is saved and used for all future connections, so you don't have to enter the information repeatedly. Whenever you request a connection to a server (for example, when you are following a link), FrontPage checks to see if your organization has servers that are inside the firewall. If the server is available internally, FrontPage makes the connection directly. If not, FrontPage first connects to the proxy server and then has the proxy server connect to the server you want to use. This means that after you supply that information for the proxy server, FrontPage automatically handles all proxy communication, and you don't even have to be aware that a proxy server is in use.

Testing Your Web

Once your Web is all nice and spiffy and you think it'll run just fine, it's always a good idea to test it. Testing can prevent a scenario like the following from happening: It's the morning when you're scheduled to present your finished, working Web to the CEO for final approval. It's a small Web, but you're mighty proud of it. Your office mate, J. G. Clueless, who's jealous over your recent raise and subsequent purchase of a shiny red convertible, drops by the office around 11:30 the night before. J.G. gets into your Web and makes a teensy-weensy change to one of your links. So instead of linking to a profile of the CEO from the See Profile button as you've set it up, the button links to the "Little Johnny Visits the Morgue" Web. As interesting as that Web may be, it's sure to make the CEO think twice about your work.

But you're craftier than Clueless, so you show up a little early the next morning to make sure that your Web runs fine. Here are three techniques you should use to check those links:

● You can check them individually, page by page. It's a slow way to check links, but if you're ever in Page view and want to make sure that a link works, you can put your mouse pointer on the link, press Ctrl, and then click the link. FrontPage takes you to the page to which the link jumps.

- You can wander through your Web using a browser, such as Microsoft Internet Explorer, Netscape Navigator, or any other popular browser, and test each of the links. This way, you can see firsthand that all of the links work, including links to other sites on the Internet.

- You can check the status of all links in Report view. This technique is explained in Chapter 3. However, it verifies only that the targets of your links exist—it doesn't verify that what you linked to is what you intended to link to!

Finally, you can check that your image files are positioned on your pages where you want them. You should do this in Page view and in the various browsers. When testing your images, you want to look for things such as download time and visual quality. For more information about optimizing graphics for the Web, see Chapter 8.

The easiest way to test your Web in a browser is to choose the Preview In Browser command from the File menu. Choosing this command allows you to select any installed browser to view your Web, even at different window sizes (also called *screen resolutions*). Remember, you must be in Page view in order to use this command. For more information on the Preview In Browser command, see Chapter 7.

When you test a Web locally, you often get results that differ from the results you get when you test the same Web over a network or over the Internet, due to variables that can affect speed and information transfer. If you can, test your Web in as many ways as possible, such as

- Locally, on your own computer
- Over a network
- Remotely, over the Internet
- Using modems and other communication devices at different speeds
- On different operating systems
- Using different browsers at different screen settings (such as different resolutions)

Going Live with Your Web

Maybe you have several thousand Benjamin Franklins to spare for the kind of party where you break bottles of champagne against your Web server, but most organizations don't. Nonetheless, going live with an intranet site or a World Wide Web site is still a milestone event, and when the moment arrives, you have to know how to do it.

111

CHAPTER 5

There are a few ways in which you can make your Web accessible to your audience. One common way is to develop your Web on the server on which it will be viewed and let people visit your site as it matures.

If you're not comfortable with people seeing your Web under construction, and if there's simply not enough content to make a visit worthwhile, you can do one of two things: develop your Web locally or limit access to the site's location.

Developing Your Web Locally

FrontPage is a disk-based Web development tool. This means that you don't need to have a server running on the computer where development is taking place. If you want, you can build and manage your FrontPage Webs while storing them on your local hard drive. This can save you plenty of time, as well as serious money on aspirin.

When your Web is complete and you're ready to go live with it, you can easily copy it to its destination Web server with the push of a button, by choosing the Publish Web command from the File menu. When you use this command, you can copy the Web to any of the most popular types of Web servers. For more information on the Publish Web command, see Chapter 3.

Updating Your Web

The World Wide Web is a perfect reflection of information technology in general today—it changes constantly. One day you can e-mail a friend about a great site you visited, and the next day your friend can't see what you saw because it's already changed. Even corporate intranets reflect this constantly changing nature. One reason that some sites change so often is that it's easy to make small changes to them. Once they're up and running, it takes little effort to replace a graphic, change a link, or even add a new page.

Another reason that sites change so often is that audiences demand it. You must keep your Web updated with the latest information, or else viewers will not return. Visiting a site is like turning up a playing card that's face down; if your audience doesn't see a different card now and then, they'll move on to a different game.

That said, you need to be careful not to make major changes too often. If you have a strong repeat viewer base, you want your Web to be a familiar place to visit. You don't want to confuse your audience by changing the location of your navigation buttons every month, or by changing the names of the departments or areas on your Web so people can't find what they're looking for. Just remember, regularly changing content (such as stories and images) is fine, but changes to the structure of a Web can be a real pain for your regular viewers.

Updating large Webs can be time-consuming, however, and the process can require even more time as the Web's size and the frequency of updating increase. You should have a plan for updating your Web even before you begin to develop your Web. If you're planning a site now, or if you need to implement an update plan, read ahead for a few ideas on how to go about it.

Updating Content

You can use a process for updating content that's similar to the one you used for gathering the content originally, but watch for ways to streamline that process. When getting approval for your content, for example, you can try routing it to people in a different order if the routing process was slow the first time around. Or you can eliminate a step in the process if you determine that the step wasn't necessary; for example, the material might need only one editing stage, not two. Also, check employee schedules to make certain that a folder that has Web-site content doesn't sit on someone's desk while he or she is lying on a beach in Tahiti.

If your company requires you to route material through a legal department, perhaps not all of it has to be routed there, or maybe some of the material that you want to put on your Web has already been approved for use elsewhere in the company. If you can avoid rerouting some of the material, you can save time and energy that you can apply elsewhere.

Never forget to plan ahead. If you put forth a major effort to implement a Web that's to be updated monthly, and if you plan to create a test Web for your new material before you go live with it every month, leave yourself plenty of time for that test. If you first went live in May and you have an update planned for June, for example, allow enough time to develop and test the update before June 1 rolls around. That might mean that all content for the June release must be finalized by mid-May so that you have enough time to test the Web and fix any errors you find.

Consider the time that you or a member of your team will need to write, edit, and approve content. You'll need resources from different departments around your company, and even if you or an assistant is the ultimate go-getter who loves to make personal office visits for every bit of information you need, be sure to allow plenty of time for gathering that material.

Updating Content Remotely

One of the greatest strengths of FrontPage is that it gives you the ability to update site content from a remote location; few other Web authoring tools offer this feature. It's easy—here's all you need to do:

CHAPTER 5

- You need to be able to connect to the Web server that contains the Web you want to update. (Preferably, the server should have the FrontPage Server Extensions installed.)

- You must have FrontPage installed on the computer that you're using remotely.

If you utter a resounding "Yes!" to these requirements, it's time to lobby your boss to allow you to work on the Web while you sip an espresso from your favorite café along the Champs Élysées.

Simultaneous authoring

FrontPage makes changing the content of your Web a simple task that multiple authors can perform at the same time. If you update content while you're on the go, piece by piece, you can be changing one page in your Web while someone else is working on another page. The danger, of course, arises when two or more authors attempt to make changes to the same page simultaneously.

To help avoid this problem, FrontPage issues a warning if someone tries to save changes to a page that another person is working on.

If you receive a warning like this, you'll need to decide which set of edits to retain. If you continue with your changes, the others might be lost. In the future, coordinate with the other person so that only one of you works on a given page at any one time.

Your organization can avoid such complications by adhering strictly to Tasks view assignments. In Tasks view, only one author is assigned a given task. If that author is not the one who should be performing that task, you should reassign the task. Even if multiple authors are changing content in a Web from separate locations, they still use the same Tasks view for that Web. You can easily avoid having two people work on the same page simultaneously if you direct them to work only on tasks assigned to them.

Another great feature in FrontPage is that it lets you take advantage of *source control*. By adding a source control program, such as Microsoft's Visual Source Safe (VSS), you can require that authors check out, and then check in, any file that needs to be worked on. You can think of source control as your online library, checking files (rather than books) out and in. The only thing missing is that cranky librarian telling you to "shhh" all the time. And when you use source control, you'll always have a record of who did what and when. When source control is running, you can access the Check Out and Check In commands by choosing them from the Edit menu in FrontPage.

PART
II

Updating for Traffic

Are you and your company prepared to receive heavy traffic on your Web? If your site becomes popular on the Web, you need to have a high-volume Web server to handle the hits. FrontPage's Publish Web command on the File menu makes it easy to move Webs from one server to another. So if a server in one location is taking a beating and you have a higher-volume server that can handle increased traffic, you can simply move your Web to the new server. It's as easy as point-and-click. For more information on the Publish Web command, see Chapter 3.

Coming Up

This wraps up Part 2, which has covered the basics of using FrontPage to view, manipulate, and manage your Web. Part 3 familiarizes you with Page view, which is where you actually "build" individual pages. Part 3 also shows you how to fine-tune your Web so that no visitor will want to leave.

CHAPTER 5

PART III

Building Your Pages

CHAPTER

6

Creating Your Pages

HTML Got You Down?

We all know that the Web is where it's at right now, and it's where you want to be too, or you wouldn't be reading this. What you may not know, though, is that way back in the Web dark ages (two or three years ago), you had to be an HTML whiz to create anything respectable for the Internet. These days, who has the time to become a whiz at anything, especially computer programming? I mean, there's always a good rerun of *I Dream of Jeannie* on TV, right?

Microsoft FrontPage 2000 makes creating pages as easy as managing Webs. FrontPage doesn't require that you know a speck of HTML in order to produce professional-looking pages for your intranet or for the Web. If you're editing a page and you want to italicize a word or change the color of a heading, you just select the text, click a button, and voilà—FrontPage creates the HTML behind the scenes. This allows you to concentrate on more important things, like creating a good Web presence. You might even have enough time left in your day to catch up on some of those old reruns on TV.

For all those people who do have the time to become an HTML whiz, or who are already experts, FrontPage didn't forget about you, either. If you want to, you can edit the HTML right in FrontPage, and you can even see how your page looks without even opening a browser.

Now it's time to get your hands dirty and find out how to use FrontPage to craft all the elements on your Web's pages to get just the look and feel you want. To illustrate the many components you can add to your pages, we'll work with the pages from an intranet Web of a fictitious company called Cascade Coffee Roasters. You'll see several examples of the integration between FrontPage and the Microsoft Office suite of applications.

Page View in Brief

One reason Page view is so easy to use is that it presents pages in WYSIWYG (what you see is what you get) format. This means that whatever you see in Page view is what you or your audience will see when they view your pages using a Web browser. In the days when every detail on a page had to be formatted with HTML code, you would painstakingly make changes to the code and then cross your fingers that the changes looked right when you actually viewed the results. Now all you need to do is make sure it looks right in FrontPage, and you're all set. What You See Is What You Get!

Working in Page view is much like using a word-processing application such as Microsoft Word. Page view includes many of the standard buttons and commands found in Word, such as buttons for bold, italic, and underline; numbered and bulleted lists; undo and redo; and so on. You type text in Page view just as you do in Word, and you can check the spelling of the files in your Web as you would a file in Word. You can also draw tables and use frames easily in Page view—with just a few clicks of the mouse.

Like Word, Page view allows you to have more than one Page open at a time. This is useful for toggling back and forth between pages to ensure consistency, accuracy of information, and so forth. In Page view, you can also copy a page (including all of its HTML) from the World Wide Web and edit it as you wish. This is useful if you own other sites and need to gather information from them quickly. Be careful, of course, about copying information from others' Web sites—there are copyright laws to heed, and plagiarism should be left to those who don't mind shelling out big bucks for a defense attorney.

So This Is Page View

To begin working in Page view is easy: just choose the Page icon from the Views menu in FrontPage. That's all there is to it; you're there, ready to go.

PART
III

Page view appears in the right window, and it has its own set of toolbars and provides numerous menu commands. Figure 6-1 shows an example of Page view, with all of its toolbars visible.

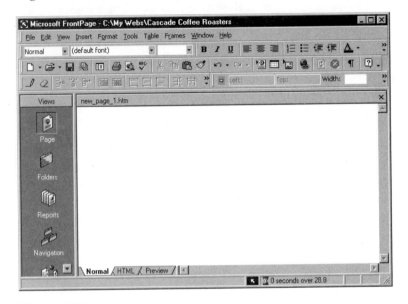

Figure 6-1
Page view's toolbars and menus.

As you can see, many of the toolbars that are unavailable in the other views, such as the Positioning toolbar, are here in Page view. It might look a tad formidable at first, but don't worry—we'll describe what many of the toolbar buttons and commands do in this chapter. If you're an Excel user, you'll notice the spreadsheet-like view tabs at the bottom of the window: Normal, HTML, and Preview. These tabs let you view your page in different ways. For now, we'll be using the Normal tab. Before you begin to use Page view, though, you should learn how to customize it so that you can use it to your best advantage.

Adjusting Settings

Surely you have a preferred way of working on your computer. For example, maybe you don't like working with toolbars—so what's the purpose of keeping them on the screen? Or maybe you like working in a smaller or larger window. Adjusting these elements in Page view is easy; here are a few ways to tailor your environment.

121

Changing the window size

It's often useful to maximize Page view to a full screen so you can get the largest view of the page you're editing. To do this, click the Maximize button, which is the middle button of the three-button set in the upper-right corner of the FrontPage title bar when the window isn't maximized. To restore FrontPage to its previous location and size, click the Restore button that appears in the same position for maximized windows. That three-button set is the same one you see in all applications for Microsoft Windows NT 4.0, Windows 95, and Windows 98.

You can close a page that's open in Page view by clicking the "X" in the upper-right corner of Page view, just above the scroll bar. You can also see which pages are open in Page view by choosing Window from the menu bar. All of the open pages are listed, and the most recently opened page is at the top of the list.

Working with toolbars

Page view includes the Standard, Formatting, DHTML, Picture, Positioning, and Table toolbars, available from the View menu. When they're all displayed, they take up a fairly large chunk of space in the window. If you don't need some of them, you can hide them. To hide a toolbar, select Toolbars from the View menu and then choose the appropriate toolbar name from the pop-up menu. Alternatively, to show a hidden toolbar, select Toolbars from the View menu and then, from the pop-up menu, choose the name of the toolbar that you want to make visible. Toolbars that are visible have a check mark beside their names. When a toolbar is made visible it appears in the same position it held before it was hidden.

You can position the FrontPage toolbars anywhere on your screen. You might, for example, prefer to work with the toolbars off to one side or at the bottom of your screen. To move a toolbar, click a region of the toolbar outside the buttons and drag it to its new position. To make a toolbar *float* (move anywhere on the screen), drag it from the toolbar region to a new position, which can be anywhere on the screen. To *dock* the toolbar again so that it remains in a stationary position in the toolbar region, drag it back to the toolbar region at the top of the FrontPage window.

Showing and hiding HTML tags

If you're one of those people (and you know who you are) who likes to see the HTML tags on the page as you're working, you're in luck. You can show or hide the HTML tags in the Page view window by choosing the Reveal Tags command from the View menu.

Now that you've learned how to adjust some basic settings, it's time to dive into Cascade Coffee Roasters' RoasterNet Web.

TIP You can click the Show/Hide Paragraph toolbar button, which looks like a paragraph symbol, to show or hide formatting marks.

Let the Construction Begin

This section describes most of the elements you can add to a page in FrontPage. You can add all of the obvious page components, such as text, links, and headings, plus some that you might not have thought of. Examples:

- Adding tables, frames, marquees, background sound, and video is discussed in this chapter.

- Adding images, another major component of a Web page, is detailed in Chapter 8.

- Adding forms and FrontPage components to a page is explained in Chapter 9.

- Adding advanced features, such as ActiveX components and Java applets, to a page is discussed in Chapter 10.

When adding elements to your pages, follow this simple guideline: think as you would when using a word processing application such as Word. Page view lets you use many of the same procedures and techniques you use in Word to add and manipulate page elements. Many of the menus and toolbars also closely resemble those in Word. If you've used any word processing application, you'll have no trouble working in Page view.

Moving Around in Page View

Once you have material on your page, you can use your keyboard to navigate in the standard ways. For example, you can use the Page Up and Page Down keys to move one screen up or down. Pressing Ctrl+Home takes you to the top of a page, and pressing Ctrl+End takes you to the end of a page. You can also use the pointer keys to navigate on your pages, and you can use a scroll bar, if one is present, to move horizontally or vertically.

TIP Page view implements the 25 most frequently used keyboard shortcuts of Microsoft Word, so Office users can feel right at home.

Text

Adding text to a page is as simple as typing it in. Let's walk through the steps needed in order to add some text to a new Human Resources page in the RoasterNet Web:

1. In Page view, to create a new blank page, click New Page on the FrontPage toolbar. A blank page appears on your screen (see Figure 6-2); the insertion pointer is blinking in the upper-left corner.

2. Type the words *Cascade Coffee Roasters*.

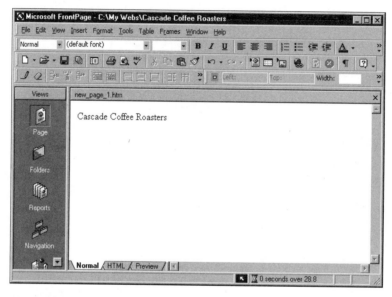

Figure 6-2

Page view showing a blank page that has title text added.

Notice that the text begins on the far left side of the current line. It doesn't have to stay there; you can indent the text, center it, or right-align it. You can also change the font and point size of the text, turn the text into a heading, and change its properties in many other ways. We'll discuss all of those formatting techniques in Chapter 7.

Whatever you type on the screen is what you see in the browser. And just as in Word, to start a new paragraph, you simply press the Enter key.

Page view uses common keyboard and toolbar shortcuts for cutting, copying, and pasting—Cut: Ctrl+X; Copy: Ctrl+C; Paste: Ctrl+V. You can also right-click to choose the Cut, Copy, and Paste commands from the pop-up menu.

Cutting, copying, and pasting text

You can cut, copy, and paste text (and any other elements, for that matter) in Page view just as you do in Office applications. FrontPage (which is one of the applications in the Premium edition of Microsoft Office 2000) uses the Clipboard in the same way that Office applications do; you can cut or copy material to other pages or to other documents in other applications. Simply cut or copy the material, move to the destination document (opening it first if necessary), and paste it in. Depending on the application you move the material to, you might lose some of the formatting when you move the material. For example, if you're moving text of varying point sizes to a file in Notepad, all the text appears in Notepad in the standard Notepad point size.

Deleting text

Deleting text or other elements is also simple, and you can do it in many ways. After you select the material you want to delete, press the Delete key or choose Clear from the Edit menu.

> **TIP** If you want to reinsert material you've just deleted, choose Undo from the Edit menu or click the Undo toolbar button. For more details, see "Undo/Redo" in Chapter 7.

You can also delete words and characters preceding and following the insertion point. To delete a word to the right of the insertion point, press Ctrl+Delete, and to delete a word to the left of the insertion point, press Ctrl+Backspace. Try these shortcuts to get comfortable with them; they're some of the least-used keyboard combinations in Page view and in Word, but they can make your editing work go much faster.

Material from Microsoft Office Files

A significant advantage in FrontPage 2000 is its ability to seamlessly incorporate material from Microsoft Office files. This integration can be a big time-saver. For example, if you have material in a Word or Excel file that you want to use on a page in a FrontPage Web, you don't have to re-create that material in FrontPage. This applies to entire documents as well; if you have documents in Word or Microsoft Excel that you want to use, you can incorporate them into FrontPage in a matter of seconds. And if your Office files contain hyperlinks, FrontPage imports them with all of their hyperlinks intact.

Copying and pasting from Office files

You can easily copy text from an Office document and paste it into FrontPage. Simply select the text in Word or in another Office program, copy it, switch to the FrontPage Page view, and paste the text wherever you want on the open page. FrontPage automatically converts the material to HTML for use on the page.

Dragging Office files into FrontPage

Now let's get on to some bigger things. Suppose Susan has typed a mountain of pages in Word instead of just a few lines. Perhaps she was intending to type in the material and then use Word to turn it into an HTML file so that she could use it in her company's intranet Web. Nice thinking, Susan—but your fellow HR, Roberta, knows that this step is unnecessary, because Cascade Coffee Roasters uses FrontPage.

Roberta shows Susan how to link to Office files or insert entire files in the FrontPage Page view and automatically convert them to HTML files:

- **Link to an Office file**. If an Office file has already been copied to a directory as a part of the FrontPage Web (in other words, for the purpose of linking to it from within the Web), you can drag that file from Folders view to a page in Page view. Just click the icon representing the file in Folders view (such as a Word or Excel icon), and while pressing and holding the left mouse button, drag the file onto the Page view icon on the Views menu. FrontPage opens the current page in Page view. Release the mouse button; FrontPage creates a link to the file, using the name of the file.

- **Insert an Office file**. You can drag an Office file from anywhere in Windows into an open page in Page view. For example, you can drag files from Windows Explorer or even from the Windows desktop. FrontPage converts the entire file to HTML and presents it on the open page at the insertion point. If the file has links, they are converted to FrontPage links, and they continue to link to the same places.

TIP

You can also insert files in a page in Page view by using the File command on the Insert menu.

When you're dragging, remember that you don't need to have Page view active on your screen when you begin. You can drag the file over the Page icon on the Views menu and wait for a moment (while continuing to press and hold the mouse button). Page view then becomes active on your screen, and you can drop the file onto the open page.

PART

III

TIP FrontPage allows you to drag or insert files that are in any document format that Office recognizes. For example, you can drag WordPerfect documents or Lotus 1-2-3 spreadsheets into Page view.

Headings

One mark of an effective Web page design is the wise use of headings. Too many large headings can make a page difficult to read, and too few headings can make a page look dull or perhaps difficult to understand. Headlines help to prioritize the levels of information on a page, just the way they do in a newspaper or magazine.

To show you a simple use of headings, let's imagine that you are a Cascade employee, Kurt, who's creating his Accounting home page. Kurt wants the names of his department's personnel to appear on the page, to serve as links to their own pages. Here's what you should do:

1. Create a new page by choosing New from the File menu and selecting Page from the submenu. In the New dialog box, select Normal Page and then click OK. A blank page appears in Page view, and the insertion pointer is blinking in the upper-left corner.

2. From the Style drop-down list on the Formatting toolbar, choose Heading 1. You'll notice there are six levels of headings in the list, plus a few other formatting choices. The page heading should be a fairly prominent one, such as Heading 1. FrontPage adds space for the heading as a separate paragraph, placing it on its own line, ready for you to type the heading text.

3. Type the main heading for the page, *Accounting,* as shown in Figure 6-3.

4. Next, add the names of your salespeople to the page. Press Enter to move the insertion point to the next line, and then choose Heading 3 from the drop-down list. A line formatted as Heading 3 appears below the title you just typed. Type *Kraig.*

5. Repeat step 4 to enter the names of your other salespeople: Donna, Diane, Blaine, Tony, Kim, Mike, and Jenny. Your page should look like Figure 6-4.

CHAPTER 6

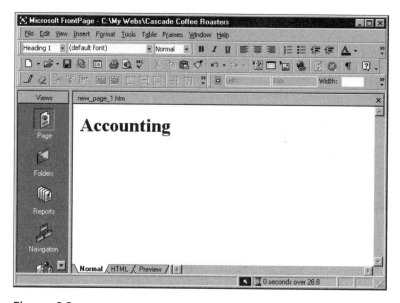

Figure 6-3

This heading is formatted as Heading 1. Notice the Heading 1 option in the Style drop-down list.

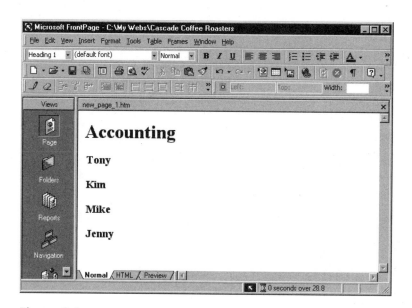

Figure 6-4

Heading 1 followed by several headings formatted as Heading 3.

Figure 6-5 shows the relative sizes of the six heading formats.

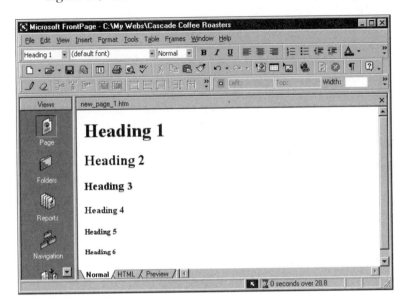

Figure 6-5

Relative sizes of heading levels.

The Web browser used by the visitors to your page determines the exact formatting of the headings and might override FrontPage-specific formatting. But in every case, the formats are designed so that the higher-level headings (starting with Heading 1) stand out more than the lower-level ones (ending with Heading 6). Generally, the more important the heading, the larger the text, the more space above and below the heading, and so on. Later, in Chapter 10, you'll learn how to customize style formatting, using style sheets.

Lists

When you're designing your pages, consider using a list instead of cramming material into paragraph form. Lists are much easier to read, so they tend to make your pages more user-friendly. If you use too many lists, though, your pages can become dry and tedious to read, and your audience will dash off to read *Particle Physics Illustrated* just to clear their minds.

It's possible to modify the numbered list attributes. For example, you can order the list using uppercase and lowercase Roman numerals and uppercase and lowercase letters. You can also modify the starting value. For more information, see "List Properties" in Chapter 7.

The Web browser your visitors use to view the page determines the exact formatting of each kind of list. Here's a rundown of the kinds of lists that are available from the Style drop-down list:

- **Numbered List.** Presents items in an ordered sequence, typically using numerals and beginning with the number 1. Numbered lists are ideal for step-by-step procedures.

- **Bulleted List.** Presents items with bullets. Bulleted lists are often used for related but nonsequential items.

- **Directory List.** Another bulleted list format. Some browsers recognize the coding for a directory list and format the list items differently than for a simple bulleted list. Generally, this format is used for short items.

- **Menu List.** Another bulleted list format supported by most browsers.

Creating a list

Back to RoasterNet. Now imagine that you are Jodi, an HR Specialist, who wants to create a numbered list to spell out the steps employees should take to declare their sick-leave days. (Of course, Cascade Coffee Roasters employees, honest folks that they are, wouldn't even think of *not* declaring those days.) Here are the steps that you should follow:

1. On the page in Page view, position the insertion point where you want the list to begin. You can position the pointer at the beginning, middle, or end of a paragraph. If you position the pointer at a line that contains text, FrontPage turns that text into the first item of the list. If you want to start a new list, position the pointer on a blank line.

You can convert existing text to a numbered or bulleted list by selecting it and then clicking the appropriate toolbar button. For more on formatting, see Chapter 7.

2. Select Numbered List from the Style drop-down list. FrontPage formats the first line of the new list with a number 1.

3. Type the text for the first item and press Enter. FrontPage inserts the next number, and you can type in the text for the next list item. Continue this process until you finish the list.

4. When you finish the list, press Ctrl+Enter. FrontPage inserts a new line following the list, assigns it the Normal style, and positions the insertion point at the start of that line.

Working with Page Files

Standard file management commands in Page view are similar to their counterparts in the other views, except that they work at the page level, not at the Web level. For example, in Page view, formatting a Theme applies only to the open page, while the Theme command in the other views applies to the entire Web. Also, you can perform a few additional tasks with files in Page view, such as printing. In this section, you'll learn how to use Page view's file management commands.

Creating New Pages

FrontPage allows you to create numerous kinds of pages easily using its templates and wizards. Most often, you'll create new pages to add them to a Web that's currently open, but you're not limited to that scenario. You can also create a new page, save it separately, and add it to any other Web later on. (See "Saving Pages" later in this chapter for more information.)

TIP You can quickly create a new Normal page by clicking the New button on the toolbar.

1. To create a new page, choose New from the File menu and Page from the submenu, or press Ctrl+N on the keyboard. You'll see the New dialog box, as shown in Figure 6-6.

   If you want to create the new page, but you'd rather work on it later instead of opening it in Page view, select Just Add Web Task, and FrontPage will add this to Tasks view. If you want the page to be opened in a frames page that's currently open in Page view, select Open In Current Frame.

   In the New dialog box, you can select any number of page templates from the General tab, or you can click the Frames Pages tab and select from the frames page templates. You can also select the Style Sheets tab and select from the FrontPage-supplied style sheets. For more information on style sheets, see Chapter 10.

CHAPTER 6

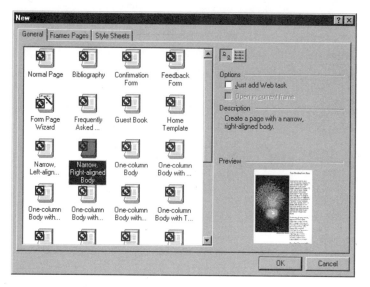

Figure 6-6

The General tab of the New dialog box.

2. After choosing a template from the list, click OK. You can find full descriptions of the templates and wizards in Chapter 4.

Opening Pages

The Open command allows you to open pages from the open Web, existing pages that are stored as files in your system, and even pages from the World Wide Web. Not only can you open pages created with FrontPage, but you can open additional file types as well. This gives you many options for adding new material to your Web.

If you have Microsoft Office installed, and if during the Office setup you selected a configuration that installs additional document converters, those converters are also accessible to FrontPage.

Opening a page from the current Web

If you need to edit a page that's part of an open Web, there are two easy ways to do it: You can go to a view (such as Folders view), find the page, and open it from there (perhaps by double-clicking it). Or, for an even easier way, you can open it in Page view by choosing the Open command from the File menu.

When you choose the Open command, you see the Open File dialog box, shown here in Figure 6-7.

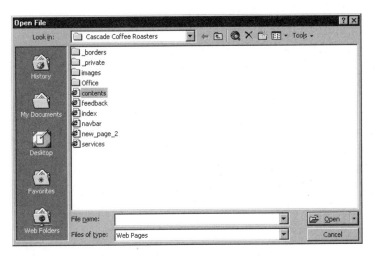

Figure 6-7
The Open File dialog box.

Select a file from the list and click OK. The page opens in a new window in Page view for you to edit to your heart's content.

Opening a page from your file system

Say you're editing your Web, and you need to add a page that's saved as a file but not saved as part of any Web. For example, suppose someone in your organization is creating custom pages for several different Webs and is saving them separately for others to add to their respective Webs as needed. If you want to add a page like this to your Web, here's how to do it:

1. Choose the Open command from the File menu. You'll see the Open File dialog box. Click the Look In: drop-down menu and find the location of the file, in a folder on your hard drive, for instance. The contents of the folder are displayed in the window of the Open File dialog box.

2. Select the file of your choice and then click Open. The file opens in Page view.

You can quickly access the Open File dialog box in any view by pressing Crtl+O or by clicking the Open button on the toolbar.

FrontPage tries to open the actual HTML files as they are, without conversions, and displays all of their elements. However, if the file contains HTML that FrontPage doesn't recognize, FrontPage preserves it.

133

Opening a page from any Web site

You can open any page from any Web site you have access to—including those on intranets and the Web. All you have to know is the page's address. Here are the details:

1. Choose Open from the File menu to bring up the Open File dialog box.

2. Click the third button/icon to the right of the Look In drop-down menu (that's the Search The Web button, that has the little globe on it). This launches your default browser.

3. Use the search tool in your browser to locate the Web page you want to open; FrontPage automatically places the address in the URL text field for you.

4. Click OK in the Open File dialog box, and the page opens in Page view, ready to be saved to your Web.

If you're attempting to open a page from the Web and you get an error message, you might not be connected to the Web. Make sure your connection is live by viewing the page with your browser, and then try again.

You can also open a Web page in Page view by typing its address in the File Name: drop-down list of the Open File dialog box. The address must be in the form of an absolute URL. An *absolute URL* is the full address of a page, including the protocol, host name, folder name, and file name, such as http://www.microsoft.com. When you use absolute URLs, you can open pages from any system that can create a connection to that site. For example, say Cascade Coffee Roasters is testing a Web called *RoasterTest1* on a local server named BeanThere, which includes a press release page (that has the page URL *PR3.htm*) that you'd like to edit. If you have access to the Web, you could open that page by typing *http://BeanThere/RoasterTest1/PR3.htm*—the absolute URL. It's that easy, even for bringing up World Wide Web pages in Page view. Notice that an address on a local server begins with a directory name; for example, a Web address would begin htttp://www..., and the host name, or domain name, would come after the www.

FrontPage might display a warning that the address you supplied isn't a valid IP address. If you see this warning, check the address and try it again. Make sure you typed the correct characters; you'll need at least the server name at the beginning of the address. Be sure to use forward slashes instead of backslashes in the address.

Closing Pages

To close a page in Page view, choose Close from the File menu. If FrontPage notices that you haven't saved the page, you'll be prompted to do so first; then FrontPage saves the page and closes it.

PART
III

Saving Pages

Save your work in the same way that people in Seattle drink their coffee: early and often. Murphy's Law will strike you when it hurts the most; there will be times when the power goes down, or when the oversized blue suede shoes of your officemate, T.R. Tripsalot, rip the power cords from the wall sockets. Page view gives you two saving options:

- **Save.** Saves the active page in HTML format to a Web or to a file.

- **Save As.** Copies and saves the active page to a new page in the current Web or to a file.

Saving for the first time

No matter which command you use, if you haven't saved the page before, you'll see the Save As dialog box, which gives you several options for saving your file. You can also use the Save As command to save a page to a different location or with a different name. Figure 6-8 shows the Save As dialog box.

Here's how to use the Save As dialog box:

- Change the default page title by clicking the Change button and typing a new File name. Give your page a unique, logical name so you can recognize it easily among other page names. After you enter that information, click OK.

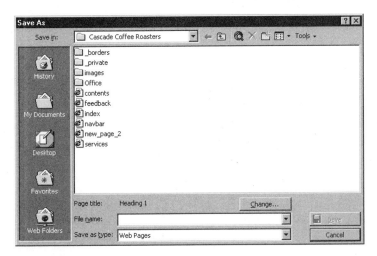

Figure 6-8
The Save As dialog box.

- You can also save the page as a template from the Save As dialog box. For details on this, see Chapter 4.

You can quickly save a page by pressing Ctrl+S or by clicking Save on the toolbar.

Printing Pages

Sometimes in the virtual world of Web development, it's good to see a hard copy of a page you're working on, even if it's just to get a different perspective on the page.

 Sometimes visitors to your Web print your pages to save them for later reading. Thus, you might want to print your pages from various browsers, too, to see what they'll look like to visitors.

FrontPage prints your pages as they appear on screen in Page view, provided that your paper size is large enough to accommodate the page. The following sections describe how you can use the Page Setup, Print Preview, and Print commands to produce a paper version of the page you're working with.

 If your page is wider than the paper you're printing on, portions of the page might not print. In these cases, try printing the page in Landscape orientation.

Page setup

While in Page view, choose Page Setup from the File menu. You'll see the standard Print Setup dialog box. You can configure the settings of the printers connected to your computer

Print preview

While in Page view or Navigation view, you can choose the Print Preview command from the File menu at any time to see what your page looks like when printed. This isn't necessarily what the page will look like in a Web browser, however, so be careful not to rely on Print Preview for that purpose.

When FrontPage shows your page in Print Preview, as shown in Figure 6-9, it presents a series of view-adjustment buttons at the top of the screen. You can zoom in or zoom out, and you can view the next page, the previous page, or a two-page side-by-side view. You can also print directly from Print Preview by clicking Print. To exit Print Preview without printing, press the Esc key or click Close.

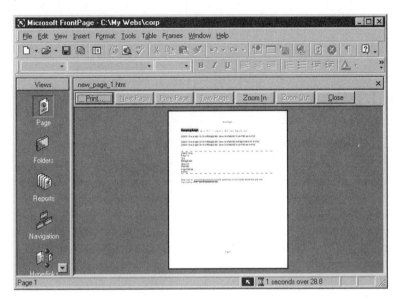

Figure 6-9
An example of a page in Print Preview.

You can click the Preview In Browser button on the toolbar to preview your page in a Web browser. For details, see "Preview in Browser" in Chapter 7.

Print

Choose Print from the File menu to print your page. The standard Print dialog box appears on your screen; if you need to change printer settings, click the Properties button. You can change printer settings in the Properties dialog box that appears. You must be in either Page view or Navigation view in order to use the Print feature.

Press Ctrl+P or click the Print button on the Standard toolbar to reach the Print dialog box quickly.

When you're satisfied with your printer settings, click OK in the Print dialog box to print your page. If your Web page runs longer than the length of paper you're using, FrontPage prints it on multiple pages.

Making Tables

Many Web sites these days use tables to present information in a neat, orderly fashion. Tables allow you design flexibility and control over the layout of your pages, so that you don't have to format text and images manually in order to make them look structured. Tables also allow for more consistency across Web sites, and especially across pages within a site. In addition, using tables increases the likelihood that information will appear the way you want, regardless of the browser a visitor to your Web is using. Most browsers treat tables in a fashion that's similar enough to ensure some consistency from browser to browser.

If you open a Word document containing a table in FrontPage, the table is converted to an HTML table and can be modified in Page view.

Tables in FrontPage have the same structure and are used in the same way as tables in a Word document. Tables consist of columns and rows of cells that can contain text, images, background images, forms, FrontPage components, or even another table. If you create a table and find later that you need to change the size of cells or add or delete rows or columns, don't fret—it's easy to customize an existing table in FrontPage. When you create a table, you don't have to consider cell width and height if you don't want to; as you add material to the cells, the width and height automatically expand to accommodate the material.

You can never have too many options, right? Well, at least not when it comes to adding a table in FrontPage. You can create a table on a page in Page view in one of two ways. Just to help keep the day interesting, you can draw one right on the page, using the Table toolbar, or you can insert a table from the Table menu. If you're someone who has trouble making decisions, don't worry; FrontPage lets you use both table options on any table, in a variety of combinations. For example, you could insert a table from the Table menu and then add rows to the table using the Table toolbar. So you can mix and match table options as you wish. For clarity of instruction, though, we'll describe each method individually, starting with the Table toolbar, and then we'll follow up with what they have in common.

Using the FrontPage Table Toolbar

FrontPage lets you draw tables in Page view in almost exactly the same way as Word lets you draw tables on a page, using the Table toolbar, as shown in Figure 6-10. To access the Table toolbar, choose Toolbars from the View menu and Table from the pop-up menu, or choose Draw Table from the Table menu.

Figure 6-10
The Table toolbar.

The Table toolbar lets you draw your table right on the page and then alter many aspects of it to suit your needs. The first button on the Table toolbar, the Draw Table button, is also what you use to take the first step in drawing your table.

1. If you chose Draw Table from the Table toolbar, the Draw Table pointer is automatically active; otherwise, click the Draw Table button from the Table toolbar. The mouse pointer becomes a pen.

2. Position the pointer where you want the table to begin, click, and then drag down and to the right to create the table. The table is automatically drawn at the left side of the page. You can change this later if you like. For more information on table properties, see "Changing Table Properties," later in this chapter.

   To help you see how large your table is going to be, FrontPage represents the table's outer border as a dotted outline as you drag the pen.

You've just drawn a single-celled table, one that has one column and one row. When you draw a table, FrontPage automatically adds a border. To remove the border, you need to access the table's properties dialog box. For more information on the Table Properties dialog box, see "Changing Table Properties," later in this chapter. Your table should look something like the table shown in Figure 6-11.

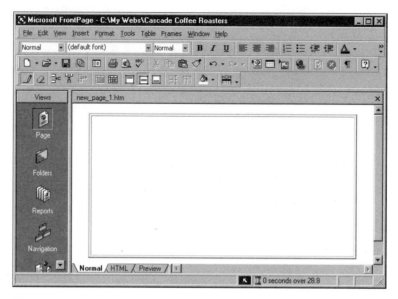

Figure 6-11

One large table that has one column and one row.

In case you didn't get it right the first time, you can easily change the size of your table without having to redraw it. Move your pointer to the border of the table. Notice how it changes to a two-sided arrow. You change the table's width by dragging the right side of the table or change its height by dragging the bottom of the table.

TIP

If you press and hold the Shift key while you drag a border, all of the cells in the direction you drag retain their current widths.

Adding rows and columns

Now that your table is the size you want, you might want to add some rows and columns.

You can easily draw a row or column, dividing your table almost any way you like, using the Draw Table pen pointer.

1. Click the Draw Table pen pointer, if it isn't already selected.

2. Position the pointer inside the cell you want to divide. Make sure that you don't touch the table border with the pointer, because that creates a new table within the cell.

PART
III

3. Drag horizontally to create a row or vertically to create a column. As you drag, a dotted line represents the new border. You don't have to worry about drawing straight; FrontPage constrains the line for you, either vertically or horizontally. All you need to do is start in the right direction.

Figure 6-12 shows the table divided into two columns, and the right column divided into two rows.

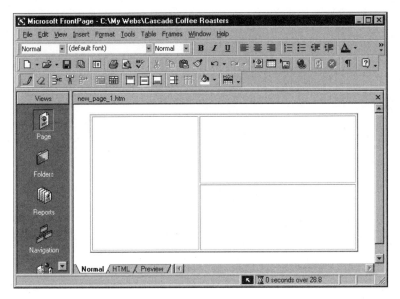

Figure 6-12

A table that has two columns; the right column has two rows.

If you want to divide the table evenly by rows or by columns, you can use the and Insert Columns buttons on the Table toolbar.

1. Place the pointer in the cell of the table you want to divide.

2. Click either the Insert Rows button or the Insert Columns button. FrontPage automatically creates a column equal to half the width of the cell, or it creates a row equal to the size of the cell. Your pointer is left blinking in the new cell.

Figure 6-13 shows the table divided by means of the Insert Column button on the Table toolbar. Notice that the table is now divided into two equal columns. By repeating the steps above, you can divide each cell as often as you like. Once you've created a table, you can move the borders around to suit your needs, no matter which method you used to create them.

141

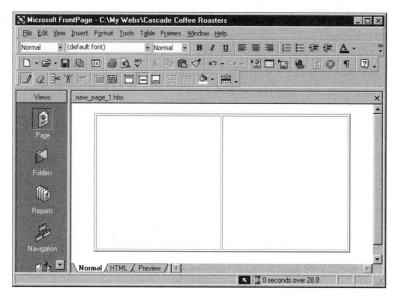

Figure 6-13

A table that has two equal columns.

Erasing a row or column

If you've created a table and then you notice that you have too many rows or columns, you can easily erase a border using the Erase button on the Table toolbar.

1. Click the Erase button on the Table toolbar. The pointer becomes an eraser.

2. Place the eraser pointer outside the border you wish to delete.

3. Drag across the border line you wish to delete. As you drag, the border is highlighted.

4. When you release the mouse button, FrontPage deletes the selected borders.

You can't erase a border if doing so would produce an incomplete cell. In other words, all border lines must touch two complete borders. As Figure 6-14 shows, the interior borders are selected to be erased. However, you couldn't erase the circled area by itself, because if you did, you would create an incomplete cell at the bottom.

PART

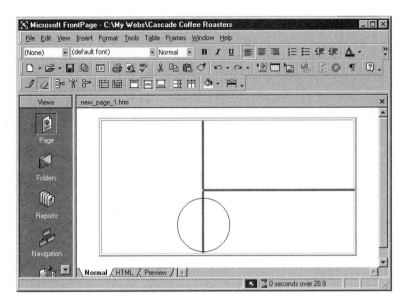

Figure 6-14

Border lines of a table selected to be erased.

The remaining Table toolbar buttons

The other buttons on the Table toolbar let you further adjust and design your tables:

- **Delete Cells.** You can delete cells by selecting the row or column containing the cells and clicking the Delete Cells button on the Table toolbar. For more information on selecting rows and columns, see "Selecting Rows and Columns," later in this chapter.

- **Merge Cells.** You can merge cells together by selecting the cells and then clicking the Merge Cells button on the Table toolbar.

- **Split Cells.** You can split cells into columns or rows by selecting the cells and then clicking the Split Cells button on the Table toolbar to display the Split Cells dialog box. For more information on this dialog box, see "Splitting Cells," later in this chapter.

- **Align Top, Center Vertically, Align Bottom.** By placing your pointer in the cell and clicking one of these buttons, you can align any text in the cell accordingly.

- **Distribute Rows and Columns Evenly.** If you want a group of rows or columns to be distributed evenly in the table, select them and then click the appropriate button.

- **Fill Color**. If you want to add color to the background of a cell, or to the entire table itself, select the area and then click the Fill Color button. This displays the Color pop-up dialog box; select a color and then click OK. Notice that the color you've chosen now appears under the Fill Color icon on the toolbar.

- **AutoFit.** If you want the cell's width to match that of whatever you insert in the cell, click the AutoFit button. For example, if you're using the table to help control the layout of your page, and you want it to conform to the image you just inserted in the cell, select AutoFit, and the table automatically adjusts its width to the width of the largest image placed in the cell.

Inserting a Table

Here is the process to follow if you want to insert your table using the FrontPage menu commands.

1. Position your pointer where you want the table to begin, and then choose Insert from the Table menu and Table from the submenu. You'll see the Insert Table dialog box, as shown here in Figure 6-15.

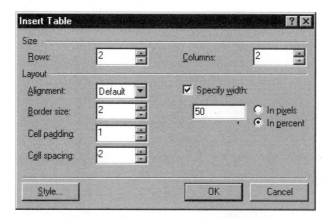

Figure 6-15

The Insert Table dialog box.

2. Enter the number of rows and columns you think you'll need in your table. You can add or delete rows and columns later.

3. Select an alignment option for the table relative to the page or to elements on the page: to the left, centered, or to the right.

4. If you want a border around the table, enter the width in pixels for the border size. This setting is for the border that surrounds the entire table; each cell in the table also has a border representing the cell spacing (see step 6). If you don't want a border, enter *0*. If you choose to surround your table with a border, you can specify border colors later on.

NOTE

If you create a borderless table, don't worry. FrontPage creates a dotted outline of the table in Page view so that you can see where it is and what you're doing. The dotted line is for layout purposes only; it doesn't show up in a Web browser.

5. Enter a number, in pixels, for the cell padding. *Cell padding* is the space between a cell's contents and each of its borders. This number pertains to all cells in the table; cell padding can't be set for individual cells. The default value is 1 pixel.

6. Enter a number, in pixels, for *cell spacing*. This value controls the spacing between the cells in a table and is represented as a border around each cell (including those at the outer edge of the table). The default value is 2 pixels.

7. Specify the width of the table. You can set the number in pixels or as a percentage of the page width. For example, if you set the table width to 50 percent, the table spans half the width of the page.

8. Click OK. FrontPage creates the table and displays it on the page, as shown in Figure 6-16. FrontPage uses the number of columns and the width of the table to calculate the size of each of the individual columns.

CHAPTER 6

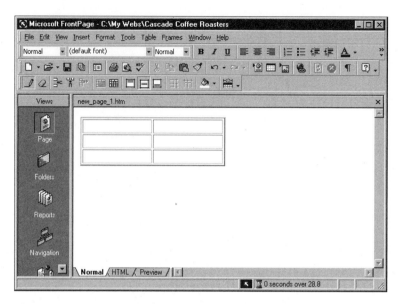

Figure 6-16

This table has three rows and two columns, is left-justified on the page, has a 2-pixel border, 1-pixel cell padding, and 2-pixel cell spacing, and has a width setting of 50 percent.

Working with Tables

Once you have a table on your page, you'll probably want to fine-tune it.

Adding text

You can type in a table cell just as you would anywhere else on a page in Page view. If you add more text than the cell is formatted to hold, the cell expands to accommodate it.

Changing table properties

At any time, you can change settings for table alignment, border size, cell padding, cell spacing, and overall table width by using the Table Properties command. Simply right-click anywhere on the table and then choose Table Properties from the pop-up menu. You can also access table properties by placing your pointer in the table and then choosing Table Properties from the Table menu. The Table Properties dialog box opens, as shown in Figure 6-17.

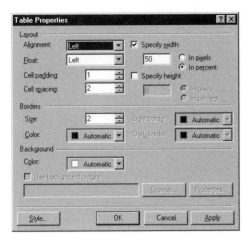

Figure 6-17

The Table Properties dialog box.

You can quickly add a table to your page: click the Insert Table button on the toolbar and then select the size of your table by clicking the appropriate box on the grid that appears. The table properties are based on the last table property setting.

To obtain a "test view" of what your table might look like with different settings, you can change some settings in the Table Properties dialog box and then click Apply. You can change the settings and then click Apply as many times as necessary.

Whenever you see the Style button in a FrontPage dialog box, it means that you can create or modify a style sheet associated with the page from within that dialog box. For more information on style sheets, see Chapter 10.

In addition, you can insert a background image or add a background color by checking the Use Background Picture check box. When you make this selection, you'll see that the Browse button becomes available. If you click Browse, you'll have a few different ways to choose an image. Do one of the following:

- If you want to use a background image that is currently in your Web, find the file in the appropriate folder and then click OK.

- If you want to use a background image from another location, such as a floppy disk, hard drive, or LAN, locate the background image in the Select Background Image dialog box and then click OK. You can also select a background image from the World Wide Web or make a hyperlink to a file on your computer.

- You can also use FrontPage-provided clip art for your background image. To do so, click the Clip Art tab, click a background image, and then click OK.

If your table has borders, you can specify their colors in the Border Colors section of the Table Properties dialog box. To use a uniform color for all borders, select that color in the Border drop-down list. Selecting colors from the Light Border and Dark Border drop-down lists allows you to give the table a three-dimensional look. The light border color specifies the highlight color, and the dark border color the shadow color. Experiment with these colors to customize the look of your tables.

NOTE

An easy way to expand the number of rows in a table is to position your pointer in the lower-right cell and then press the Tab key.

Changing cell properties

You can change some properties of cells, such as the alignment of text within them, their minimum width, the number of rows or columns they span, and their background images or colors. Here's how to view and change these properties:

1. Position your pointer in a cell with properties you want to change. To change the properties for multiple cells at once, you need to select those cells first. To do so, position your pointer in one of the cells and then choose Select Cell from the Table menu. Then press and hold the Ctrl or Shift key to select additional cells with the pointer. Holding down the Ctrl key also lets you deselect selected cells. For information on methods for easily selecting entire rows or columns, see "Selecting Rows and Columns" later in this chapter.

PART

III

2. Choose Cell Properties from the Table menu or right-click the selected cell(s) and choose Cell Properties from the pop-up menu. The Cell Properties dialog box appears, as shown in Figure 6-18.

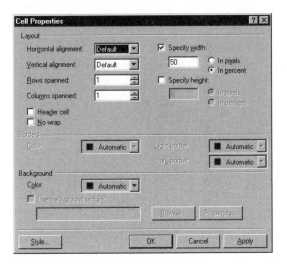

Figure 6-18
The Cell Properties dialog box.

3. To change the alignment of text within the cell(s), alter the settings in the Layout section. For example, to align the text in the exact center of a cell, select Center for the Horizontal Alignment and Middle for the Vertical Alignment.

4. Enter new numbers in the Specify Width and Specify Height text boxes to change the width and height of the cell(s), respectively. You can set the number in pixels or as a percentage of the table width. For example, if you set the cell width to 50 percent, the cell spans half the width of the table.

5. Use the Rows Spanned and Columns Spanned text boxes to enter the number of rows or columns you want a cell to span. Changing this setting expands the cell to cross that number of rows or columns. This causes cells in the column to the right or the rows below to move accordingly to make room for the enlarged cell. One reason you might want to expand a cell in this fashion is to fill the area with an image.

For example, suppose you have a two-row, two-column table, and you want an image to fill the area below the top two cells. You can expand the bottom left cell so that it spans the two columns. To insert a background image or add background color to the cell(s), choose the appropriate options in the Custom Background section.

6. To add colored borders to the cell(s), select those colors in the Borders and Background areas of the dialog box.

7. Click Apply to view your changed settings before closing the dialog box. When the settings are the way you want them, click OK to exit the Cell Properties dialog box.

Creating header cells

Header cells are marked for special formatting; in FrontPage tables, the text is made bold and centered in the cell. A header cell is often useful as a title at the top of a column or at the left end of a row, but it can be any cell that you want to make prominent in your table. You can turn any regular cell into a header cell by doing the following:

1. Select the cell you want to turn into a header cell. To select multiple cells, select the first cell and then press and hold the Ctrl or Shift key while you click additional cells.

2. Choose Properties from the Table menu and Cell from the submenu, or right-click the selected cell(s) and choose Cell Properties from the pop-up menu. In the Cell Properties dialog box, check the Header Cell check box and then click OK.

That cell becomes a header cell, and any existing text in the cell is shown in bold and centered. Any additional text you type in the cell will also be bold and centered. Be aware that different browsers might treat header cell formatting in different ways.

Selecting rows and columns

To select a row or a column, position the mouse pointer near the top of a column or near the left border of a row until it turns into a solid arrow, and then click. You can also place your pointer in a cell, choose Select from the Table menu, and then choose Table, Column, Row, or Cell from the pop-up menu.

Moving around within a table

You use the arrow keys to move from character to character (or element to element) within a cell and the Tab key to move from cell to cell.

Adding cells

If you need to add a piece of information in your table but have nowhere to add it, you can always insert a blank cell. Inserting a cell in a table adds one more cell to the row into which you insert it and can extend the row outside the original table boundary. Figure 6-19 shows a cell added to the right of the cell that has 6 in it.

As you can see, inserting cells can make your tables asymmetrical, but that just might be your goal. To insert a cell, position your pointer in the cell directly to the left of where you want the new cell to appear. Then choose Insert from the Table menu and Cell from the pop-up menu.

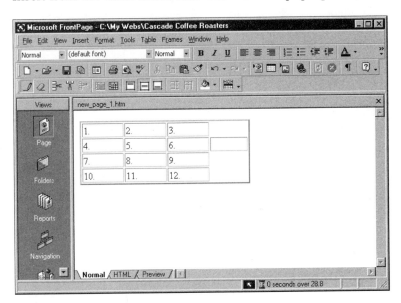

Figure 6-19

A table that's had a cell added to the right.

Adding rows

To add a row or rows to your table, do the following:

1. Position your pointer in the row above or below where you want the new row(s) to appear.

2. Choose Insert from the Table menu and Rows Or Columns from the submenu. You'll see the Insert Rows Or Columns dialog box, shown here in Figure 6-20.

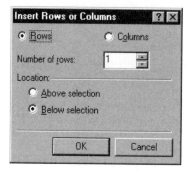

Figure 6-20

The Insert Rows Or Columns dialog box.

3. Select the Rows option and enter the number of rows you want to insert. Then specify whether you want the row(s) to be inserted above or below the row you selected, and click OK.

Adding columns

To add one or more columns to a table, position your pointer in the column next to where you want the new column or columns to appear. Then follow the same procedure outlined above in "Adding Rows," but select the Columns option and enter the number of columns you want to insert.

> To add a blank paragraph after a table, position the pointer at the end of the lower-right cell and then press Ctrl+Enter.

Deleting rows or columns

To delete a row or a column, select the row or column you want to delete, and then choose Delete Cells from the Table menu.

Inserting a caption

A *table caption* is a descriptive headline that appears at the top of your table. To insert a caption for the table, choose Insert from the Table menu and Caption from the pop-up menu. Your pointer will be blinking at the top of the table, ready for you to start typing. If you want to switch the caption to the bottom of the table, right-click the caption and choose Caption Properties from the pop-up menu. In the Caption Properties dialog box that appears, select either Top of Table or Bottom of Table. You can format the caption text just as you would any other text on a page.

PART
III

Moving rows or columns

Here's how to move a row or a column to another place in a table. In FrontPage (as in Excel), when you paste a portion of a table, the pasted information replaces whatever was in the new location. Therefore, to move a row or a column without losing any existing information, you must first insert a blank row or column into which you'll paste the row or column you want to move. For this example, we'll move a row, but the same procedure works for columns:

1. If there are no blank rows in the table, insert a row to serve as the destination row for the material you want to move.

2. Select the row you want to move, and then choose Cut from the Edit menu or press Ctrl+X.

3. Select the blank row you want to move the material to, and then choose Paste from the Edit menu or press Ctrl+V. The material is pasted in the new row.

This procedure also works for material you want to copy from one row or column to another. You can cut and copy multiple rows and columns at once in the same way.

Splitting cells

To provide more detailed information in your table, or to clean up the formatting on a page, you might want to split a cell. When you split a cell, you divide a single cell into as many rows or columns as you need. Here's how:

1. Position your pointer in the cell you want to split.

2. Choose Split Cells from the Table menu. The Split Cells dialog box appears, as shown in Figure 6-21.

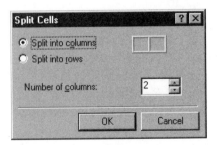

Figure 6-21

The Split Cells dialog box.

3. Specify whether you want to split the cell into columns or rows, and then enter the number of new columns or rows you want in that cell. Click OK.

Figure 6-22 shows an example of a three-column table that has its center column split into three rows:

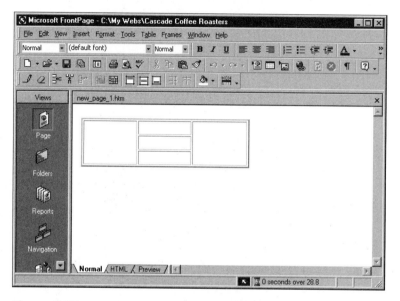

Figure 6-22

A table with its center column split into three rows.

Merging cells

There might be times when you want to combine material from several neighboring cells into one cell. This is called *merging cells*. Here's how to do it:

1. Select the cells you want to merge. To select multiple cells, select the first cell and then click in the next cell while pressing and holding the Ctrl or Shift key. When merging cells, you can select as many cells as you want, but ultimately you must select a rectangular area.

2. Choose Merge Cells from the Table menu, and FrontPage merges the cells, removing any cell borders shared by the merged cells. The result is a larger cell, as shown in Figure 6-23. The content of each cell is retained and formatted as a separate paragraph.

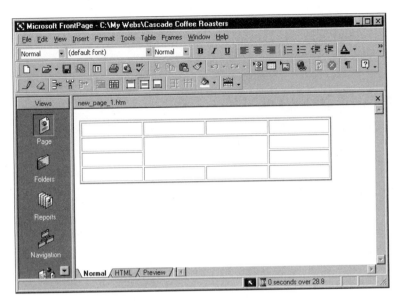

Figure 6-23

A table with its four centermost cells merged.

Adding images to cells

To add an image to a table cell, position your pointer in the cell, choose Picture from the Insert menu, and then choose either Clip Art or From File from the pop-up menu. You can also drag an image from Windows Explorer. For detailed information on inserting images, see Chapter 8.

Inserting tables within tables

FrontPage allows you to insert a table within a table. You might want to use a table within a table to arrange your data in a special way. Or you might want the look of several bordered tables on a page. If you use tables to present thumbnail images that users can click to obtain a larger version of the image, using a table within a table might help you present the thumbnails in a more logical or graphically pleasing way than in an ordinary table.

Before you use the table-within-a-table strategy, consider whether you can obtain the same results by splitting cells. Keeping your table design as simple as possible can save you time when you troubleshoot any problems on your pages.

To insert a table within a table, first position the pointer in the cell where you want the new table to appear. Then create the new table by choosing

CHAPTER 6

Insert from the Table menu and then Table from the submenu or by clicking the Insert Table button on the toolbar. This process was described in
"Inserting a Table," earlier in this chapter.

Using WYSIWYG Frames

Frames are rectangular regions on a Web page in which you can display other
pages or images. In FrontPage, you can create frames pages using the frames
templates as described in Chapter 4.

Uses for Frames

You can use frames in a variety of ways limited only by your imagination.
You should use a frame whenever you want particular content on a page
to remain static while other content on the page changes. Page designers
often insert a company logo in a frame at the top of a page and divide the
rest of the page among frames for other content.

Another way to use frames might be to present a list of your company's
products in a frame on the left side of a page and then to include a description
of each product appearing on a page in a frame on the right side. The page
in the left frame is static; you want the list of products to appear all the time.
The page that appears in the right frame changes according to the product
the user clicks in the left frame. You can associate each of the links on the
page in the left frame with a target frame, which in this case is the right frame.
Thus, when a user clicks a link on a page in the left frame, the appropriate
page appears in the target frame on the right side of the page.

For example, in the left frame of one page of Cascade Coffee Roasters' RoasterNet Web, you might present a list of the months of the year. You
could link each month to a sales report page for that particular month that
would appear in the right frame. Or, in a frame near the top of the page,
you could place a list of forms that employees need to submit periodically;
you could put the forms themselves in a larger window near the bottom of
the page. The following figure shows an example of a Web page in progress,
containing three frames displayed in Page view.

As you can see in Figure 6-24, the page is divided into three sections,
each separated by a gray border. Notice that it appears in Page view in the
same way as it would appear in a user's browser.

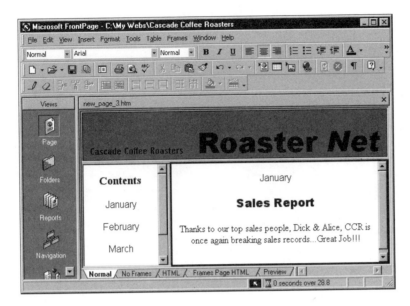

Figure 6-24
Page view showing three frames.

Framesets

A *frameset* is actually a separate page that contains the combined information of the pages in the set. The frameset page communicates with the server to display the pages in a browser. In the previous example, there are three pages visible; add to that the frameset page, and the total number of pages required for displaying the frames is four. This means that four hits to the server are necessary before the server can display the pages, which suggests why it's a good idea to limit the number of frames in each frameset.

FrontPage displays all of the pages in a frameset together in Page view. You can create, manipulate, and view frames pages in FrontPage. This WYSIWYG viewing is extremely helpful when you design with frames. In the "old" days, you had to open each page individually in order to work on it, and you could view the finished results only in a browser.

Working with Frames

When you use the frames templates (described in Chapter 4) to create frames, FrontPage automatically creates the individual pages and the frameset, and it displays all of the frames in Page view. Now, isn't that nice?

Define your new frames page

When you first create a frames page in FrontPage, as shown in Figure 6-25, the pages aren't set for you. You need to make some quick choices before you can begin to populate them with content:

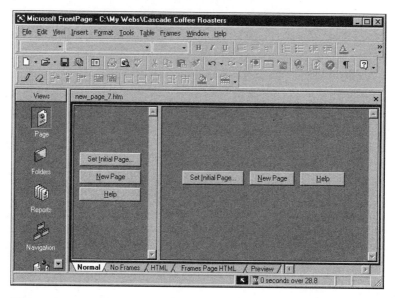

Figure 6-25

A new frames page created with the Contents frame template.

- **Set Initial Page.** The *initial page* is the page initially displayed in a frame when a user first opens the frame. Each page in a frameset needs to be set separately. When you click this button, it brings up the Create Hyperlink dialog box. Here, you can create a new page and a link to it or, if you have existing pages in your Web, you can set the initial page to any page currently saved in your Web. For more information on the Create Hyperlink dialog box, see the "Links" section in Chapter 7.

- **New Page.** When you click this button, a new page is displayed in the frame. This is an unsaved page created with the Normal template. For more information on page templates, see Chapter 4.

Once you define your pages in the frameset, you're ready to begin adding content and laying out the page. Figure 6-26 shows a frame that has a new page created, ready for content and layout.

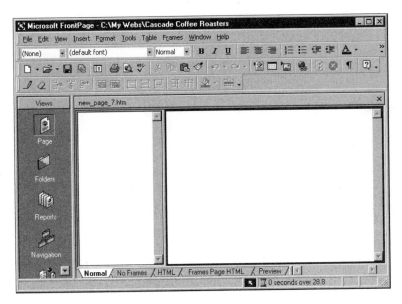

Figure 6-26

A frameset with a new page created.

Selecting a page or a frameset

When you click anywhere in a frame, the page it contains becomes the active page. A colored border around a page signals that it's the active page. Click anywhere on an outer border of the frameset to select the entire frameset.

Setting frame properties

Select a single frame page and choose Frame Properties from the Frames menu or right-click on the page and choose Frame Properties from the pop-up menu. This displays the Frame Properties dialog box, as Figure 6-27, on the next page, shows.

From here, you make changes to an individual frames page. Just in case you weren't happy with your earlier choices, you can give the page a new name by typing the name in the Name: text box. You can also set a new initial page by typing directly into the Initial Page: text box, or by clicking the Browse button. Clicking Browse brings up the Edit Hyperlink dialog box, which (as the Create Hyperlink dialog box, which is identical) is described in detail in Chapter 7.

There are three other areas of this dialog box that let you further customize your frames page: Frame Size, Margins, and Options.

- **Frame Size.** Here you can adjust the Width or Row Height of the frame.

CHAPTER 6

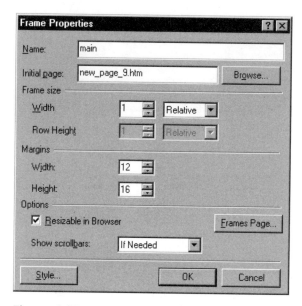

Figure 6-27

The Frame Properties dialog box.

● **Width:** If the frame page is in a column alongside another frame, these options are available. Choose Relative if you want the frame size to be based on the other frames in the column; for example, a relative value of 1 means that the frames in the column will be of equal size. A relative value of 3 in one frame and 1 in the second frame means that the first frame will be three times wider than the other. Choose Percent if you want the frame to occupy a certain percentage of the total window when it's displayed in a browser. And if you want to define an exact size for the frame, insert a value and choose Pixels.

● **Row Height:** These options are available if the frame is in a row that has another row of frames to its left or right. You define the values in the same way as for Width.

FrontPage changes all frames in a row or column uniformly when you change any one of the frames pages in that row or column.

● **Margins.** If you want to adjust the margins within the page, enter the value in the Width and Height text boxes. Anything displayed on the page is offset by the value entered here, in pixels.

- **Options.** Here you can specify whether the frame is automatically resized by the browser, based on the browser the visitor is using. The box is checked by default and, for most pages, that's a good idea. You can also decide when to show scroll bars: If Needed, Never, or Always. If Needed is selected by default; it's a good idea not to change this unless you're certain that the content won't need to scroll. If you select Always, the page will have scroll bars no matter how much content is on the page and no matter what resolution the user has set. Unnecessary scroll bars not only look unprofessional, but they also can put viewers in a bad mood and make them want to leave your site—and we want them to stay, right?

- **Frames page properties.** You can make changes to the frameset by selecting a page in the frameset and then choosing Frame Properties from the Frame menu. This brings up the Frame Properties dialog box; click the Frames Page button. The Page Properties dialog box appears; select the Frames tab. You have two options here:

  - **Frame Spacing.** You can add spacing between the frames, in pixels, by typing a number in the Frame Spacing box.

  - **Show Borders.** You can show or hide frame borders by checking or clearing the Show Borders check box.

  For more information on the Page Properties dialog box, see Chapter 7.

  If you want to create or edit a style sheet associated with the page, click Style to display the Style dialog box. For more information on this dialog box, see Chapter 7.

  When you finish making changes to the frame, click OK.

Setting page properties

You can change the properties of a page by right-clicking it and choosing Page Properties from the pop-up menu. The Page Properties dialog box appears. For more information on the Page Properties dialog box, see Chapter 7. You can also change the default target frame. For instructions on doing this, see "Assigning Default Target Frames," later in this chapter.

Saving frames and framesets for the first time

Saving the frames pages for the first time, and the frameset page itself, works in exactly the same way as saving a regular page for the first time, with one cool difference. When you save a frame for the first time, the Save As dialog box displays a thumbnail version of your frameset in which the current

CHAPTER 6

page is highlighted, ready to be saved, as shown in Figure 6-28 on the next page. This lets you know exactly which frame is being saved and what its name is.

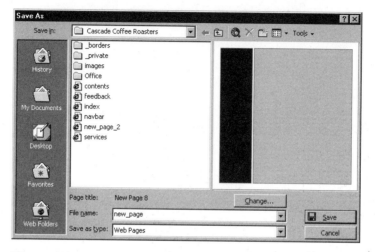

Figure 6-28

The Save As dialog box highlighting the frame to be saved.

When you name the page and click OK, the next page is highlighted in the thumbnail, ready to be saved. Once you've saved the frames, you'll be asked to save the frameset page.

NOTE

It's a good idea, especially when saving frames pages and the frameset page that controls them, to use names that are easy to remember. Later on, you'll want links from one frame to open pages in another frame. Without logically named pages, this linking process can get confusing.

Saving when the page has been saved previously

Once you've saved the page for the first time, every subsequent save occurs in the background.

Deleting a frame

If you want to delete a frame from the frameset, select the frame and choose Delete Frame from the Frames menu. The frame is deleted and the remaining frames expand to fill the window.

PART
III

Opening a page in a new window

If you want to view a frame page in its own window outside the frameset, right-click the page and choose Open Page In New Window from the pop-up menu, or choose Open Page In New Window from the Frames menu.

Splitting a page in a frameset

After you've created a frameset by using a Frames template, you may decide that you need another frame. You can generate one quickly from the Frame menu.

1. Select the frames page you want to split by clicking inside the page. The page should now be outlined in color.

2. Choose Split Frame from the Frame menu to see the Split Frame dialog box, shown in Figure 6-29. This dialog box works in exactly the same way as the Insert Rows Or Columns dialog box does, as explained in "Adding rows and columns" earlier in this chapter.

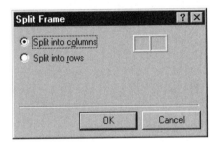

Figure 6-29

The Split Frame dialog box.

3. Select Split Into Columns or Split Into Rows and then click OK.

Displaying a Page in a Frame

To designate a page to appear in a frame, you can create a link to the page and associate the link with the frame. This all happens in the Create Hyperlink or Edit Hyperlink dialog box. For example, suppose RoasterNet has a Table of Contents page that contains the word "Sales" in the frame on the left, which is already linked to a page containing sales information. You want to click the Sales link and have the Sales page appear in the frame on the right. Here's how to set this up:

1. Open your frameset in Page view.

2. On the Table of Contents page, right-click the Sales link and choose Hyperlink Properties from the pop-up menu to open the Edit Hyperlink dialog box, as Figure 6-30 on the next page shows.

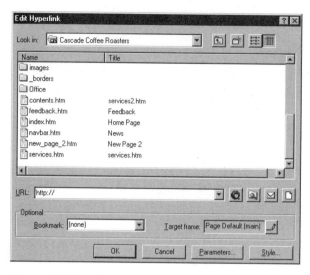

Figure 6-30

The Edit Hyperlink dialog box.

3. Specify the URL in the URL text box or use the drop-down list to view the files most recently used by FrontPage. For more information on the other options in the Edit Hyperlink dialog box, see Chapter 7.

4. Click the button to the right of the Target Frame text box to see the Target Frame dialog box, shown here in Figure 6-31. Enter the name of the frame you want the Sales page to appear in. You can also click the frameset thumbnail (the picture that represents your frameset) to select the target frame.

You can skip step 4 if you've already set a default target frame for the page and you're happy with it. For more information on setting the default target frame, see "Assigning Default Target Frames," later in this chapter.

5. Click OK in each dialog box to return to Page view.

Back in Page view, you can follow the Sales link in the left frame, which opens the Sales page in the right frame. To follow a link in Page view, make sure the Normal view tab is selected, and then right-click the link and choose Follow Hyperlink from the pop-up menu, or Ctrl+click the link.

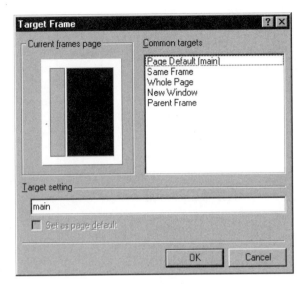

Figure 6-31

The Target Frame dialog box.

Displaying Form Submission Results in a Frame

In the same way that you can direct a standard page to appear in a frame, you can direct the results of a form submission to appear in a frame. This result is typically used with the Custom ISAPI, NSAPI, or CGI script, or with Database Region Wizard form handlers. For more information on these topics, see Chapter 10. Here's how to set this up:

1. In Page view, right-click any form field and choose Form Properties from the pop-up menu to open the Form Properties dialog box, shown in Figure 6-32.

2. Click the button to the right of the Target Frame text box to display the Target Frame dialog box. Enter the name of the frame in which you want the form results to appear.

3. Click OK to close the Target Frame dialog box, and then click OK to close the Form Properties dialog box.

For more information on creating and using forms, see the section named accordingly in Chapter 9.

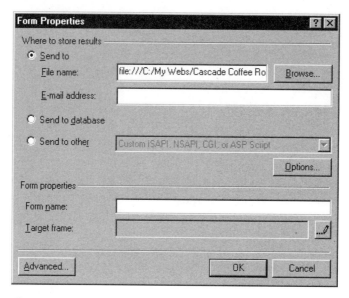

Figure 6-32

The Form Properties dialog box.

Assigning Default Target Frames

If you have a page that contains many links and you don't want to assign a target frame to each one of them, you can associate them all with a default target frame. Default target frames specify a frame for any links on a page (including clickable images) that aren't associated with a specific target frame. To assign a default target frame, do the following:

1. When the page is open in Page view, right-click anywhere on the page and choose Page Properties from the pop-up menu.

2. In the Page Properties dialog box, click the General tab, and then click the button to the right of the Default Target Frame text box to display the Target Frame dialog box. Enter the name of the frame in which you want the form results to appear, and then click OK.

    You can still edit an individual hyperlink to point to a target frame other than the default target. This process is described previously in this chapter in "Displaying a Page in a Frame."

Using Frames View Tabs

When you first open a frameset in Page view, you may notice a new series of view tabs at the bottom of the window. Each of these tabs gives you a different look, behind the scenes of your frameset and frames pages.

PART

III

● **Normal.** The Normal tab is selected by default. This is your "working" view in FrontPage, the view we've been working in thus far.

● **No Frames.** If users try to open your frames Web but have a browser that doesn't support frames, they'll see the text on this page automatically. You can change this as you like.

● **HTML.** This tab shows the HTML for all the frames in the current frameset. This is a fully functioning HTML editor, so be careful what you change.

● **Frames Page HTML.** Here, you'll be able to edit and view the HTML for the frameset. Be careful here, too: Don't change anything unless you're experienced in using HTML and frames.

● **Preview.** You can preview your page right in FrontPage by selecting this tab. FrontPage does its best to display the pages as they would appear in a browser, but for the most accurate representation, you should use the Preview in Browser feature described earlier in this chapter.

Coming Up

With that, the grand discussion of creating your pages in Page view comes to an end. In the next chapter, you'll learn how to format your pages, and you'll also learn about some of the utilities and useful commands in Page view.

Fine-Tuning Your Pages

I Wonder What This Would Look Like...

Once you've got the material you want on your pages, more than likely you'll want to fine-tune it. Your paragraphs don't have to stay left-aligned, your text doesn't all have to remain the same size and color, and the links and background of your pages don't have to stay the same, either. When you use Microsoft FrontPage 2000, you can easily change all of this and more. And with the advent of the Positioning toolbar, you have even more precise control over the elements on your pages.

You've probably noticed many Web pages that use plain black text in a single size, which makes for plain, boring paragraphs. Even though the trend is moving in the other direction, we still have a long way to go before the majority of Web pages are pleasing to the eye. Using FrontPage, you can format your pages so they really stand out in comparison to the competition—like a Ferrari next to a beat-up, rusted 1973 Pinto. Your pages will catch more eyes and generate a positive reception if they're lively as well as clean.

Now that FrontPage is integrated with Microsoft Office, you have much more flexibility in formatting your pages than you had in earlier versions of FrontPage. You can do most formatting simply by using the Formatting toolbar (Figure 7-1); you can turn it on and off by choosing Toolbars from the View menu and then choosing Formatting from the pop-up menu.

Figure 7-1

The Formatting toolbar.

We'll begin with an exploration of how to use Themes in FrontPage, and then we'll continue with the formatting basics, starting with fonts.

Working with Themes

How many times have you visited a Web, only to find it just plain old ugly? There are no interesting colors or buttons, and the only thing consistent between the pages is that they're consistently bad. Have you ever felt as if you'd like to put together a great, professional-looking Web, one that looks like the pages go together, but you're concerned that you simply might not have the time or the talent to produce pages like a professional graphic designer? Well, FrontPage is going to make your day, because using Themes, you can do all that and more. No one ever has to know that you didn't spend years in art school.

Using Themes

The developers of FrontPage have designed Themes with the new or business user in mind. (Professional graphic designers will probably want to create their own graphics from scratch. For more information on creating graphics for the Web, see Chapter 8.) When you apply a theme to your Web, you get professionally designed buttons, banners, backgrounds, text, and link colors, all of them developed to look good and work together to form a consistent-looking Web. You also get the added feature of being able to modify the colors, graphics, or styles in a theme, just in case you want to play graphic designer for a day.

To see the Themes dialog box, as shown in Figure 7-2, choose Theme from the Format menu.

If no theme has been applied to your Web or page, (No Theme) is selected in the list box on the left side of the dialog box. If a theme currently is applied to your Web, its name is highlighted in the list.

The right portion of the Themes view contains a Theme Preview window. As you select the various themes in the list, FrontPage displays them in this window. You can scroll through this preview window to view all of the options in the selected theme. FrontPage comes with plenty of themes to choose from, so have some fun and look around. As always, consider who you're creating the Web for and how a given theme might affect the user experience.

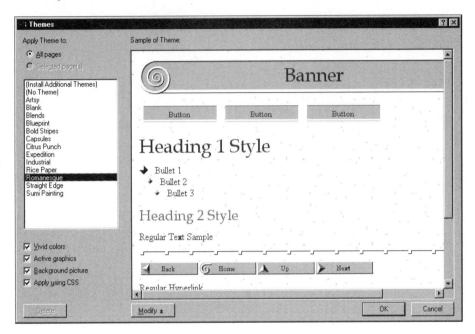

Figure 7-2

The Themes dialog box.

Using a Theme: the Basics

To ensure that themes within a Web remain consistent and work together properly, FrontPage doesn't let you pick and choose pieces of one theme and add them to another theme. However, you *can* alter the way a particular theme looks. When you choose a theme, you have a few basic options that affect the way the browser presents that theme.

- **Vivid Colors.** Select this check box to make the colors of the various buttons, backgrounds, and other elements stand out more vividly. When this check box is unselected, most of the elements appear as black and white, with color enhancing only a few pieces.

- **Active Graphics.** Select this check box to populate your Web with more interactive graphics. Some elements, like bullets, become animated. Navigation buttons change appearance as the user moves the mouse over or clicks them. Be careful not to overdo

171

animation, because too much action on a page can distract users. If Active Graphics is unselected, the elements on the page aren't interactive; they have a more subtle elegance, and they'll appear more quickly in the user's browser.

- **Background Image.** This check box acts as a toggle to switch between having a background image and having a background color. All of the themes have a tiled background designed to fit with the theme. If you select Vivid Colors but not Background Image, FrontPage chooses an appropriate background color for your theme.

- **Apply Theme Using CSS.** If you want your theme to use Cascading Style Sheets (CSS) to customize the fonts, sizes, colors, and positioning, check the Apply Theme Using CSS check box. For more information on CSS, see Chapter 10.

You have two options when it comes to applying a theme. If you want to apply the theme to the entire Web, select the All Pages option under the heading Apply Theme To in the Themes dialog box. If you want to apply the theme to a single page, or to a selection of pages, first select the pages in FrontPage (in the Folders view, for example). Then open the Themes dialog box and activate the Selected Page(s) option. Click OK to have FrontPage apply the theme automatically to the entire Web or to a selection of pages.

Using a Theme: Advanced

Okay, so you've looked through the supplied themes, and they're all pretty cool, but you want something a little different, more *you*. If you had the ability to just alter the theme—change a color here, a font there, or maybe throw in one of your own graphics—now, that would be cool. Well, it looks like this is your day. By taking advantage of the advanced themes features in FrontPage, you open a whole world of possibilities.

To begin using the advanced themes features, click Modify at the bottom of the Themes dialog box. Remember, though, that if you only want to apply these changes to selected pages, you must select them before you open the Themes dialog box.

When you click Modify, FrontPage presents you with three new options: Colors, Graphics, and Styles. Clicking any of these buttons opens a unique dialog box that offers a series of customization options, described next.

Modifying the colors

You've selected a theme that you really like, except for one thing—the colors. If you could only change the color of the fonts, that would be great. By selecting Colors and using the Modify Theme dialog box shown in Figure 7-3, you can do just that.

When you first open this dialog box, you'll notice a few interesting things about the themes. Each theme is listed in the left column and has a series of colors next to its name. These colors are the *color schemes* or "color palette" used in the theme. Each theme is made up of a series of six colors, all from the color safety palette. The *safety palette* is a collection of 256 standard colors that have been determined to appear correctly in most browsers. For more information on the safety palette, see Chapter 8. By knowing the colors in a given theme's palette, you can easily create any additional graphics using the same palette, ensuring that they work with your new theme. Select any of the themes that you want to modify.

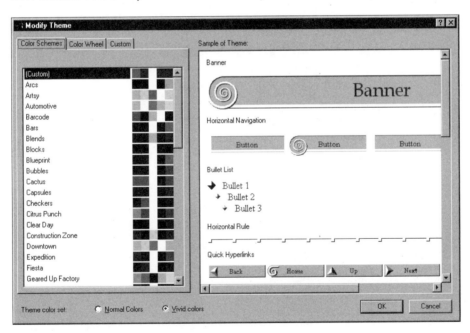

Figure 7-3
The Color Schemes tab of the Modify Theme dialog box.

CHAPTER

7

Once you've selected a theme to modify, click the Color Wheel tab in the Modify Theme dialog box (shown in Figure 7-4) to get started altering the color palette in that theme.

By clicking in different areas of the color wheel, you'll see that both the palette for a given color scheme and the colors in the theme sample change. Experiment to your heart's content. When you've made a decision, you can use the Brightness slider bar to adjust the brightness of the palette. Of course, if all you want to do is adjust the brightness, you can do that without modifying the color scheme.

The final tab in the Modify Theme dialog box, the Custom tab shown in Figure 7-5, lets you modify the colors of the fonts used in the theme. Pretty cool, eh?

Make a selection from the Item drop-down list, and then select a color from the Color drop-down list. The theme sample automatically reflects your changes, so you can see just exactly what you've done. You can select one of the 16 standard colors, or you can select More Colors to view the Color dialog box. For more information about the Color dialog box, see Chapter 8.

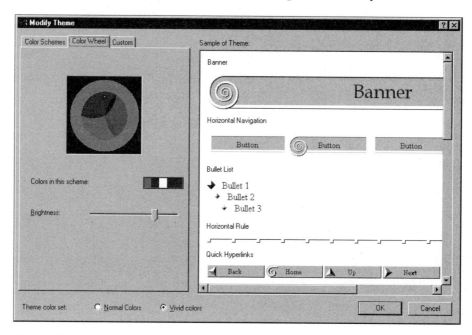

Figure 7-4

The Color Wheel tab of the Modify Theme dialog box.

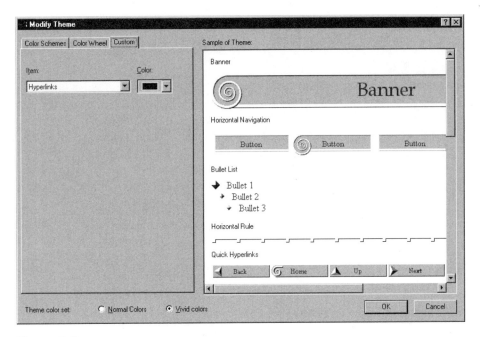

Figure 7-5
The Custom tab of the Modify Theme dialog box.

Of course, it's a good idea to use discrimination when changing the colors of the fonts, or you might end up with a circus on your hands. Remember, the idea is that themes are supposed to make the pages more interesting—not to sacrifice the usability of the page.

Modifying the graphics
This is where you really get the chance to show your stuff—to bring out the graphic designer in you and impress your friends and neighbors. Well, it's pretty doggone cool.

To modify the graphics in a theme, click the Graphics button in the Modify Theme dialog box, as shown in Figure 7-6, on the next page.

You select an item to modify from the Item drop-down list. Enter the name of the new graphic in the text field, or browse to find the image, and whammo, you're finished. You've just modified a graphic in your theme.

When you select an item from the list, it appears automatically in the Sample Of Theme window, and its file name appears in the text field with a description above it. The Sample Of Theme window lets you keep track of everything you're doing and see what you're getting before you click OK.

If you've selected an item that uses fonts, click the Font tab to see your font choices.

CHAPTER 7

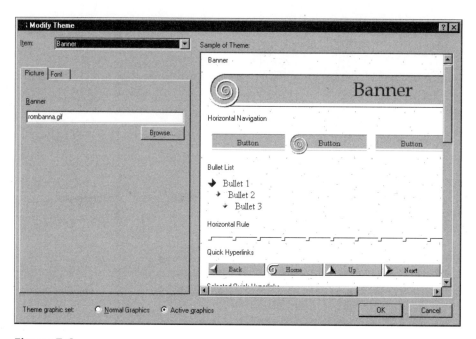

Figure 7-6

The Modify Theme dialog box after the Graphics button is clicked.

On the Font tab, you can change the font, its style, its size, and its horizontal and vertical alignment. The Sample Of Theme window reflects each change you make.

There are a couple of things to keep in mind when making changes to the fonts. Don't go too crazy selecting tons of different fonts. Just a couple of different fonts per theme is plenty. And remember that in order for users to view these cool fonts, they'll need to have them installed on their own computers. So it's a good idea to stick to the standard fonts supplied with your operating system, unless you're sure that visitors to your Web have the fonts you'll be using.

Modifying styles

Clicking the third Modify button brings you to the dialog box shown in Figure 7-7, where you can change the styles associated with a certain item. Select an item from the Item drop-down list, choose a new font from the Font window, and before you know it, you're manipulating styles.

When you're selecting fonts for styles, keep in mind that the same rules apply as mentioned previously—don't go too crazy here.

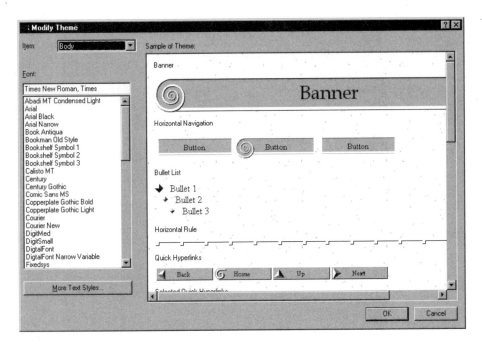

Figure 7-7

The Modify Theme dialog box after the Text button is clicked.

If you want to make even more changes to styles, perhaps by adjusting their alignment on the page, click the More Styles button to open the Style dialog box, as shown in Figure 7-8. For more information about using the Style dialog box and Cascading Style Sheets, see Chapter 10.

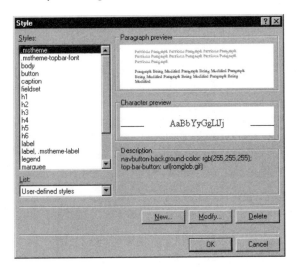

Figure 7-8

The Style dialog box.

After you've made changes to a theme using the Modify buttons, click OK. You can then click Save As in the Themes dialog box to save the theme for later use.

Formatting Fonts

FrontPage gives you many options for formatting characters in different sizes, colors, and styles. You can change most of this formatting by using the buttons on the Formatting toolbar, but you can make the same changes by choosing various menu commands. You can, however, use style sheets to define custom heading sizes and other font and paragraph attributes. For more information about using style sheets, see "Cascading Style Sheets" in Chapter 10. The following sections provide a primer on your character-formatting options.

Choosing Heading Size

FrontPage follows the HTML standard of using headings to determine the size of the fonts on a page. The headings determine the size at which the fonts are displayed in the browser, and the smaller the heading number, the larger the size. For example, a heading 1 is larger than a heading 2, and so on.

You define the size of a heading on your page by selecting the appropriate heading from the Style drop-down list on the Formatting toolbar.

Choosing Text Size

In addition to changing the heading sizes, you can also change the point size of the text on your page; the higher the point size, the larger the text. The default point size is 12, which works well for reading text on a computer screen.

Here's the easiest way to change the size of your text: Select the text you want to change—it can be a single letter or word, a line, a paragraph, or an entire page (to select the page, press Ctrl+A). Then click the Font Size drop-down list on the Formatting toolbar and choose the font size you want. Alternatively, you can use the Font command on the Format menu to change text size.

Choosing Text Color

An occasional change of color in your text can attract attention, but we stress "occasional." Too many different text colors can make a page look busy and cluttered. One good way to use a second text color is to make the first words of important paragraphs a different color. This can help to "index" the page; readers pay attention to anomalies, and a different text color is just that if you use it sparingly.

Changing text color

You can make your text any of 16 standard colors supplied by FrontPage, or any other custom color. To change the color of your text, select the text you want to change and then click the Font Color button on the Formatting toolbar.

In the pop-up dialog box that appears, click the color you want. If you want to use a custom color, click the More Colors button to display the Color dialog box, from which you can define the new color. You can even define colors using Hex color values, so the possibilities are endless. If you're designing your Web using a 256-color "safety" palette, be sure, when you create a custom color, to make it part of that palette. For more information on the Color dialog box, Hex color values, and color palettes, see Chapter 8.

Choosing Font Type

With a wide range of fonts and several styling options to choose from, you can easily craft the effect that you want for your pages. However, you should strive for consistency—don't use too many different fonts or font styles on a page. If you get carried away, your visitors will run screaming from your pages faster than a runaway semi down Teton Pass.

TIP

Remember that in order for a font to appear in the viewer's browser, it must be available on the viewer's computer system. If you choose a font that's not installed on the viewer's system, the browser defaults to another font, usually Times. If you really want to use a particular font, and you don't want to run the risk that viewers won't have it, make the text a graphic.

Changing fonts

You have oodles of fonts to choose from in FrontPage. If you've used the Font drop-down list in Microsoft Word, you'll have an easy transition to FrontPage.

C
H
A
P
T
E
R
7

To change fonts, select the text you want to change, and then click the Font Size drop-down list on the Formatting toolbar and select the font you want. If you're not sure what a particular font looks like, don't worry; FrontPage displays each font in the list as it will appear on the page.

Choosing Font Style

A change in font style (**bold**, *italics,* or underline, for example) can add just the right emphasis to words, phrases, or even entire paragraphs on your pages. Be objective in your use of style changes and consider how site visitors will see your pages. For example, consider those visitors to your Web who have less-than-perfect vision. Those people will have trouble reading an entire paragraph of italic text; that's why overusing italics and bold on computer screens is a big no-no.

Changing font style

You can easily change font style—to bold, italic, or underline—by clicking a toolbar button. FrontPage includes these buttons on the Formatting toolbar.

To change font style, select the text you want to change and then click one of the buttons.

Using font effects

FrontPage includes some additional styles called *Effects*. FrontPage supports these because the pages you open might contain special styles. Try to use regular styles, not special styles, when you create new text. The special styles might not appear in a browser as they do in Page view, because some browsers don't support many of them. If you want to apply a font effect to selected text, choose Font from the Format menu. In the Font dialog box, click the Font tab, as shown in Figure 7-9.

There are many font effects available. Selecting a check box displays an example of the style in the Sample section. To apply a special style, select the style and then click OK.

You can also select multiple styles. For example, selecting both Italic and Keyboard results in an italicized Keyboard style.

Changing character spacing

The second tab of the Font dialog box, the Character Spacing tab, lets you define the space between the letters (*characters*) in a word. This could come in handy if you're looking for that something extra to add a little zip to a headline or page title.

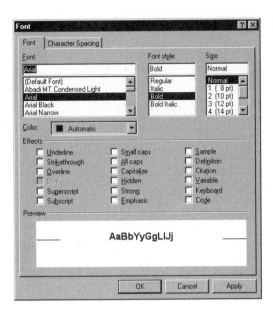

Figure 7-9

The Font tab of the Font dialog box.

If you want to change the character spacing of some selected text, choose Font from the Format menu. In the Font dialog box, click the Character Spacing tab. You can define the spacing of the letters by selecting an option in the By: drop-down list or by simply typing a value in the text field. You can also define the position of the text, either raised or lowered from the baseline, by choosing the appropriate values in the Position drop-down list.

Using Symbols

Symbols are also called *special characters;* they contain characters beyond those found in the standard seven-bit ASCII character set. Say what? All you need to know is that the *ASCII character set* is the most widely used character-coding system in the world, although it doesn't include all of the characters from European languages that use accent marks, many other foreign characters, and symbols such as the copyright mark and the trademark. But you can still use many of these special characters in FrontPage, and here's how:

1. Position the insertion pointer where you want the symbol to appear on your page.

2. Choose Symbol from the Insert menu to display the Symbol dialog box, shown in Figure 7-10, on the next page.

CHAPTER 7

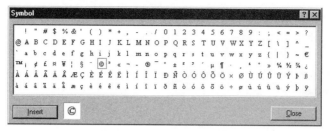

Figure 7-10

The Symbol dialog box.

3. Click a symbol and then click Insert. FrontPage inserts the symbol on the page but does not close the dialog box. You can insert more symbols directly following the symbol you just inserted by repeating this step.

4. Click Close when you're finished.

Once you've inserted a symbol on your page, you can format it just like any other text on your page. For example, if you insert a trademark symbol next to a word on your page, you might choose to take advantage of the superscript formatting option in the Font dialog box in order to raise the symbol next to the trademarked word.

Formatting Paragraphs

The other major type of formatting in FrontPage is paragraph-level formatting. You can format lines, sentences, and entire paragraphs, and you can implement such features as justification, list styles, line breaks, and exact page positioning. The following sections provide a collection of paragraph-level formatting options, many of which can help give your pages a flash-and-dazzle touch.

Creating a New Paragraph

Let's start at the simplest level. To create a new paragraph, press the Enter key. A blank line appears, and the new paragraph defaults to the Normal style.

To insert a new paragraph that has a different style, do the following:

1. Position the insertion point where you want the next paragraph to begin. If the insertion point is at the end of a line, press the Enter key once. If the insertion point is in the middle of a paragraph, press the Enter key twice and the Up arrow key once.

2. Select a new style from the Style drop-down list. Anything you type in the new paragraph appears in the style you've chosen.

PART
III

If you insert a new paragraph in the middle of an existing paragraph, FrontPage splits the original paragraph into two parts and adds the new paragraph between the two, keeping the original style for both parts. For example, if you insert a formatted paragraph in a Normal paragraph, you'll have a paragraph containing the first portion of the Normal paragraph, then the new Formatted paragraph, and finally the remaining portion of the original Normal paragraph.

Paragraph Properties

Web developers have always wanted to be able to make their pages stand out. They've always asked for more control over the way text appears on the page. One way that FrontPage has addressed these issues is by giving you more flexibility in the way you can position and space individual paragraphs. You can manipulate the content on your pages even more precisely by using the Position dialog box and the Positioning toolbar. For more information on those features, see "Using Exact Positioning," later in this chapter.

In order to see all the paragraph-formatting options, you need to open the Paragraph dialog box. You can do that in Page view by first placing the insertion point anywhere in the paragraph you want to change and then choosing Paragraph from the Format menu. The Paragraph dialog box, shown in Figure 7-11, appears.

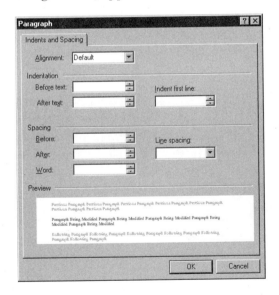

Figure 7-11

The Paragraph dialog box.

C
H
A
P
T
E
R

7

In the Paragraph dialog box, you can adjust paragraph alignment by selecting one of the options in the Alignment drop-down list: Left, Right, Center, or Justified. By default, paragraphs are left-aligned. In the other two sections of the Paragraph dialog box, Indentation and Spacing, you can either make a selection from the drop-down list or type directly in the text boxes.

The Preview window at the bottom of the Paragraph dialog box shows you what the paragraph will look like after you click OK. When you have the paragraph just the way you want it, click OK to see your changes applied to the paragraph in Page view.

Indenting a paragraph

When you want to indent a paragraph by hand in Page view, you can position the insertion point anywhere in the paragraph and click the Increase Indent button on the Formatting toolbar. To remove an indent, click the Decrease Indent button on the Formatting toolbar.

Aligning a paragraph

You can left-, center-, or right-align a paragraph by clicking a toolbar button. Just position the insertion point anywhere in the paragraph and then click the Align Left, Center, or Align Right button on the Formatting toolbar.

Use these buttons to align paragraphs on a page or to align text in a table cell. Left-aligning a paragraph leaves a ragged right margin; right-aligning a paragraph leaves a ragged left margin; and centering a paragraph leaves both sides ragged and centers the paragraph within its margins.

Changing Paragraph Styles

Suppose you want to change the style of a paragraph from Normal to Heading 3. You can do this with a click or two of the mouse. First select the paragraph whose style you want to change (or simply place the insertion point anywhere within the paragraph), and then, from the Style drop-down list, choose a new paragraph style.

List Properties

FrontPage gives you a vast array of list style options, including several varieties of bulleted lists and numbered lists, and an option for using an image as a bullet. In Chapter 6, you learned how to create a list item by item; here you'll learn how to change the style of your lists once they're on the page.

Assigning a list style to text

Suppose you have a number of lines on your page that you'd like to turn into a list. You don't have to follow the process in Chapter 6 to re-create that list. You can simply select all the elements of text you want to format as a list and then choose Bullets And Numbering from the Format menu. You'll see the Bullets And Numbering dialog box, shown here in Figure 7-12.

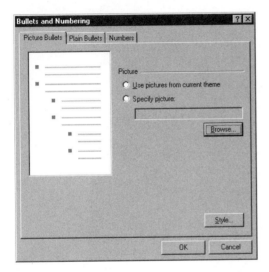

Figure 7-12
The Picture Bullets tab of the Bullets And Numbering dialog box.

The Bullets And Numbering dialog box has three tabs. The Picture Bullets tab lets you use an image for a bullet. If you're already applying a theme to the page, FrontPage can use images from that theme to format your list. You can also specify an image by clicking Browse and then choosing an image from a file. Of course, the image you choose should be small enough to use as a bullet character.

The other two tabs let you format either Plain Bullets or Numbers, giving you a variety of choices displayed as thumbnails. To turn your text into a bulleted list, click the Plain Bullets tab, select one of the styles, and then click OK. The default style applies no formatting. If you want to turn text into a numbered list, click the Numbers tab. You can begin your list with a number other than "1" (or if you want a lettered list, a letter other than "A"). All you need to do is select one of the styles on the Numbers tab and then select or enter a number in the Start At box. Then click OK.

CHAPTER 7

Changing the style of an entire list

To change a list from one style to another, right-click the list and then choose List Properties from the pop-up menu. You'll see the List Properties dialog box, which is exactly the same as the Bullets and Numbering dialog box except that it has an extra tab called Other. You can choose from image bullets, bulleted, or numbered styles on the Picture Bullets, Plain Bullets, and Numbers tabs, or you can choose a standard bulleted list, definition list, directory list, menu list, or numbered list style on the Other tab, as shown in Figure 7-13. When you select a style and click OK, FrontPage changes your existing list to that style.

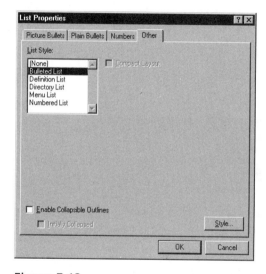

Figure 7-13

The Other tab of the List Properties dialog box.

Changing the style of individual list items

From a page design standpoint, it's a good practice to keep all items in a list consistent. But if you ever want to change an individual entry to a different style, here's how: Right-click on a list item and then choose List Item Properties from the pop-up menu. You'll see the List Item Properties dialog box, which will have a single tab pertaining to the type of list item that you assigned previously. Select a different style and then click OK to exit the List Item Properties dialog box.

PART
III

Line Breaks

A line break forms a new line on a page without creating a new paragraph or inserting a blank line. In other words, when you insert a line break, the next line starts below the previous line but has the same formatting as the other lines within the paragraph. In contrast, when you start a new paragraph, it too begins on the next line but could have paragraph formatting that differs from that of the previous paragraph.

Inserting a line break

To insert a line break, position the insertion point where you want the line break to appear and then choose Break from the Insert menu to display the Break Properties dialog box, shown here in Figure 7-14.

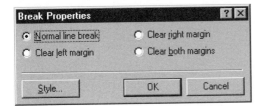

Figure 7-14
The Break Properties dialog box.

In the Break Properties dialog box, select one of the following options:

- **Normal Line Break.** Adds a line break exactly where you position the insertion point. The line break doesn't move based on the presence of any images in the left or right margins. In other words, even if an image is in the right or the left margin, the new line starts immediately below the line break. (You can insert a Normal line break by pressing Shift+Enter.)

- **Clear Left Margin.** Adds a line break and, if an image is in the left margin, moves the line following the line break down until the left margin is clear.

- **Clear Right Margin.** Adds a line break and, if an image is in the right margin, moves the line following the line break down until the right margin is clear.

- **Clear Both Margins.** Adds a line break and, if an image is in one or both margins, moves the line following the line break down until both margins are clear.

Deleting a line break

You can treat a line break like any other character and delete it by pressing the Backspace or Delete key.

Horizontal Lines

Using horizontal lines on a page is a neat way to separate sections, topics, or other elements. You can insert shaded or solid horizontal lines and format them using one of several available options.

Inserting a horizontal line

To insert a horizontal line, position the insertion point where you want the line to appear and then choose Horizontal Line from the Insert menu. A line appears, formatted the same way as the last horizontal line that you inserted. The horizontal line conforms to any page margins or other formatting that you've already set for the page. If you place horizontal lines inside table cells, they follow the formatting already applied to the table cells.

Formatting a horizontal line

To change the appearance of a horizontal line, right-click it and then choose Horizontal Line Properties from the pop-up menu. The Horizontal Line Properties dialog box appears, as shown in Figure 7-15.

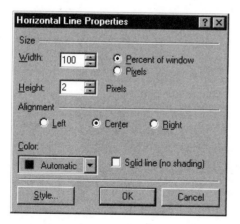

Figure 7-15

The Horizontal Line Properties dialog box.

PART
III

You can also use an image as a horizontal line. Choose Picture from the Insert menu and then choose Clipart or From File from the pop-up menu, and select the image you want to use as a horizontal line. Because these lines are actually images rather than standard HTML horizontal lines, you must specify their properties differently, using the Image Properties dialog box instead of the Horizontal Line Properties dialog box. For more information, see Chapter 8.

In the Width section of the dialog box, specify the length of your line in pixels or as a percentage of the browser window width (or in frames, as a percentage of the frame width). Then enter the line's thickness in pixels in the Height section of the dialog box. In the Alignment section, specify Left, Center, or Right alignment. From the Color drop-down list, select a color for the line. You also can specify whether the line should be displayed with no shading by selecting the Solid Line check box. Solid lines set to the default color typically appear in gray, and shaded lines set to the default color appear shaded with the page's background color. Click OK to accept your settings and close the dialog box.

Deleting a horizontal line

To delete a horizontal line, select it and then press the Delete key or the Backspace key.

Using Exact Positioning

So, you're like every other Web developer on the planet. You want, you crave, you need more control over the positioning of the elements on your pages. You want total 2-D layout control, don't you? In the old days (about a year ago), that would have been too much to ask for, or it would have created a complete mess in the HTML code for the page. But when you use FrontPage 2000, clean, exact, 2-D positioning is a reality. You'll also be happy to learn that, like everything else in FrontPage, exact 2-D positioning is as easy as pie to implement on your pages.

You control the positioning of elements in FrontPage by using the Position dialog box and the Positioning toolbar. Let's examine the Position dialog box first.

CHAPTER
7

To access the Position dialog box, you must have something on a page in Page view to manipulate. Select an object, such as an image or a selection of text, and then choose Position from the Format menu. The Position dialog box appears, as shown in Figure 7-16.

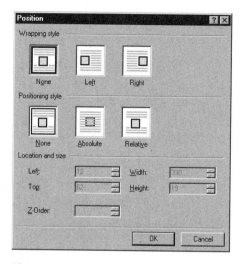

Figure 7-16

The Position dialog box.

The Position dialog box gives you a broad variety of choices in the positioning of the selected element. Here's the lowdown on your options:

- **Wrapping style**. You can select among three options. Depending on which choice you make, the text around the selected element wraps to the left, to the right, or not at all.

- **Positioning Style—Location and Size**. Here you can adjust the positioning of the element as either Absolute (precisely, using specific *x* and *y* coordinates) or Relative (positioned a specific distance from other elements that surround it). You can also adjust the Z-Order of the element, which is useful when you want to overlap elements, one layered on top of another. An element that has a higher Z-Order number is positioned on top of an element that has a lower number. You can also use a negative number in the Z-Order text box.

Figure 7-17 shows one example of the exact positioning you can achieve by using the Position dialog box.

You can see that the image is selected and that the Positioning toolbar is visible. The image has an Absolute position—it has a left margin of 34 pixels and a top margin of 8 pixels. It has a Z-index of –1, which allows the text to overlay the image.

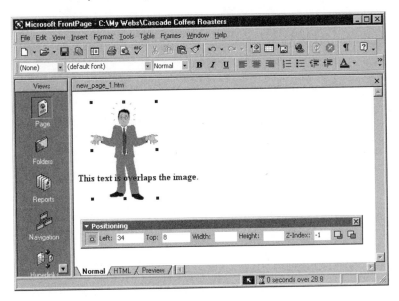

Figure 7-17
Page view showing exact positioning of text and image elements.

Figure 7-18, on the next page, shows what the Position dialog box looks like for the image in Figure 7-17. As you can see, just as on the Positioning toolbar, the image has an Absolute Positioning Style, and its location is 34 pixels from the left margin and 8 pixels from the top margin. The Z-Order value is shown, as are the width and height of the image.

TIP

If an image is set to Absolute, you can set its location either in the Position dialog box or by using the Positioning toolbar. But there's an even easier and cooler way to do it. Select the image; you'll see squares around the image indicating that it's selected. Next, click and hold the mouse button over the image. Now you can drag the image anywhere on the page, or even off the page if you like. The Position dialog box and Positioning toolbar adjust themselves accordingly.

CHAPTER 7

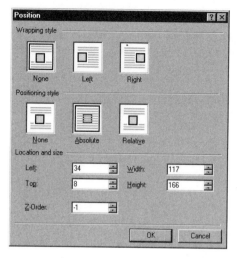

Figure 7-18

The Positioning dialog box settings for the image in Figure 7-10.

The Positioning toolbar works basically the same way as the Position dialog box. Its main advantage is that, because it's a toolbar, it's easy to access. You can also quickly set an image back or forward by one layer in the Z-order by clicking either the Bring Forward or the Send Backward button on the Positioning toolbar. If you want to make a quick adjustment to an element, just get busy on the Positioning toolbar, and you're on your way in a flash.

Enhancing Your Pages

Now that we've covered some ways to format your pages, let's look into some other features—bookmarks, links, sound, and themes—that you can use to enhance your pages.

Applying a Theme to a Page

As we discussed earlier, themes offer a great tool for creating a consistent, professional look, even for non-designer types. In "Working with Themes," earlier in this chapter, you learned how to apply a theme to the entire Web. In Page view, you can apply a theme to a single page or modify the theme that you've already applied. For example, let's say you choose a cool theme for your Web and it includes a background image. When you begin working on the feedback form on your Web, you decide that the background image distracts too much from the form you want people to use. You can remove just the background image on that page, keeping the rest of the theme intact.

Choose Theme from the Format menu to open the Themes dialog box. This dialog box works in exactly the same way as it does when you're setting a Theme for the entire Web, giving you the option to choose a theme (if one isn't already selected), use the theme from the current Web, or select a new theme. Remember that any changes you make here apply only to the page you're working on, not to the entire Web.

Using AutoThumbnail

Occasionally, you'll have no choice but to use a large image, or perhaps you'll find yourself faced with having to put a large number of images on a page. As you probably know by now, using too many images (especially big ones) is no way to make happy surfers out of your visitors. Using the Auto Thumbnail command, you can have FrontPage create a small version of a graphic, one that automatically links to the larger version. This saves file size, which in turn reduces the time it takes to load a page. If you use the AutoThumbnail feature consistently, all of the images in your Web will appear quickly. Visitors still have the option to click an image and display the large version in its own window.

AutoThumbnail is an excellent feature when you can get away with showing a small version of the image. If you were creating a Web catalog, for example, you'd probably want to have many product pictures. Using the Auto Thumbnail feature, you could create small pictures and display many of them on a single page. Visitors to your Web could then choose to view an enlarged version of only those products in which they're interested.

To make a thumbnail version of an image, first select the image and then do one of the following: either choose Auto Thumbnail from the Picture toolbar or press Ctrl+K. FrontPage creates the thumbnail and displays it in Page view as a hyperlinked image. The way the thumbnail appears to the user is based on the choices you made in the Options dialog box. For more information about setting the options for Auto Thumbnail, see "Setting AutoThumbnail Options," later in this chapter.

When you make an image a thumbnail, FrontPage creates a new, smaller version of the image, and when you save the page, you'll be asked to save the new image along with it. Although this method does create two different graphics of the same image, it also boosts viewing speed on your Web and puts control in the hands of the visitors; they decide whether to view the full-sized image. Remember though, that this feature is best used when a small version of the picture is necessary or appropriate, and it shouldn't be used as a standard throughout your site.

CHAPTER 7

Using Bookmarks

A *bookmark*, also known as an *anchor*, is a set of one or more characters on a page that serves as the target of a link. Using links to bookmarks allows a visitor to your Web to jump to any point within a page (not just to the beginning of a page).

For example, suppose one of the pages in the RoasterNet Web consists of a long, five-section document on the bright future of coffee bean sales in Seattle, and you link to that page from somewhere else within your Web. When a visitor follows that link, the top of the page (that is, the top of the document) appears in the browser. But if you include bookmarks at the beginning of each section of the document, you can create links directly to those bookmarks. That way, a visitor can jump directly to any of those sections instead of having to jump to the top of the document and then scroll down.

Bookmarks appear in Page view as text that has dashed underlines, not to be confused with the squiggly red underlines that indicate spelling errors. See "Using Links," later in this chapter, for information about linking to bookmarks.

Creating a bookmark

To create a bookmark, do the following:

1. Select one or more characters of text that will become the bookmark (the text you want to jump to).

2. Choose Bookmark from the Insert menu. The Bookmark dialog box appears, as shown in Figure 7-19.

3. Enter a unique name for the bookmark in the Bookmark Name: box. Try to name your bookmarks intuitively, because later, when you create a link to a bookmark, you'll need to enter the bookmark name or select it from a list. It'll help to be able to easily distinguish one bookmark from another. If your page already includes other bookmarks, they appear in the dialog box.

4. Click OK after you enter the bookmark name. In Page view, the selected text now appears with a dashed underline, indicating that it's a bookmark.

TIP You can access the Bookmark Properties dialog box by right-clicking any bookmark and choosing Bookmark Properties from the pop-up menu. You can also press the Alt+Enter keys at any selected bookmark to open the Bookmark Properties dialog box.

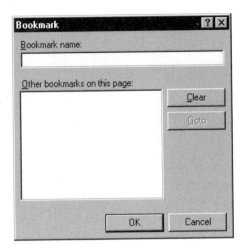

Figure 7-19

The Bookmark dialog box.

Finding a bookmark

Suppose you have a list of bookmarks on the current page in the Bookmark dialog box, and you want to find one of them. To find any bookmark in the list, select the bookmark and then click Goto. The page scrolls to the bookmark location, and the bookmark is selected. This is a quick and handy alternative to scrolling up and down a page to locate your bookmarks.

Clearing a bookmark

To remove a bookmark, select it and then choose Bookmark from the Insert menu, or right-click the bookmark and then choose Bookmark Properties. In the Bookmark dialog box, click Clear. The dialog box closes, and the bookmark is removed. This procedure removes only the bookmark reference, not any associated text.

Using Links

Links, also known as *hyperlinks*, are connections from one point to another. Visitors to a Web can click a link and jump to wherever it points to; this location is represented in HTML as a URL. You can link to and from text, images, other files (such as Microsoft Office files), or bookmarks. For information on creating links from images, see Chapter 8. To learn about changing the color of a link, see "Setting Page Properties," later in this chapter.

If you have an intranet site populated with Office documents, those documents can be interconnected by means of links. For example, a Word file can have a link that jumps to an Excel file. When you click that link, the Excel file appears in Excel. You can link between Office files and

195

FrontPage HTML files easily, creating a dynamic and powerful Office-style intranet site. This book describes how to create links from FrontPage to Office files. For information on creating links within Office files only, see the documentation or online help for the individual Office applications.

Creating a link to pages or bookmarks

To create a link, select the text or image you want to link from and then press Ctrl+K, or choose Hyperlink from the Insert menu. The Create Hyperlink dialog box appears, as shown in Figure 7-20.

TIP

You can quickly create or edit a link by selecting the text or link and then clicking the Create Or Edit Hyperlink button on the toolbar.

You can create hyperlinks in a few different ways: you can link to any page in the current Web, to any URL through your Web browser, to any file on your computer, or to any e-mail address. You can also create a new page and link to that. Further, you can link to a bookmark and set the target frame where you want the link to appear. Here's how to create hyperlinks in each of these ways:

- **To a page from within an open Web.** When you're working on a Web in FrontPage, you see all the pages in the current Web listed in the dialog box, each one available for linking. Note that once you select a file, FrontPage places its URL in the URL text box of the Create Hyperlink dialog box.

- **To any World Wide Web URL.** Just as selecting a file places the URL in the URL text box, you can type the URL directly in the text box. Or you could click the Use Your Web Browser To Select A Page or File button. Your browser will launch, prompting you to go to the page you want to link to. When you find the page on the Web, FrontPage automatically places the URL in the URL text box for you.

- **To any file on your computer.** If the file you want to link to is located on your computer, you can select it by clicking the Make A Hyperlink To A File On Your Computer button. You'll see the Select File dialog box, where you can choose the file you need.

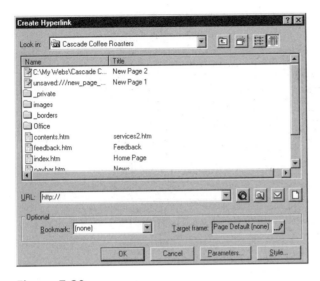

Figure 7-20

The Create Hyperlink dialog box.

- **To an e-mail address.** If you want your link to allow visitors to send e-mail to a certain address, click the Make A Hyperlink That Sends E-mail button. You'll see the Create E-mail Hyperlink dialog box, as shown in Figure 7-21.

    Just enter the address in the text box, and whammo, it's done.

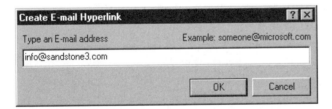

Figure 7-21

The Create E-mail Hyperlink dialog box.

- **To a new page.** This allows you to link to a page in the current Web that has not yet been created. Click the Create A Page And Link To The New Page button to display the New dialog box. Select the type of page you want to create from the list of templates. FrontPage creates the new page and either opens it for you or assigns it as a Task, depending on the choices you've made. For more information about the New dialog box and using templates, see Chapter 4.

You can also choose from these two options in the Create Hyperlink dialog box:

- **Bookmark.** If your target link is a bookmark, you can enter its name in the Bookmark text box for the selected page.

- **Target Frame.** To specify a target frame for the page to appear in, enter the frame name in the Target Frame text box.

After you've made your link selections, click OK to return to Page view. Your link is now highlighted in the link color set for the page. You can test your new link by pressing and holding the Ctrl key and clicking the link.

Selecting a link

Once you've created a link and you want to modify it, you must first select it. All you need to do to select a link is to click anywhere within the link. You can also select the text associated with a link, but you don't need to. If the insertion point is in a link, the toolbar buttons and menu items pertaining to links are available.

Removing a link

To remove a link, select it and then choose Hyperlink from the Insert menu. In the URL text box, delete the text and then click OK. The link is removed, but the text or image associated with the former link remains.

Automatically created links

Whenever you type in a supported protocol in Page view and follow it with a destination URL, FrontPage detects that you want to make a link from the text and automatically creates one for you. All you need to do is simply type the text, like *www.sandstone3.com,* on a page. Because *www* prefaces only World Wide Web addresses, FrontPage assumes that the HTTP protocol is to be used, so you don't have to enter that. You can also create other supported links, like *mailto:*, by just typing the link starting with the correct protocol.

Editing a link

To change a link's properties, select it and then choose Hyperlink from the Insert menu or Properties from the Format menu. Alternatively, you can right-click the link and then choose Hyperlink Properties from the pop-up menu. You can change any of the link's properties in the Edit Hyperlink dialog box that appears. For more information, see "Creating a Link to Pages or Bookmarks," earlier in this chapter.

PART
III

Dragging a link from another view

Here's another neat feature in FrontPage: if you want to create a link to a page in your Web, you can drag the page from a view in FrontPage (such as Folders view) to a page in Page view. Here's how to do it:

1. Make sure the page where you want to create the link is open in Page view.

2. Go to another view in FrontPage. You can use either Folders, Reports (only in a report that lists files, like the All Files report), Navigation, or Hyperlinks view.

3. Click the icon or file in the view of your choice that will be the link's target, and drag it onto the Page view icon on the Views menu. Make sure that you keep the mouse button depressed. After a second, FrontPage switches you automatically to Page view. Position the insertion point at the exact spot where you want the link to appear on the page, and then release the mouse button. FrontPage inserts the name of the target and creates a link from that text to the target itself. The link you created is just like any other link you might have added manually, and you can edit it in the same way.

Creating links to the Web using a browser

In FrontPage, you don't have to recall and retype Web addresses if you want to link to a page on the Web. You can easily create such a link in one of two ways:

●   Position your insertion point on the page where you want to create the link, click the Hyperlink button on the toolbar, and then click the World Wide Web tab (as explained earlier in this section).

●   While you're browsing in Microsoft Internet Explorer or Netscape Navigator, simply click any link you see on a page, hold the mouse button down, and then drag that link onto a page in Page view. Ta Da! FrontPage automatically creates a link to that page.

Using Navigation Bars

You may be wondering why you spent all that time building a structure in Navigation view. Well, in addition to being a whole lot of fun, it's also the foundation you use to create navigation bars on the pages in your Web. *Navigation bars* are a graphical representation of the structure of a Web. They're placed on the page in Page view, and they appear as navigation buttons or as hyperlinked text in the browser. You can create them in two different ways: you can design the structure in Navigation view yourself, or, if you use a Web wizard to create your Web, they'll be created for you. If you used a Web wizard, the navigation bars are based on the choices you made during the setup process. If you designed the structure yourself, the pages are automatically linked on the navigation bar, based on their position in that structure.

If you've created or modified a navigation structure in Navigation view, you can use that structure to create navigation bars automatically on a page in Page view. If you want to create a navigation structure for a home page that has a feedback page set up as its peer, for example, the process goes like this:

1. Create the structure in Navigation view, as shown in Figure 7-22. The Home page and Feedback pages are peers, and we want them to appear together as a navigation bar on a page.

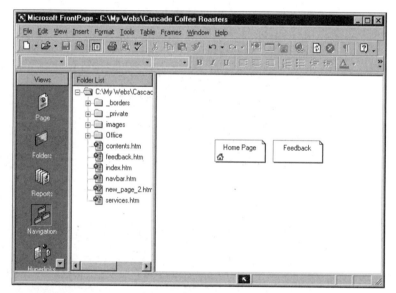

Figure 7-22

A structure created in Navigation view; the Home Page and the Feedback page are peers.

2. Make decisions about the way you want the navigation bar to look by using the Navigation Bar Properties dialog box. To open the dialog box from Page view, choose Navigation Bar from the Insert menu. Figure 7-23 shows that our navigation bars will appear at the Top level; the Home page is displayed horizontally on the page and shown as text.

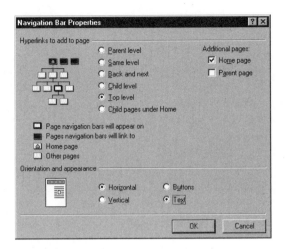

Figure 7-23

The Navigation Bar Properties dialog box showing current settings.

3. View your finished navigation bar, which appears at the top of the page.

Of course, you can get a lot fancier than the example shown here. If your Web has a theme applied to it, for example, and you choose to display the structure as buttons, FrontPage chooses the appropriate button style and creates your navigation bars using those cool theme buttons.

Once the navigation bar is on your page, you can modify it in Page view using the Navigation Bar Properties dialog box. You can modify only the way the structure is displayed, however, not the structure itself. You must make any structural changes in Navigation view. For more information about Navigation view, see Chapter 3.

You can insert or modify a navigation bar on your page in your choice of the following ways:

● While you're in Page view, choose Navigation Bar from the Insert menu.

● If you currently have a navigation bar on the page, right-click the bar and then choose Navigation Bar Properties from the pop-up menu.

● Double-click the navigation bar.

● Select the bar and press Alt+Enter.

The Navigation Bar Properties dialog box (shown in Figure 7-24, on the next page) offers you a variety of options for displaying the navigation bar on the page.

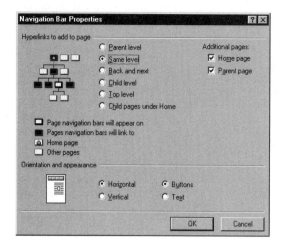

Figure 7-24

The Navigation Bar Properties dialog box.

The dialog box is divided into two sections:

● **Hyperlinks to add to page.** Here you select which pages to include in the navigation bar. As you select the various options, they are highlighted in the structure thumbnail on the left side of the dialog box. The list below the structure is a legend that defines what the pages are. Many times, you'll be using navigation bars as your only source of navigation on a page, and you'll want to display the home page on the navigation bar. In these cases, select the Home Page check box. You can also choose to include the parent page of a selected level by selecting the Parent Page check box.

● **Orientation and appearance.** You can position the navigation bar in either a Horizontal or Vertical position on the page. If you're not using a theme on the page, or if you just prefer text, select the Text check box, and the navigation bar will appear as hyperlinked text only.

Modifying navigation bars

Because FrontPage creates navigation bars automatically based on decisions you've made, you'll probably be happy with them just the way they are. If not, you can modify them in a few different ways.

- The text labels on a navigation bar are based on the page titles. If you decide that you don't like one of the names, rename the page title of the file and then apply changes.

- If the navigation bar was created automatically by a wizard and you want to change its destination, open the page in Page view and then open the Navigation Bar Properties dialog box. Here you can adjust the settings.

- If you're not happy with the colors, button types, or fonts used in the navigation bar, you need to select a different theme. If you change the theme in Page view, your changes apply to the current page only.

Deleting navigation bars

If you need to delete a navigation bar from a page, select the navigation bar and then press the Delete key or choose Cut from the Edit menu. You can also right-click the navigation bar and then choose Cut from the pop-up menu.

Setting Page Options

You can customize the look of certain behind-the-scenes elements on your Web globally. In FrontPage, you make the adjustment once, and it's applied to every page that contains that element and that hasn't been adjusted separately.

You make these changes in the Options dialog box, which you access by choosing Page Options from the Tools menu. There are several tabs from which to choose, allowing you to make several types of modifications. We'll examine each one individually, just because we like you that much.

Setting color coding options

If you like to tinker with the HTML, you'll find it much easier when the various HTML tags and attributes are color coded. As Figure 7-25 shows, you can define the colors for the Normal text, Tags, Attribute names, Attribute values, Comments, and Scripts here.

You can also choose to have no color coding at all, by clearing the Show Color Coding check box. If you start changing a lot of colors and then decide later that you want to use the default colors, click the Reset Colors button to reactivate the default settings.

These colors are visible only when you're working in Page view and you have selected the HTML tab. For more information on the view tabs in Page view, see "Using the Page View Tabs," later in this chapter.

CHAPTER 7

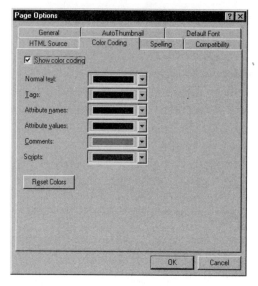

Figure 7-25

The Color Coding tab of the Page Options dialog box.

Setting spelling options

The Spelling tab on the Page Options dialog box includes two different options. You can configure FrontPage to check your spelling as you type, and you can decide whether or not to show spelling errors in your documents. Remember those little red squiggly lines that appear under misspelled words? Well, if you select Hide Spelling Errors In All Documents, that red line won't show up. Of course, if you make a spelling error, you won't catch it as easily, so clear this check box at your own spelling risk. Select either check box to enable each feature, or clear the check·box to disable it.

Setting compatibility options

If you want to enable the menu commands of a certain browser, version of a browser, or specific server, you can do that on the Compatibility tab of the Page Options dialog box, as shown in Figure 7-26.

Select your options from the drop-down lists and then click OK.

If you want to exclude the use of certain technologies in the pages of your Web, you can activate or deactivate them as needed. They're all activated by default, and it's not a bad idea to leave it this way.

Figure 7-26

The Compatibility tab of the Page Options dialog box.

Setting general options

The General tab of the Page Options dialog box offers you two options: you can enable the use of DIV tags—tags that let you define variables for the browser to follow. You can also automatically enclose Form fields within a form, which means that if you begin to create a form one piece at a time and forget to add a surrounding form, FrontPage adds it for you. Select either check box to enable each feature, or clear the check box to disable it.

Setting AutoThumbnail options

To set the parameters for the AutoThumbnail feature, click the AutoThumbnail tab on the Options dialog box. For more information about using an AutoThumbnail, see "Using AutoThumbnail" earlier in this chapter. Figure 7-27, on the next page, shows the AutoThumbnail tab.

Here, you can set the default size for the thumbnail image in pixels. You can define values for Width, Height, Shortest Side, or Longest Side. FrontPage creates the thumbnail based on your settings and on the sizes of the thumbnail images in proportion to the original. For example, if you set the width to 50 pixels, all thumbnails will be 50 pixels wide, and their heights will vary depending on the original image.

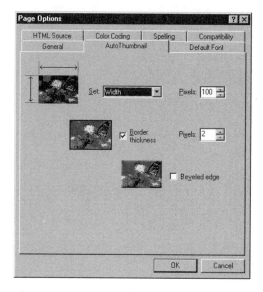

Figure 7-27

The AutoThumbnail tab of the Page Options dialog box.

You can also choose to apply a border around the image, and you can adjust the border thickness that appears on the thumbnail hyperlink. Select the Beveled Edge check box if you want to create thumbnails that have a beveled edge.

Setting default font options

The Default Font tab lets you choose a default font language, such as US/ Western European, when no other font is defined for text. These settings don't affect the HTML encoding; they affect only the font display in Page view. You can also select the default proportional font, as well as the default fixed-width font.

Setting HTML source code options

If you've always fancied yourself an HTML guru, and you like being in control, then this is the dialog box for you. You can set several options that define the way the HTML code appears in HTML view or when the HTML is viewed from within a browser. Figure 7-28 shows the HTML Source tab of the Page Options dialog box.

You can adjust options for saving the files, formatting the HTML (for example, by defining indents and line breaks), and defining the display of a specific tag. If you've created some wonderful HTML code and want all

PART
III

of your pages to be formatted to match those specifications, click the Base On Current Page button. Of course, you must open a page in Page view first, if you want this setting to take effect. If you make a lot of changes and then decide later that what you really did was make a mess, you can easily clean up that mess by clicking the Reset button, which changes all the settings back to their default values.

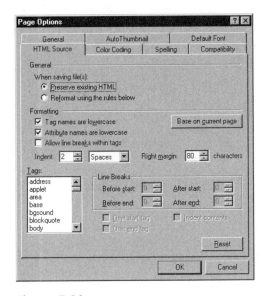

Figure 7-28
The HTML Source tab of the Page Options dialog box.

Using Shared Borders

Let's say that you want your company's logo to appear at the bottom of every page on your Web. You might think that you'd have to add it to each page individually, or that you'd have to use frames—but wait! You have another, much easier, option. You can use a shared border at the bottom of the page, and every page that has a bottom-shared border will display the same information. This means that you only need to add your logo once, on one shared border page. If you modify the information in a shared border, you need to do that only once too; and you can do it on any of the pages in your Web that have the same shared border location.

To use shared borders, choose Shared Borders from the Format menu; you'll see the Shared Borders dialog box, shown in Figure 7-29, on the next page.

CHAPTER 7

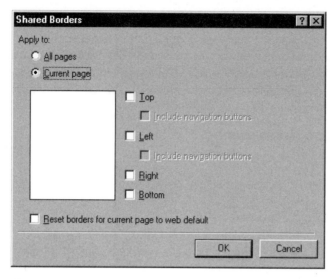

Figure 7-29

The Shared Borders dialog box.

You can specify whether you want to include the shared borders on all pages in the Web, or on just the current page, by clicking the appropriate option button. You also have the option of displaying the shared border at the top, left, right, or bottom of each page. Figure 7-30 shows a page that contains a shared border at the top of the page, so any text or image that you insert in the shared border appears on all pages in the Web that use a top-shared border. The border around the shared border area doesn't appear in the visitor's browser; it's there only for layout purposes.

NOTE

Because using a shared border creates a new page, we don't recommend using a shared border on a frames page.

To use shared borders, check one or more borders to include, and then click OK. You can also set the borders for the current page to the default for the Web by selecting the Reset Borders For Current Page To Web Default check box. If you want to remove a shared border from a page, open the Shared Borders dialog box and clear that border's check box.

PART
III

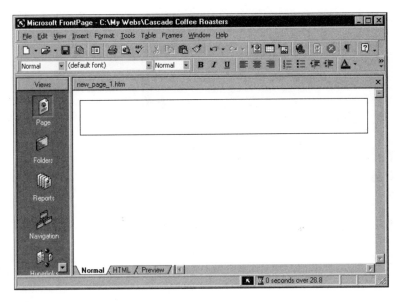

Figure 7-30

Page view showing a shared border ready for input.

Adding Sounds

A background sound can add a multimedia dimension to your Web. *Background sounds* play whenever someone visits the page the sound is on, and the sound can play a specified number of times or loop continuously. Just as hearing a certain song can put us in a certain mood, a background sound can set the tone for your viewers—it can also annoy them if it's overused. Use background sound sparingly and wisely.

FrontPage supports several types of sound files, ranging from wave sounds (which have WAV extensions) to midi sequences (MID), AIFF sounds (AIF, AIFC, AIFF), and AU sounds (AU, SND).

You insert a background sound and set its properties in the Page Properties dialog box. For more information on the other options in the Page Properties dialog box, see "Setting Page Properties," later in this chapter.

Here's how to insert the sound:

1. Right-click anywhere in the page and then choose Page Properties from the pop-up menu (or choose Properties from the File menu). The Page Properties dialog box appears, as shown in Figure 7-31, on the next page.

CHAPTER 7

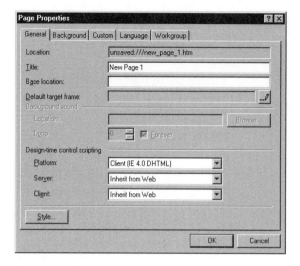

Figure 7-31

The General tab of the Page Properties dialog box.

2. In the Location text box (under the Background Sound heading) on the General tab, type the path to the sound you want to use. You can also select a background sound by clicking the Browse button. The Background Sound dialog box appears, as shown in Figure 7-32.

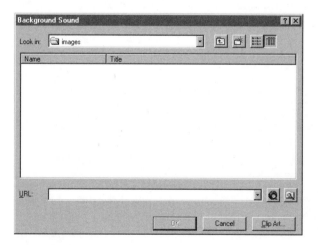

Figure 7-32

The Background Sound dialog box.

You can select a sound from the current Web, use your browser to select a sound from the World Wide Web, or choose a sound from a local drive on your computer. When you've finished, click OK to return to the Page Properties dialog box.

3. In the Page Properties dialog box, specify in the Loop: text box the number of times you want the sound to play. If you want the sound to loop endlessly, select the Forever check box.

4. Click OK to exit the Page Properties dialog box.

Using Active Elements

Maybe you're tired of seeing all of those static Web sites: you know, the ones that just sit there and do nothing. But you're thinking, "In order to have some fun on my page, I'll need to hire some ten-year-old kid to write me some code." Not to worry—FrontPage has some built-in features that let you add extra zip to your pages without having to spend a lot of dough on that little programming genius.

We discuss four active components in this chapter: *Banner Ad Manager, Hit Counter, Hover Button,* and *Marquees.* You can use each of these features by choosing Component from the Insert menu and making the appropriate selection from the pop-up menu. FrontPage also includes many other components that you can access by choosing the Component command on the Insert menu. Those components, such as Scheduled Image, Search Form, and Table of Contents, are discussed in Chapter 9.

Using the Banner Ad Manager

One of the most popular ways people make money on the Web today is by selling ads on their pages. You've seen these banners all over the place, right? Have you ever noticed that sometimes, if you stay on the page long enough, you see a succession of different ads rotating in the same place? Well, using the Banner Ad Manager, you can rotate multiple banners on any page, just like the big boys.

Of course, you aren't limited to rotating ads. You can rotate any image you like and even apply transition effects between multiple images. You could, for example, create your own little slide show and tell a story as each new image shows itself.

FrontPage creates the rotating banners by using a Java applet, and you configure their properties in the Banner Ad Manager Properties dialog box, shown in Figure 7-33, on the next page. You can access the Banner Ad Manager Properties dialog box by choosing the Component command from the Insert menu list or by double-clicking an existing banner. You can also

CHAPTER 7

right-click an existing banner (or press Alt+Enter) and then choose Java
Applet Properties from the pop-up menu.

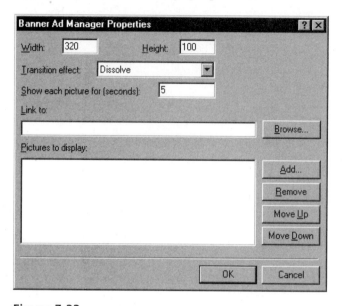

Figure 7-33

The Banner Ad Manager Properties dialog box.

Here, you can configure the way your banners appear in the browser.
You have a variety of choices.

- **Width, Height.** Be sure to enter a value that's equal to the size
  of the largest image being rotated. All other images will be centered in the space and will appear on a neutral-colored background. If you really want to make the most of this feature, try
  to make all of your images the same approximate size.

- **Transition Effect.** You can choose among a variety of effects.
  Selecting None displays the images in sequence without a transition effect. You can also set a time, in seconds, for the banner
  to appear before the next one comes in. If your banner contains
  text, be sure to leave enough time for the visitor to read it. It's a
  good idea to keep the time under ten seconds. If you don't think
  that's enough time for anyone to read your banner, you probably
  have too much text on it. Think of these banners as if they were
  billboards you see when you're driving. You have only a second
  or two to read a billboard, and they're designed with that short
  time span in mind, just as you should design yours here.

- **Link To.** If you want the banner to be a hyperlink, add the URL for the link here. Try to anticipate what visitors will do when they come to a page. If you make your banner look like an ad, your visitors will think it's an ad, and they'll want to click it—and you don't want them to click if nothing's going to happen. You can use the standard Browse button to locate your link destination.

- **Pictures To Display.** Here you can add and remove images to be rotated. Click Add to add an image to the list or click Remove to remove a selected image. The images play in a top-down order: the image listed first appears first, and so on. You can adjust the order of the images by selecting an image in the list and clicking the Move Up or Move Down buttons as necessary.

The Banner Ad Manager rotates through the list of images indefinitely as long as the visitor is on the page.

Adding a Hit Counter

Adding a *hit counter* is a popular way to show how many visitors have been to your page. Most of the time, you'll see hit counters on the home page, and they're usually at the bottom of the page. You can add a hit counter to your page by choosing Component from the Insert menu and then choosing Hit Counter from the pop-up menu. You'll be greeted by the Hit Counter Properties dialog box, shown in Figure 7-34.

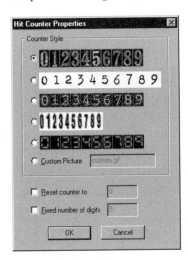

Figure 7-34
The Hit Counter Properties dialog box.

You can choose from one of five predefined Counter Styles, or you can create your own Custom Picture. A hit counter isn't the type of thing you'll want to put on every page in your Web; after all, it shows how many people have not visited your Web! If visitors come to your page and see a bunch of zeros on the counter, they might think that there's nothing good to see there and move on. By checking the Reset Counter To check box and putting in a number, you can make it look like plenty of people have been to your Web. Think of it as a little white lie. You can also fix the number of digits displayed by checking the Fixed Number Of Digits check box and entering a number.

Using Hover Buttons

Have you ever wondered how they get those cool buttons on a Web page—you know, the ones that change color or bevel when you roll your mouse over them? Well, you need a degree in computer code writing and graphic design to get those effects. But you know that with FrontPage, you're not going to have to get a fancy degree, and you won't need the aesthetic sense of Picasso. The only thing you need is the Hover Button feature.

Using the Hover Button feature in FrontPage, all you need to do is make a few simple choices, and wham-bam, there she is, a fully functional animated button, complete with mouseover effects and hyperlinks. To begin, choose Component from the Insert menu, and then choose Hover Button from the pop-up menu. You can also right-click an existing Hover button and choose Java Applet Properties from the pop-up menu, or you can double-click a Hover button, or press Alt+Enter when a Hover button is selected. When you use any of these methods, you display the Hover Button Properties dialog box, shown in Figure 7-35.

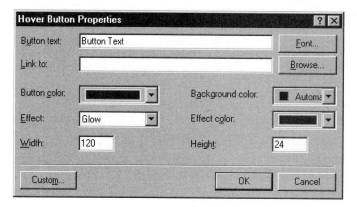

Figure 7-35
The Hover Button Properties dialog box.

You have several standard options to choose from, as well as some interesting custom options that let you do things such as play a sound or display an image as a button. The standard options include:

- **Button Text.** Most buttons on a Web page have text on them, telling visitors what to expect when they click it. In the Button Text text box, type the text you would like to appear on the button. Click the Font button to select the font type, style, size, and color for the button text.

- **Link To.** If you want your button to be a hyperlink, type the URL in this text box, or click the Browse button to locate the URL. Remember that most people naturally expect a button to be a hyperlink, so it's a good idea not to disappoint them.

- **Button Color, Background Color.** Use the drop-down Color list to pick a button color or a background color. If you choose an image for the button in the Custom dialog box, you don't need to enter a color here.

- **Effect, Effect Color.** Select from the various visual effects in the Effect drop-down list. When you have selected an effect, you can select the color of the button to use when the effect is activated. Select a color in the Effect Color drop-down list. You have quite a few interesting options here, so experiment and choose the one that best suits the mood you're trying to create on that page.

- **Width, Height.** Type in the button's Width and Height values (in pixels), respectively. If you choose to use an image as a button, make sure you enter the size of the image here.

To access the custom options available for a Hover Button, click Custom at the bottom of the Hover Button Properties dialog box. Figure 7-36, on the next page, shows the resulting Custom dialog box.

The Custom dialog box is divided into two sections.

- **Play Sound.** In this section, you can choose to play a sound when visitors click the button in the browser or when they move the mouse pointer over the button (*mouseover*). Technically, you could have a sound play using both techniques, click and mouseover, at the same time, but we know that that wouldn't be a very good idea, don't we? Use the standard browse buttons to locate your sounds.

- **Custom Image.** If you'd rather have your button in the form of an image, click Browse and choose an image for the button. If you'd like an image to appear when the visitor hovers the mouse over the button, click Browse and locate an On Hover image. Remember to enter the correct width and height in the Hover Button Properties dialog box for any image you choose.

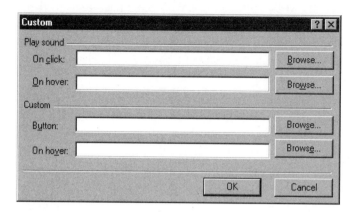

Figure 7-36

The Custom dialog box.

Adding Marquees

Marquees can turn people's heads and get them to pay more attention to your Web. As Sheriff Buford T. Justice, of the movie *Smokey and the Bandit,* would say, they're "attention gettas." But as you would with any other catchy design element in your Web, be careful not to overuse them—visitors might find them annoying or might ignore their messages.

Marquees are HTML elements that allow text to move on a page. They turn an otherwise static page into one that's dynamic and lively. Let's use another example from RoasterNet to show what marquees can do for a page.

Mila, who's in charge of the National Sales department at Cascade Coffee Roasters, realizes the importance of evangelizing the sales message within the company, so she has instructed her department to create a Sales section for RoasterNet. She plans to have sections detailing general sales patterns, news from the competition and reactions to it, and up-to-the-minute news of the big "scores" the department makes. In the early stages, these pages are under construction, and she doesn't have as much time to build them as she'd like. But one of her salespeople, Cody, has just made the company's largest-ever sale, and Mila wants the news to go up on a page on RoasterNet. If she just types the news on the page, it will look static and people might read past it, especially since the page is under construction. They might think that nothing has changed unless they look carefully. So Mila will use a marquee to get their attention. Here's the process she'll use to insert it:

1. Position the insertion point where you want the marquee to appear. Choose Component from the Insert menu and then choose Marquee from the pop-up menu. You'll see the Marquee Properties dialog box, as shown in Figure 7-37.

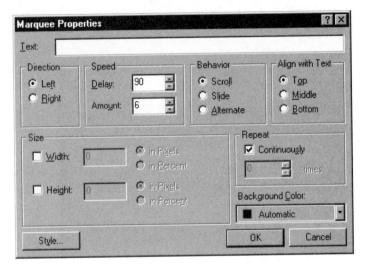

Figure 7-37
The Marquee Properties dialog box.

2. In the Text text box, type the text you want displayed by the marquee.

3. In the Direction section, specify whether you want the marquee to move toward the left or the right. (If you select Alternate in the Behavior section in step 5, you won't need to specify a direction here.)

4. In the Speed section of the dialog box, specify values for Delay and Amount. Delay sets the length of time in milliseconds between each movement of the marquee. The higher the number, the longer the delay, and the slower the marquee moves. Amount refers to the distance in pixels between each movement of the marquee. You can make your marquee move faster, therefore, by increasing this number. You can adjust the Delay and Amount values to make your marquees move at any speed, from very fast to very slow.

5. In the Behavior section of the dialog box, select one of the following options:

- **Scroll.** This moves the text across the screen in the direction that you specified in the Direction section. Text appears and disappears from the sides of the marquee area.

- **Slide.** This also moves the text across the screen in the direction you specified in the Direction section. But instead of scrolling off the screen, the text stops when it reaches the end of the screen and remains on screen. If you designate your marquee to repeat a specified number of times, the slide process begins again after the text reaches the end of the screen.

- **Alternate.** This moves the text back and forth across the screen. The text never leaves the screen when you select Alternate.

6. In the Align With Text section of the dialog box, specify how you want the text to align within the marquee area. (You set the marquee area in the Size section.) You can align the text at the top of the marquee area, in the middle, or at the bottom.

7. In the Size section of the dialog box, set the size of the marquee area. To specify the width of the marquee area, select the Width check box. If you want to specify the width of the marquee area in pixels, enter a number and then click In Pixels. If you want to set the width as a percentage of the screen, enter the number and then click In Percent.

   Select the Height check box if you want to set the marquee area height. This number determines the amount of room, from top to bottom, within which the text in the marquee area moves. Enter a number and click either In Pixels to specify the height in pixels, or In Percent to specify the height as a percentage of the page. The marquee will always be as large as it needs to be to hold the font size of the text, no matter how small you set the marquee height.

TIP

To give your marquee space to breathe from top to bottom so it can be easier to read, specify an ample height and select Middle in the Align With Text section of the Marquee Properties dialog box. This centers the marquee from top to bottom in the area you've specified.

PART
III

8. In the Repeat section of the dialog box, select the Continuously check box if you want the marquee to run all the time. If you want the marquee to move only a certain number of times when a visitor comes to your page, clear the Continuously check box and enter the number of times in the Times text box below it.

9. If you want the marquee to move against a colored background, select a Background Color. Sometimes using a background color that's different from the rest of the page can have a pleasing effect, but beware of "overstunning" your audience with this option. The movement of the marquee might be enough to grab their attention. If you select a Background Color, be sure to select a compatible font color.

10. When you're satisfied with all your settings, click OK to exit the Marquee Properties dialog box.

Changing marquee settings

To change the settings of a marquee on your page, right-click the marquee and choose Marquee Properties from the pop-up menu. In the Marquee Properties dialog box that appears, change the settings and then click OK. You can also double-click the Marquee to access the Marquee Properties dialog box. To change the font type, style, size, and color of the marquee text, right-click the marquee and then click Font.

Inserting Videos

Another great way to liven up your Webs is to add video to them. As you might know, however, video files tend to be huge, and even though the bandwidth of the Internet is increasing gradually, it's not yet sufficient to transfer large video files in a speedy way. The situation can be different within a corporation if its intranet uses local connections where bandwidth is less of a concern.

TIP

In Page view, the time it takes to download a page is displayed (in seconds) in the lower right part of the screen. Click the current download time, and you'll see a pop-up menu that lets you change the time to reflect various connection speeds, such as T1 and ISDN. As you change your page—adding or deleting videos, sounds, images, and other elements—the download time is updated accordingly.

FrontPage supports the viewing of Windows-based AVI files in its Webs. First you insert the video file on your page, and then you set its properties.

CHAPTER 7

Place the insertion point on the page where you want to insert the video, choose Picture from the Insert menu, and then choose Video from the pop-up menu. You'll see the Video dialog box. This dialog box lets you select a video located in the current Web, use your browser to locate a video, or select a video from a local drive. Select your video file and then click OK.

The opening frame of the video file will appear on the page as a place-holder until the video downloads and plays in the visitor's browser.

TIP

If you double-click the placeholder, FrontPage tries to launch a video-editing ap-plication. Unless you have one installed, you'll get a message that says that there is no editor configured.

Once you've inserted the video file, you might need to adjust its prop-erties. Here's how:

1. Right-click the video file placeholder on the page and choose Image Properties from the pop-up menu. The Video tab of the Picture Properties dialog box appears, as shown in Figure 7-38.

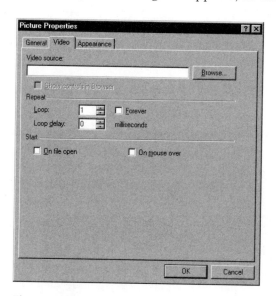

Figure 7-38

The Video tab of the Picture Properties dialog box.

2. If you want to replace the current video with another, click Browse, locate the replacement AVI file in the Video dialog box, and then click OK.

PART

III

3. Select the Show Controls In Browser check box if you want to provide a set of controls—Play, Stop, and a slider—along with the video when it's displayed in the browser at runtime.

4. In the Repeat section of the dialog box, specify in the Loop text box how many times you want the video file to play, and specify in the Loop Delay text box the amount of time (in milliseconds) between repeats of the video. If you want the video to play endlessly, select the Forever check box.

5. In the Start section of the dialog box, specify when you want the video to begin playing. Specifying On File Open starts the video whenever a visitor opens the page it's on, and specifying On Mouse Over starts the video whenever a visitor moves the mouse pointer over the video in the browser.

6. When you're satisfied with your settings, click OK to exit the Picture Properties dialog box. For more information on the Picture Properties dialog box, see Chapter 8.

Setting Page Properties

You can set the properties for a page in Page view by choosing the Properties command from the File menu or from the pop-up menu that appears when you right-click the page. In the Page Properties dialog box, you can:

● Change general file information such as the page's title

● Set a page's background image, color, or sound

● Set default colors for text and links

● Specify workgroup categories

You must open a page in Page view in order to set these properties. (To open a page or create a new page, see Chapter 6.) Here's a primer on the properties, starting with those you can set on the General tab, shown in Figure 7-39, on the next page.

You can change the page's title by entering a new title in the Title text box and you can change the optional base URL by entering it in the Base Location text box.. To assign a frame as the default target for all the links on the page, enter its name in the Default Target Frame text box or click Target Frame to display the Target Frame dialog box. (For more information on working with frames, see Chapter 6.)

In the Background Sound section, you can change the properties for a background sound. For details on this, see "Adding Sounds," earlier in this chapter. You can also define the Design Time Control Scripting for the Platform, Server, and Client.

221

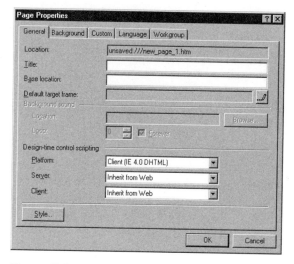

Figure 7-39

The General tab of the Page Properties dialog box.

NOTE

Design Time Controls (DTCs) are controls that are added at design time (when the page is created) and that can be displayed at run time (when the page is viewed in a browser), from either the client or the server, depending on how they're implemented.

On the Background tab, shown in Figure 7-40, you can specify background colors and colors for various links.

In the Formatting section of the dialog box, you can set the following properties:

● **Background Picture formatting.** By checking the Background Picture check box, you can specify an image to use as your page background; most browsers tile this image automatically. You've probably seen this on the Web; a tiled background can be effective if it adds to the "viewability" of a page and doesn't impair viewing of text or other images on the page.

TIP

To adjust the properties of an existing background image, open the Page Properties dialog box and click the Properties button in the Formatting section to display the Image Properties dialog box. See Chapter 8 for information about this dialog box.

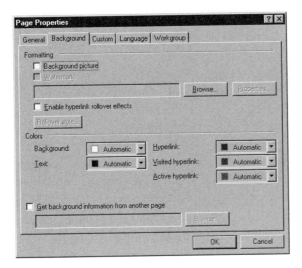

Figure 7-40
The Background tab of the Page Properties dialog box.

● **Watermark formatting.** A *watermark* is a background image that doesn't scroll when you scroll the page. Select the Watermark check box if you want to use this feature. Click Browse to specify the image. (Note: In certain browsers, this may not work the way you expect.)

● **Enable Hyperlink Rollover Effects.** Selecting the Enable Hyperlink Rollover Effects check box enables rollover hyperlink effects on your pages. Selecting this check box enables the Rollover Style button. Clicking Rollover Style displays the Font dialog box, from which you can select the style for your rollovers.

● **Background color.** You can specify a background color for your page if you don't want to use a tiled image. You might consider using a color that has more flair. Just make sure your text and images are easy to read against whatever color you select. Use the Background drop-down list to select your color.

● **Text color.** You can use the Text drop-down list to specify the default color of the text that appears on your page. Black is a safe standard, but don't hesitate to experiment using other colors that might look good against the background you've selected. Any text that's formatted in a different color in Page view overrides the default color specified here.

- **Hyperlink color.** You can use the Hyperlink drop-down list to specify a color to use for all links that have not been visited on a page.

- **Visited Hyperlink color.** Links change to this color after they have been used. If a link appears on more than one page, following one instance of the link triggers the visited link color for all instances of that link in your Web. You can specify the visited link color by using the Visited Hyperlink drop-down list.

  The default Hyperlink color is Blue, and the default Visited Hyperlink color is purple. It's a good idea to change both of these, just so that people know that you're paying attention to the details.

- **Active Hyperlink color.** The active link color is the color of a link as it's being clicked. To specify a color here, use the Active Hyperlink drop-down list.

In the Get Background Information from Another Page section of the dialog box, you can specify the use of the same background color, background image, text color, and link colors as the ones you used on another page. Select the option button and then click Browse to indicate the page from the current Web that you want to use for this purpose. If you've already set up those properties elsewhere, you've saved time because you don't have to set them up again for the current page.

TIP

The Get Background Information From Another Page option is a feature unique to FrontPage and is a great way to set up a "style page," or a page properties template if you will. For example, if you make changes to the background and colors on the style page, the changes will be reflected on all of the pages that use this style page when you reopen them.

The Custom tab displays a list of meta tags, or system variables, that are used on your page. *Meta tags* live in the page's HTML source code and contain information about the page, for example, the content type, the character set, and the application that generated the HTML code. They are never displayed in the visitor's browser, but these variables do appear in the HTML code of the pages in your Web, and they can supply information to a browser that recognizes them. You can add, modify, or remove meta tags for system variables and user variables on this tab. You can also define the User Variables, such as the Generator.

The Language tab is used to specify settings to control the language used for checking spelling, the HTML encoding for saving the page, and the HTML encoding for loading the page. These settings are used for Web pages in different languages.

Using the Page View Tabs

Because most people like to see things from different angles, and because a lot of people like to get a behind-the-scenes view of their Web, FrontPage gives you a couple of different ways to look at a page. The view tabs are located at the bottom of the FrontPage window while you're in Page view.

Using Normal View

For most people, HTML can be a scary thing. That's one of the reasons you're using FrontPage in the first place, right? So, for those of you who don't want to have anything to do with that HTML stuff, you'll want to be working in Page view, using Normal view.

Normal view is the view we've been using throughout most of this book, and if you never want to see any code, it's the place you'll want to stay.

Using HTML view

When you're working in FrontPage, you may feel like you're in the "HTML free zone," and you can stay there forever, never looking at any HTML, if that's what gets you going. If you're an HTML enthusiast, though, or in case you're just curious, we don't want you to feel neglected, so you can view and edit the HTML right in Page view. To view the HTML for any given page open in Page view, click the HTML view tab at the bottom of the FrontPage window. Figure 7-41 shows a page when the HTML view tab is selected.

You can edit the code you see in HTML view, using the same keyboard shortcuts you use on any page, such as those for copying, cutting, and pasting. The HTML view is colored coded; that is, it separates things like HTML tags, attributes, JavaScript, and page text into different colors. This makes sorting though the code a little easier to manage.

HTML view is a fully functioning HTML editor. If you make a mistake or get in over your head, remember those Undo/Redo commands. FrontPage will not attempt to correct the HTML that you add in this view, so be careful when you make changes.

CHAPTER 7

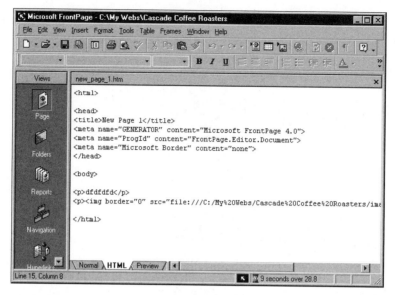

Figure 7-41

Page view when the HTML tab is selected.

TIP

If you're a bit overwhelmed looking at all that code and you're trying to find a certain place in the code to edit, you can try this little trick. In Normal view , place the insertion point in the area you want to edit, and then switch to HTML view. The area that your insertion point was placed in is right where HTML view opens. The insertion point will be blinking, ready to go. If you highlight a selection of text or an image while in Page view, and you then switch to HTML view, the area that you selected is highlighted in the code.

The Preview View

Let's say you're working on a Web off line. Maybe you're using a laptop in the middle of the beach, on some remote tropical island with no phones. Although, if you were in that situation, I don't know why in the world you'd be working on your Web—but let's just pretend, okay? Once you begin building your pages, you might want to see how they're going to look, but with no phones and no way to post the pages to your server, what will you do? Enter the Preview view in Page view. To see a preview of a page in your Web, click the Preview tab.

I know what you're thinking: "If I haven't saved the file to the server, then what am I looking at?" Well, when FrontPage edits a file, it's editing locally on your machine. The file is stored locally until you actually save it to your Internet server. When you use the Preview tab in Page view, what you're seeing is that local file, presented as if it were on a server. Because you're not actually "on" a server, though, some of the active elements you may have on your page won't work. The Preview view is a great place for offline viewing of your Web, but to get the real deal, especially when testing, you'll want to view the Web in a browser connected to the Internet. Alternatively, you can quickly see how your Web will look in a browser using the Preview in Browser menu command. For more information on this command, see "Previewing in a Browser" in Chapter 3.

If you're building a Web that uses frames, you'll see additional view tabs at the bottom of the window in Page view. For explanations about these frames view tabs, see Chapter 6.

Utilities and Useful Commands

You'll find numerous utilities and other commands in FrontPage to make your work a little easier. They might even save your bacon if you make a mistake somewhere along the line.

Previewing in a Browser

Believe it or not, many people use browsers other than Internet Explorer and Netscape Navigator. If your site is going to be accessible to the world, you should test it in as many browsers as possible. Therefore, you might want to install a variety of browsers on your computer and view your site using each one. You should also consider testing your site using different browser versions.

At any time, you can see the progress of your work and the way it will appear to the throngs that rush to see your pages online. You can choose the Preview In Browser command from the File menu to have FrontPage launch the current page in the Web browser of your choice. When you choose the command from the File menu, you'll see the Preview In Browser dialog box, shown in Figure 7-42, on the next page.

Select an available browser in the Browser section. You can add new browsers to the list by clicking the Add button. You'll then see the Add Browser dialog box, where you'll need to enter a name for the browser and the path and name of the executable file (which has the .EXE file extension). You can click Browse in the Add Browser dialog box to find the executable file for browsers you want to add.

CHAPTER 7

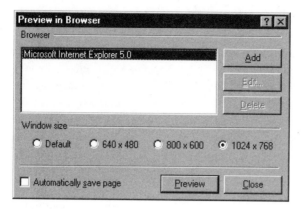

Figure 7-42

The Preview In Browser dialog box.

In the Preview In Browser dialog box, you can also edit or delete browsers you have added to your list.

To edit a browser, select it from the list and click Edit. To delete a browser, select it from the list and click Delete. If FrontPage has automatically added a browser to the Preview In Browser dialog box, the Edit and Delete buttons are typically not available for it.

You can also set the browser window size by selecting one of the option buttons in the Window Size section. This is a great reason to use the Preview In Browser command—so you can test your site in different browser window sizes. Maybe you designed your Web pages using 1024 by 768 resolution but you want to see what the browser window size will look like to visitors who use normal VGA (640 by 480) resolution. In order for the different window sizes to work properly, your display must have the same screen resolution as the one you select, or a higher one. Clicking the Preview button causes the current page to be displayed in the selected browser and window size.

Using Undo and Redo

The 3-2 hanging curve balls, interceptions in the end zone, and missed layups are on the record books to stay, but not the mistakes you make while working in Page view. The Undo command can save you on the job. Use Undo to reverse the last action you made on a page, up to the last 30 actions. To undo an action, choose Undo from the Edit menu or click the Undo button on the Standard toolbar.

To reverse the effect of an Undo command, you can choose Redo from the Edit menu or click the Redo button on the Standard toolbar. You can redo up to the last 30 Undo commands.

For a quicker way to Undo, press Ctrl+Z. For a quicker Redo, press Ctrl+Y.

Following a Link

You can use Page view as a mini-browser by using the Follow Hyperlink command. To see the actual page, file, or bookmark that a link goes to, press the Ctrl key and click the link, or right-click the link and choose Follow Hyperlink from the pop-up menu.

If the link leads to another page, FrontPage opens that page. If the link is to a file, such as a Microsoft Excel document, FrontPage opens the application configured for the file type and presents the file in its native environment.

Creating a Task

If you want to add a task to Tasks view, choose Task from the Edit menu and then choose Add Task from the pop-up menu.

In the New Task dialog box that appears (see Figure 7-43), you can add details to the task that appears in Tasks view, such as the task name, the task owner, the priority of the task, and a description. The task will be linked to the active page. Chapter 3 discusses the use of Tasks view.

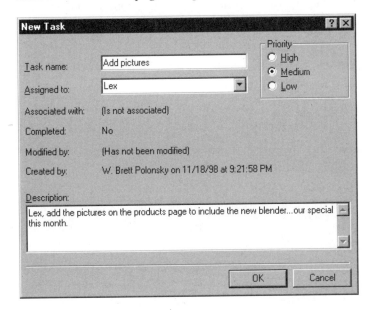

Figure 7-43
The New Task dialog box.

Using the Spelling Checker

FrontPage is equipped with the Microsoft Office spelling checker, which provides outstanding consistency between Office documents and FrontPage Web sites. You can check the spelling of selected text, selected pages, or all the HTML pages in your Web site.

TIP

You can quickly access the spelling checker by clicking the Check Spelling button on the Standard toolbar.

Checking Spelling on an Open Page

Here are the steps for checking an open page:

1. To check the spelling of a selection of text, select it first. To check the entire page, you don't have to select anything.

2. Choose Spelling from the Tools menu, or press F7. If no text is selected, the spelling checker begins checking at the top of the page. If it finds no unrecognized words, it presents a dialog box informing you that the spelling check is complete.

3. If the spelling checker finds words that it doesn't recognize, you'll see the Spelling dialog box. Use the dialog box options as follows:

   - **Not In Dictionary.** This text box displays words that aren't in the Office dictionary or the custom dictionary.

   - **Ignore.** Click this button to ignore the current word and search for the next unrecognized word.

   - **Ignore All**. Click this button to ignore all instances of the current word on the page and continue with the spelling check.

   - **Change**. Click this button to replace the unrecognized word in the Not In Dictionary text box with the selection in the Change To box.

   - **Change All**. Click this button to replace all instances of the current word on the page with the contents of the Change To box.

   - **Add**. Click this button to add the selection in the Not In Dictionary box to the custom dictionary and make no changes to the word. (Note: FrontPage shares the custom dictionary with Office, so any custom words you add while using Office applications are available in FrontPage, and vice versa.)

PART

III

● **Suggest**. When this button is enabled, you can click it to list alternative words in the Suggestions list, based on the word in the Change To box.

● **Cancel**. Click this button to close the dialog box and quit the spelling check. Changes that have been made to the page and to the custom dictionary remain.

The spelling checker doesn't check the spelling in a file included on the page by a FrontPage Include Component. You must open those files separately to check their spelling. For more information on FrontPage Components, see Chapter 9.

Checking the Spelling on All Pages in a Site

To check the spelling on all the HTML files in a site, choose Spelling from the Tools menu in any view other than Page view, or press F7. In the Spelling dialog box, specify whether you want FrontPage to check the spelling of all the HTML pages in the site or of just the ones you've selected. (To select multiple pages, press the Ctrl key while you click individual page icons in Folder view.) Then click Start.

In the Spelling dialog box, FrontPage presents the results of the spelling check. In this dialog box, you can see details such as the pages containing misspelled words, as well as the number of misspelled words per page. If you find yourself saying "Whoopsie," and you want to correct the error right away, double-click the page in the list. You'll be transported to that page in Page view, and you'll be given the opportunity to make any changes you like. If you don't feel like making the changes right then, or if you'd rather have Jeff down the hall do it because the game starts in half an hour and you've got to pick up the pizza on the way home, click Add A Task For Each Page With Misspellings to add the tasks to Tasks view. (In Tasks view, you can assign Jeff's name to the tasks.) When you're finished using the Check Spelling dialog box, click Close.

Using Find and Replace

You can use Find and Replace to search for and replace words on the current page or to search for and replace words across multiple HTML pages in your site. Take a second to imagine how useful this feature can be. If your site contains dozens of instances of the word *board* that happen to be spelled *bored*, you have a big problem on your hands. But luckily, you have a tool for searching the pages across your site and fixing any errors you know of in a straightforward fashion.

CHAPTER 7

- **Find.** Choose Find from the Edit menu to display the Find dialog box. Type the text you want to find and whether you want to have FrontPage look only in selected pages or in the entire web. If you want to find only whole words, check the Match Whole Word Only check box. For example, if every word on your page is *the*, and you search for *t*, you won't find any instance of *t* if the Match Whole Word Only check box is checked. If the box is not checked, every instance of the letter *t* will be found.

  Select the Match Case check box if you only want to find text that exactly matches the case of the selection you're searching for. You can specify the direction of the search, Up or Down, relative to the insertion point. When an instance of the selection is found, click the Find Next button to continue searching. Click Cancel to close the dialog box and stop the search.

- **Replace.** To replace text with other specified text, use the Replace command on the Edit menu, or press Ctrl+H. The Replace dialog box appears.

  Type the text you want to replace in the Find What text box, and enter your replacement text in the Replace With box. To find text only if it matches a whole word or only if it matches the case of the text you're searching for, check the appropriate check box. To replace all instances of the text on the page, click the Replace All button. To locate the first matching instance, click the Find Next button to begin the search. When FrontPage finds an instance of the text you're looking for, it selects the text on the page. To replace the text, click the Replace button. To move on without replacing the text, click Find Next.

Using the Thesaurus

You now have the power of the Microsoft Office thesaurus in FrontPage. The thesaurus comes in handy on those rainy days when you're sitting at your desk trying to find the right word that's on the tip of your tongue, and it doesn't help that your mind continually drifts back to the vacation you just spent in Cabo.

To use the thesaurus for help on a specific word, select the word and choose Thesaurus from the Tools menu, or press Shift+F7. You'll see the Thesaurus dialog box, which you use in the same way that you use one in an Office application.

PART
III

- The Looked Up text box displays the word you're currently checking.

- The Meanings list displays meanings for the word you're looking up. If you select a meaning here, you'll see a list of synonyms in the Replace With Related Word list.

- Click a word in the Replace With Related Word list if you want to use it in place of the selected word in Page view, or if you want to use that word to search further. To use the word right away, click Replace, and you'll be returned to Page view with the new word in place. To keep on searching using the selected word as the new word you're looking up, click Look Up.

- If you don't want to use any new words from the thesaurus, click Cancel.

- If the Previous button is enabled, you can click it to return to the previous word you looked up.

Moving Among Currently Open Pages

Use the Back button on the Standard toolbar to move back among pages that are currently open in the Page view. When you click the arrow to the right of the back button, a drop-down list appears showing you the pages you can go back to.

Refreshing a Page

To refresh an active page in Page view by substituting the last saved version of that page, click the Refresh button on the Standard toolbar or choose the Refresh command from the View menu. If you've made changes since the last save, a dialog box appears asking whether you want to save the changes. Click Yes or No, and FrontPage refreshes the page. The Refresh command is handy when you've made changes to a page that you don't want to save, and you want to start over from the last version that was saved. It's also handy for viewing changes made to a page by another person. You can also re-fresh the page at any time by pressing the F5 function key.

Stopping an Action

To stop an action, click the Stop button on the toolbar (if it's enabled). This command is handy for ending actions that are taking a long time to finish or that might be hung up.

CHAPTER

7

Customizing Toolbars

You can customize each toolbar in FrontPage to include only the buttons you want visible on the selected toolbar. Each toolbar has its own set of potential buttons from which to choose. Click the Down arrow to the right of a toolbar to display the Add Or Remove Buttons pop-up. Clicking the Add Or Remove Buttons pop-up displays a list of the available buttons for that toolbar. Buttons that have a check mark next to them are already on the toolbar. You can clear or check buttons any way you like.

Coming Up

With that, the grand discussion of formatting and using FrontPage's file commands and utilities comes to an end. In the next chapter, you'll learn how you can use FrontPage to work with images.

CHAPTER 8

Getting Into Graphics

Images: A Balancing Act

As any writer will tell you, "Content is king." And any graphic artist will tell you, "Content is one thing, but if you want anyone to read it, you'd better add some graphics." As a Web developer, you'll be walking this fine line and addressing the content vs. graphics issue for every page in your Web.

When you deal with graphics in a Web, the number one issue is file size, which translates directly to how long an image takes to appear in the average browser. You can discuss graphic file formats, resolution, image editing software, color palettes, browsers, and so forth until you're blue in the face, but the bottom line is that the best graphics are the ones that have both reasonable image quality and small file sizes.

Because many people are still using 14.4 KB modems, many Web developers limit the size of their pages. Typically, a page in your Web, including any images on that page, should not exceed 35 to 40 KB. That loud noise you just heard was a collective scream of "Yeah, right!" from the graphic designers of the world. That size doesn't sound like much to work with, and it's not, but with some helpful tips to optimize your images, you'll be surprised at what you can do.

This chapter discusses four aspects of using images in your Webs:

● The types of graphic file formats used in Web development

● How to optimize those formats, using color management, to achieve fast-loading images that still look good

● Using Microsoft FrontPage 2000 to handle your images, including placing images, creating image maps, overlaying text on GIFs, and creating transparent GIFs directly in FrontPage

● The new and improved Picture toolbar, which lets you adjust contrast and brightness and also lets you flip, rotate, and crop images, all from within FrontPage

Graphic File Formats

As you might know, graphic file formats are all referred to by an acronym or by the file extension associated with the format, and the names can get a little confusing. You've got BMP, GIF, EPS, PNG, TIF, JPEG, WMF, and many others. While working on your Web in FrontPage, however, you'll be dealing primarily with two types of image files: JPEG and GIF. Both are compressed graphic file formats, and they're the ones most commonly used in Web development.

But what if you have some graphics that are not JPEGs or GIFs, and you want to use them on a Web page? Well, you're in luck, because FrontPage can import many graphic file formats, which are listed here:

CompuServe GIF (GIF)

JPEG (JPG)

Bitmap (BMP)

TIFF (TIF)

Ping (PNG)

Windows Metafile (WMF)

Sun Raster (RAS)

Encapsulated PostScript (EPS)

Paintbrush (PCX)

Targa (TGA)

When you save a page that contains images you've inserted but haven't saved yet, FrontPage asks you whether you want to save each image to the current Web. By default, FrontPage saves each non-GIF or non-JPEG image as a GIF. If you want the image saved as a JPEG, be sure to specify this in the Picture Properties dialog box before you save the page.

The JPEG (Joint Photographic Experts Group) file format is a scalable compressed format that can deliver high compression with very little image degradation. It's not uncommon for an image to lose some of its crispness in electronic form, especially when it's converted from one format to another. Because JPEG images handle compression and image degradation well, they're ideal for a Web environment in which they are often resized, converted, or otherwise altered. The JPEG format is most suitable for photographs or images that contain more than 256 colors. FrontPage looks at the number of bits used to represent each color in the image, also known as the file's *bit depth*. Images with eight bits of color information per pixel are capable of supporting 256 different colors. More bits means more colors supported (see Figure 8-1).

Bit depth	Number of colors
8 bit	256 Colors
7 bit	128 Colors
6 bit	64 Colors
5 bit	32 Colors
4 bit	16 Colors
3 bit	8 Colors

Figure 8-1

Relationship between image bit depth and number of colors.

The GIF (Graphics Interchange Format) file format is a compressed format for images that contain 256 or fewer colors. It is typically used with images that contain primarily solid colors, such as illustrations. The GIF format also can support transparency and interlacing.

In FrontPage, you can do a little something extra to a GIF image. With the click of the mouse, you can make one color in a GIF transparent. You can also type text anywhere on top of a GIF, in any color, font, or size. We'll get into all of that in "Cool Stuff You Can Do to an Image," later in this chapter.

You may also come across the PNG (Portable Network Graphics) file format, pronounced "ping". The PNG format, like GIF and JPEG, is a compressed file format. You can think of PNG as an alternative to the GIF file format, in that you can set a color in PNG format to be transparent. Although the most recent versions of Microsoft's Internet Explorer and Netscape's Navigator browsers support the PNG file format, be aware that some browsers may not display PNG files correctly without a plug-in.

Color Management

The idea of color management might be new to a lot of graphic artists, but if you plan on being successful with your Web, it will become your new best friend. The basic issue in color management is this: How can you decrease the number of colors in your images and still have them look good? Decreasing the number of colors decreases the file size of the image, and smaller files download faster in a browser.

> **TIP**
>
> Start with a good color palette, which is a collection of colors (usually 256) that is designed to perform well across a variety of browsers and platforms. These palettes, called "safety palettes," are readily available on the Web.

If you want users to see those impressive graphics you're about to create, you need to make sure they're built for speed. The last thing you want is for users to become frustrated as they watch their screens draw and redraw a bunch of graphics with large file sizes. Keep in mind the following tips for making your image file sizes smaller:

- Typically, the JPEG format works well for photographic, or *raster*, images, and the GIF format works well for images containing solid colors or for *vector* images, such as illustrations and line art.

- Size your images using your image-editing software. Even though you can dimensionally size images in FrontPage, this doesn't actually change the image file size. For example, if you insert a 2-inch square image that has a file size of 10 KB in FrontPage and you size it to a 1-inch square in Page view, the image file size is still 10 KB.

- If you're creating an image that contains only black and white, save it as a black-and-white image to make the image file size smaller.

- If you're creating an image that will be saved as a GIF and it contains a blend of colors (also known as a *gradient)* or straight lines, try to make them horizontal. Because the GIF format performs its compression by looking at each horizontal line, it can make the file size smaller if an entire line has the same color value.

- Experiment with the various JPEG compression levels. Try to use as much compression as possible while still retaining acceptable image quality.

PART

III

- View your images at different resolutions and bit depths, and view them in different browsers. A JPEG image that has a depth of more than 8 bits dithers when displayed on a monitor that supports only 256 colors.

- If you're using Adobe Photoshop and you want to save an image as a GIF, change the RGB Color mode to Indexed Color mode, specify the bit depth (the smaller the better), and then select the adaptive palette with no dither.

- If you're using Photoshop and saving images as GIFs, and if you know that your image uses fewer than 256 colors, try using the Exact palette. Exact palettes contain exactly the number of colors in your image and thus decrease the image file size.

The key is to experiment. You might notice some flattening of colors, but you'll also notice a decrease in image file size. It's a judgment call, but it's one you'll have to make if you want to display graphics faster in a browser.

As crazy as this might sound, some people don't like to wait for graphics at all, so remember to take advantage of the alternative text feature (explained later in this chapter, in "Changing Picture Properties"). Think about designing your pages so those "graphics haters" out there can still navigate through your Web.

Defining Colors in HTML

If you're new to HTML and you've always wondered how colors are defined in the code to be displayed in a browser, you're in luck, because that's exactly what you're about to find out.

You may already know that your monitor uses RGB (Red, Green, and Blue) values to display all of the colors you see on your screen. Because HTML can't understand the RGB values your monitor uses, HTML uses a hexadecimal (hex) color value to display colors in a browser. You might be asking yourself, "So, what the heck are hex color values, and why should I care?" If you're creating original graphics and don't want them to dither, or if you just want a little insight into the HTML for color, you'll want to know this stuff. Because we already know that it's a good idea to use a 256-color "safety" palette, we'll concentrate on the hex and on the RGB values that make up that palette.

If you look at the HTML for a page (by using the HTML tab in Page view, for example), you might notice the *color* tag. For instance, if you have black text on your page that says "Hello," the code would look like this: <font color="#000000">Hello</font>. The hexadecimal number system is a base-16 system, with numbers ranging from 0 to F. Hex colors are a series of three sets of two numbers or letters. Each set of two relates to an R, G, and B value, which is why you end up with a total of six. In the example above, 000000 represents black, which is the absence of all color. The other extreme is FFFFFF, which is all colors, making white. In an RGB value system, black would be 0,0,0, and white would be 255,255,255. In reality, you could type in just about any combination of six numbers or letters (from A to F) and come up with a hex color, but in order to stay within our 256-color palette, we'll use only hex values that match an RGB value of 255 or less. Of course, 255 plus 0 (black) is how we come up with the 256 colors in the "safety" palette.

Here's the simple method for determining whether your color is part of the 256-color palette: the hex value for each of those colors must be either 00, 33, 66, 99, CC, or FF, and they can be in any combination of three sets. The RGB equivalent is a value of 0, 51, 102, 153, 204, or 255. So, for example, if you wanted to use a safe orange color for the word "Hello," its RGB value would be 255,102,51, and its hex value would be FF, 66, 33. In HTML it would look like this: <font color="#FF6633">Hello</font>. The illustration in Figure 8-2 shows hex/RGB values for the 256-color palette.

256 color value chart						
HEX	00	33	66	99	CC	FF
RGB	0	51	102	153	204	255

Figure 8-2
Hex/RGB values for the 256-color palette.

Now when you're working with your favorite image editing software, you can create RGB colors with confidence, knowing that they're part of the 256-color palette. And if you're the type of person who likes to fiddle with the HTML code, you'll know exactly what all of those color tags mean, and how to change them if you want.

Optimizing Your Backgrounds

If you want that cool background to appear quickly and still have acceptable quality, these tips can help you:

● Because a background image is just a tiled graphic, follow the guidelines described in the previous section to decrease the file size.

● Decrease the physical dimensions of the background image to decrease the file size.

- Don't put too much detail in a background. Remember that, in most cases, text has to be read on top of it.

- Experiment with the backgrounds that FrontPage provides. Many of these backgrounds are very small in file size. (See the next section for information on inserting them.) You can also use your favorite Web search engine and search on the word *backgrounds*—you'll get plenty of hits and find lots of pages offering free backgrounds.

- Consider using a background color instead of a background image. This decreases download time, sometimes significantly.

Bringing In Those Images

Okay, now that you know a little bit about graphic file formats and color management, it's time to find out how to get images on your pages. You do this in Page view, by choosing the Image command from the Insert menu and then choosing From File from the pop-up menu. Just follow these steps:

1. In Page view, place the pointer where you want the image to appear.

2. Choose Picture from the Insert menu and then choose From File from the pop-up menu. If the image is already part of your Web in FrontPage, you'll see the Picture dialog box, shown in Figure 8-3.

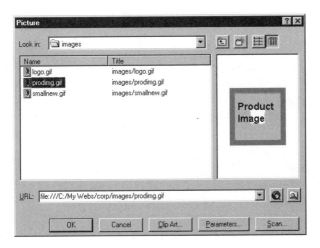

Figure 8-3
The Picture dialog box, showing the From File options.

CHAPTER 8

Here you can select from any file currently in the open Web and browse throughout the folders in that Web. Just click the file to see a preview displayed in the area on the right side of the dialog box. If you know its URL, you can just enter it in the text box. You can also use your Web browser to select an image or select a file on your computer by clicking either of the buttons to the right of the URL text box.

If you want to insert an image that isn't part of the current Web, or if you click the Select File button on the Image dialog box, you'll see the Select File dialog box, shown in Figure 8-4.

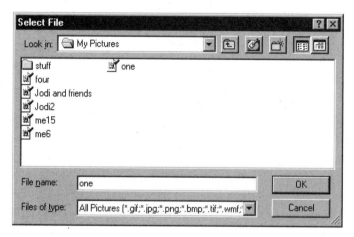

Figure 8-4

The Select File dialog box.

From this dialog box, you can select any file on your local machine. If you click Cancel, you'll see the Picture dialog box again.

If you're connected to a scanner or digital camera, you have a very cool feature at your disposal. Whenever you're in the Picture dialog box, you'll have the option to click the Scan button to launch any input device you're connected to. You can then scan an image directly into FrontPage, where you can give it any name you choose and put it into any folder you like. If you don't feel like making that decision, FrontPage names the file for you and places it in the Temp folder, located in the directory in which you installed FrontPage.

Saving Images

Images on a page aren't saved within the file that contains the HTML. They're saved as separate files in their image formats (GIF or JPEG). The HTML only references the location of the image.

If you're working with an image you've inserted from any location other than the Web open in FrontPage, you'll be asked to save the image the next time you save the page. You save these new images using the Save Embedded Files dialog box, shown in Figure 8-5.

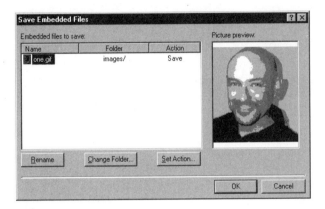

Figure 8-5
The Save Embedded Files dialog box.

You'll see the files that need to be saved listed on the left, together with their location and the action that takes place when you click OK. If you click a file in the list, you'll see a thumbnail of the image in the Picture Preview window. You can also rename the file, change its folder, or set a new save action by clicking the appropriate button. When you're finished, click OK, and FrontPage saves the images.

Using Clip Art

FrontPage has a collection of hundreds of clip art images, and it also provides access to the Microsoft Office clip art library, if you have Office installed. You can access clip art in two ways: click Clip Art in the Image dialog box, or choose Picture from the Insert menu and then choose Clip Art from the pop-up menu. In either case, you'll see the Clip Art Gallery dialog box, shown in Figure 8-6, on the next page.

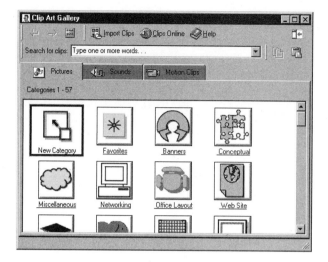

Figure 8-6

The Clip Art Gallery dialog box.

Select the category you want from one of the three tabs: Pictures, Sounds, or Motion Clips. When you find an image you want, click the image in the preview window and then click Insert. If you're looking through the Sounds or Motion Clips, you can play them on the spot, before you insert them, by clicking Play. If you don't find anything you like here, you can click the Clips Online button at the top of the dialog box. You'll be transported to a clip art area at **www.Microsoft.com,** where you'll find dozens of free clips. Any images you select here are added to your Clip Art Gallery automatically.

You can also add clip art to your gallery by clicking Import Clips (also at the top of the dialog box) and locating the images. If you need help using this dialog box, click Help, and if you want to search for a clip, type the words you want to search for in the text box. If you're poking around through a lot of clip galleries and you want to find your way back, just click the Back button.

The Images Are In—Now What?

After you insert an image, FrontPage gives you many ways to manipulate it with the Picture Properties dialog box. Here, you'll find useful information about your image, such as its type, dimensions, and much more. You also have a whole suite of image-editing tools available on the Picture toolbar. (These are discussed in detail later in this chapter.)

Changing Picture Properties

If you want to alter an image and the way it appears on a page, here's what to do:

1. Select an image in Page view by clicking it. Notice that the Picture toolbar is highlighted as soon as you select an image.

2. Choose Properties from the Format menu. You'll see the Picture Properties dialog box, shown in Figure 8-7, which has three tabs: General, Video, and Appearance.

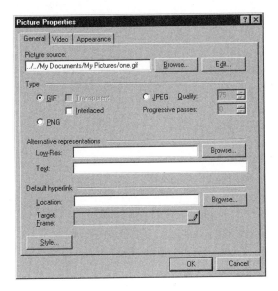

Figure 8-7
The General tab of the Picture Properties dialog box.

3. Adjust the settings as necessary, and then click OK. Remember that the settings aren't permanent and that you can always return to the Picture Properties dialog box to change them.

The following is a detailed look at the settings in the dialog box, starting with the General tab.

TIP

You can right-click an image and choose Picture Properties from the pop-up menu to reach the Picture Properties dialog box. If you've already selected an image, you can reach the Picture Properties dialog box quickly by pressing Alt+Enter.

CHAPTER 8

General tab

Your options on the General tab are as follows:

- **Picture Source.** This text box displays the image's page URL if the image is in the current Web, its absolute URL if the image is from the World Wide Web, or its path and file name if the image is in a file. If you want to change the image, click Browse to display the Picture dialog box. If you want to open the image to work on it in your image editor, click Edit.

- **Type.** This section displays the graphic format of the selected image, either GIF, JPEG, or PNG. The selected option is the image's current format. By selecting one of the other options, you can convert the image to that format.

  When the GIF option button is selected, you have two options for presenting the image: Transparent and Interlaced. You can use one or use both at the same time.

  - **Transparent.** Available only for GIF images, this check box is selected if a color in the image is currently specified as transparent. Clear the check box to return the transparent portions of the image to their normal color and make the image non-transparent. Later in this chapter, you'll find out how to make a color transparent and why you might want to specify a transparent color.

  - **Interlaced.** If the Interlaced check box is selected, the image renders progressively in the browser. A progressively rendered image slowly comes into focus as it appears in a browser.

    If the JPEG option button is selected, the Quality and Progressive Passes text boxes become available.

  - **Quality.** You can adjust the image quality by entering a number between 1 and 100. A higher number means less compression, resulting in a better-quality image, but it also means a larger image and slower performance. (Larger files take longer for the browser to download and display.) A lower number means more compression, resulting in lower image quality but a smaller file size. By default, the Quality setting is 75.

  - **Progressive Passes.** Entering a number in the Progressive passes text box tells the browser how many times to pass the image through the server before the image is completely rendered. Certain browsers do not support the progressive pass feature. The default Progressive Passes is set to 0.

- **Alternative Representations.** Not all browsers support images, and most browsers can be set to disable images. Some browsers can display a low-resolution image in place of a high-resolution image while downloading the high-resolution image from the server. You can also specify text to appear in place of the graphic, in case visitors have graphics turned off in their browsers. For all these cases, you can supply an alternative representation for the image.

    - **Low-Res.** Specifies a lower-resolution image to appear in place of a high-resolution image while the latter is downloading. Click the Browse button, select an alternate image, and then click OK. For you HTML buffs, this alternative image is the same as using the LOWSRC attribute in HTML.

NOTE

Neither FrontPage nor the browser checks to ensure that the low-res image is actually a low-res version of the real image.

    - **Text.** Specifies alternative text that appears instead of the image if the user's browser cannot display images or is set to disable the displaying of images. This is useful if you anticipate that some users will view your Web without its graphics. This "alt" text is useful to disabled users who can't see, but who still want to "hear" what's on the page using a page reader. This text also appears to users when they hover the pointer over the image in the browser. So it's always a good idea to add alternative text to every image in your Web, and to make that text short yet descriptive. In some browsers, this text appears while the image is loading. By default, FrontPage inserts the name of the image in this field, along with its size in bytes. You can, however, change this to anything you like.

- **Default Hyperlink.** You can turn part or all of your image into a hotspot that links to other locations. (See "Creating Image Maps," later in this chapter, to learn how.) If an image has multiple hotspots, you can set a default link for the parts of the image that aren't covered by a hotspot.

- **Location.** To set a default link, click Browse, and you'll see the Edit Hyperlink dialog box. For your link, you can select from a list of currently open pages, pages or files from World Wide Web, Gopher, Newsgroup, or FTP sites, or a new page. By clicking the Mail button in the Edit Hyperlink dialog box, you can also set a hyperlink that sends mail. Set your link, and then click OK to return to the Picture Properties dialog box.

    If the image already has a default link, you'll see the Edit Hyperlink dialog box when you click the Browse button. You can change the link in exactly the same way that you set it. Edit the link, and then click OK to return to the Picture Properties dialog box.

- **Target Frame.** You can also specify a target frame for the default link in the Target Frame text box. For more information on setting a target frame, see Chapter 6.

- **Style.** Click the Style button to attach or edit a cascading style sheet associated with the image. For more information on cascading style sheets, see Chapter 10.

Video tab

The second tab of the Picture Properties dialog box, Video, shown in Figure 8-8, lets you insert an AVI (Audio Video) file on your page. The image file you designated on the General tab is used as a placeholder that is displayed until the AVI is loaded and ready to run. (Adding a video to your page by choosing the Picture command on the Insert menu and then choosing Video from the submenu is a slightly different process. For more information on using the Video command, see Chapter 7.)

- **Video Source.** You can type the path and file name for your video in the Video Source text box, or you can use the Browse button to locate the video file.

- **Show Controls in Browser.** Select this check box to show a set of controls (Play, Stop, and a slider) along with the video when it's displayed in the browser at run time.

- **Repeat.** This section of the dialog box lets you set how often and when the video plays.

    - **Loop.** Enter a number for the number of times you want the video to play.

Figure 8-8
The Video tab of the Picture Properties dialog box.

- **Loop Delay.** Enter a number to specify a delay between each playing of the video. The delay is specified in milliseconds.

- **Forever.** Select this check box if you want the video to loop indefinitely while the page is displayed.

- **Start.** The options in this section of the dialog box let you determine when the video will be played.

  - **On File Open.** Select this check box to have the video play as soon as it's been downloaded in the browser.

  - **On Mouse Over.** Select this check box to have the video play when the user positions the mouse pointer over the image.

Appearance tab
The third tab of the Picture Properties dialog box, Appearance (shown in Figure 8-9, on the next page), lets you manipulate the appearance of your image in a number of ways:

- **Layout.** In this section of the dialog box, you control the position of the image on the page.

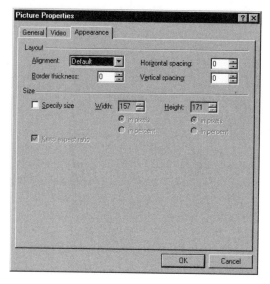

Figure 8-9

The Appearance tab of the Picture Properties dialog box.

- **Alignment.** Specifies a type of alignment between the image and the text around it. This is defined by the "align =" tag in HTML. You can align the image in several ways:

    Default. Adds no alignment tag to the image in the HTML.

    Left. Places the image in the left margin and wraps the text preceding the image down the right side of the image.

    Right. Places the image in the right margin and wraps the text preceding the image down the left side of the image.

    Top. Aligns the text with the top of the image.

    Texttop. Aligns the top of the image with the top of the tallest text in the line.

    Middle. Aligns the text with the middle of the image.

    Absmiddle. Aligns the image with the middle of the current line.

    Baseline. Aligns the image with the baseline of the current line.

    Bottom. Aligns the text with the bottom of the image so that the text begins at the bottom of the image.

Absbottom. Aligns the image with the bottom of the current line.

Center. Aligns the image in the center of the page.

These settings apply only to images that appear on the same line as text. If an image is the only element on a line, the setting defaults to Bottom.

- **Border Thickness.** Specifies a black border around the image; the width of the border is expressed in pixels. To change the width, select the number in the text box and type in the new number.

- **Horizontal Spacing.** Sets a specified horizontal spacing in pixels from the image to the nearest image or text on the current line, on both sides of the image.

- **Vertical Spacing.** Sets a specified vertical spacing in pixels from the image to the nearest image or text on the line above and below it.

- **Size.** This section of the dialog box displays the height and width of the image in pixels. Select the Specify Size check box to include width and height tags in the HTML code, or change the Width and Height of your image by entering new numbers yourself. Sizes are specified either in pixels or as a percentage of the current image size.

  - **Keep Aspect Ratio.** Check this box to maintain the image's ratio of width to height if you change one of the two dimensions. In other words, if you change the width or height, but not both, checking this box maintains the proportions of the image.

You can resize an image by selecting it and then dragging the sides or corners of the image. If you drag from the corners, the image is resized proportionally. Remember, this affects only the image display dimensions, not the file size.

NOTE

They say that size doesn't matter, but here it does. It's always a good idea to check the Specify Size check box on the Appearance tab of the Picture Properties dialog box. When a browser begins to load a page, it looks for tags in the HTML. One of those tags references any images on the page. When you specify an image's width and height, the browser leaves room for it on the page, even before it downloads the image. In the absence of the width and height tags, the browser has to wait for the image to download before it makes room for it on the page. When this happens, you'll see text and other elements on the page jump and move to make room for the image.

Cool Stuff You Can Do to an Image

Once an image is on your page, you can do many cool things with it beyond setting or changing its properties, and you'll do all of these cool things by using the Picture toolbar, as shown in Figure 8-10. You can make the toolbar visible, if it's not already, by choosing Toolbars from the View menu and then choosing Picture from the submenu. The toolbar floats, which means you can move it anywhere you want on your screen, even outside the FrontPage window. To move the toolbar, click inside the toolbar in an area not occupied by a button, and then drag the toolbar to its destination. You can dock the toolbar by dragging it to any location within the toolbar region of FrontPage. The Picture toolbar automatically becomes active when you select an image in Page view.

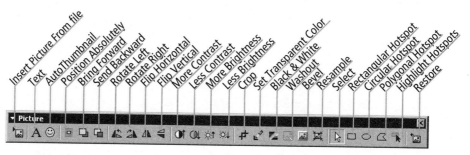

Figure 8-10

The Picture toolbar.

When you use the Picture toolbar, you have a miniature image-editing studio right at your fingertips. You can create image maps and transparent GIFs, type text on a GIF, crop images, and make adjustments to image quality, as well as do a few other things. We'll walk through each of these features, starting with the first button on the Picture toolbar, Insert Picture From File.

Insert Picture From File

Clicking the Insert Picture From File button on the Picture toolbar brings up the Image dialog box, described in the "Bringing In Those Images" section of this chapter. This is a quick method, especially if you're going to be inserting a lot of pictures on the current page.

Text

Let's say that you're in charge of putting the pages together for your company Web, and this whole Web thing is confusing enough. You've already proven your intelligence—you've chosen to use FrontPage to create the Web. Then all of a sudden your boss looks at the page and says, "Hey! We wanted that illustration of the hamburger at the top to say, 'Eat at Jeff's—You won't be sorry!' the company's slogan, and we want it to link to our nutritional facts page." And you're already over budget on the graphics. You can't afford to have the illustrator do it, but you remember that you can type the text in yourself in Page view, right on top of the image, and even make the text a hyperlink. When you click the Text button on the Picture toolbar, the problem's solved and everyone's happy—even your cranky boss, Jeff.

This is one of the coolest features on the Picture toolbar. The Text tool lets you type formatted text right on top of any image, and you can even turn that text overlay into a hotspot, using the Create Hyperlink dialog box. This is a great way to incorporate text in an image whenever you need it.

To use the Text tool, you must first insert an image on your page while in Page view. Then select the image by clicking it; the Picture toolbar becomes active. Click the Text button on the Picture toolbar, and FrontPage automatically creates a text region centered on the image. The insertion pointer is blinking in the text region, ready for you to add text.

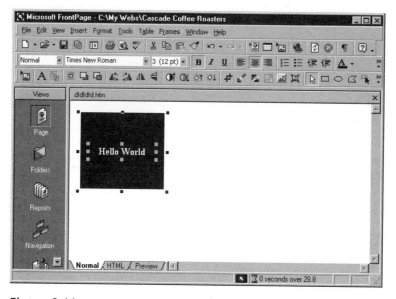

Figure 8-11

Text placed as an overlay on an image.

Formatting the text

Figure 8-11 above shows a selected image, after we've clicked the Text button on the Picture toolbar and typed in and formatted some text. The rectangular area in the middle of the square is the text field. As soon as you click the Text button, you can start typing in your text. The default text is 12 pt Arial Black, center aligned, but you can easily change those attributes. You can also change fonts, colors, size, and alignment by selecting the text and using any of the buttons on the Format toolbar. For information on the Format toolbar, see Chapter 7.

The text is displayed in a single line, so if you want it to wrap, you'll need to adjust the width to suit your needs. You do this by resizing the text region, anywhere within the boundaries of the image. Select a border anchor (the little boxes in the corners and in the middle of borders) and drag them out. Top and bottom border anchors adjust the height, left and right border anchors adjust the width, and corner border anchors adjust the height and width together. You can also move the text region to another location on the image by clicking a border and then dragging it around into place, but you must stay within the image.

Making the text a hyperlink

If you want the text to be hot (a hyperlink), right-click the text region and then choose Hyperlink from the pop-up menu. This launches the Create Hyperlink dialog box. You can also create a hyperlink by selecting the text area and pressing Alt+Enter, or by double-clicking the border. In the Create Hyperlink dialog box, you can easily make the text area of the image a hotspot. For more information on using the Create Hyperlink dialog box, see Chapter 7.

Deleting the text

You can easily delete any text that you've placed on an image. All you have to do is select the text region and press the Delete key.

AutoThumbnail

If you have many large images on your page, you might want to consider making some or all of them *thumbnails*, small versions of the original image that link to the larger image. Making a thumbnail actually creates another image entirely, one that's smaller not only in dimensions, but also in file size.

To make a thumbnail from an image, select the image in Page view, and then click the AutoThumbnail button on the Picture toolbar. FrontPage creates the thumbnail based on the parameters that you set on the Thumbnails tab of the Options dialog box. For more information on that tab of the Options dialog box, see Chapter 7.

As soon as you click the Thumbnail button, the image is automatically converted and a hyperlink is created, linking to the larger, original image. You can't use the thumbnail feature if you've placed text on the image, as described in "Text," or if you've created a hotspot on the image. For more information on creating hotspots on an image, see "Image Maps" later in this chapter.

Image Positioning

If you want to move an image on your page anywhere you want, select the image, and then click the Position Absolutely button on the Picture toolbar. This places a position box around the image, allowing you to move it to any location on the page, hence the term "absolutely positioned." For more information on positioning of elements on a page, see Chapter 7.

If you have a lot of images on a page, and you want to change their Z-order (their layering order) quickly, select either the Bring Forward or Send Backward button on the Picture toolbar. Of course, you must select each image before you can select a toolbar button. For more information on Z-ordering and layering, see Chapter 7.

CHAPTER 8

Image Manipulation

Most of the time when you insert an image, it will look just the way you want it. It will be at the right size, it will have perfect color, clarity, and orientation, and you won't need to do anything to it. But in those cases when the image does need a little tweaking, you'll be happy to learn that FrontPage has included a mini-editing suite on the Picture toolbar. By clicking a button, you can fine-tune each image to get the look you're after. With a little experimentation, you might even create a whole new look, taking you in a direction you might not have thought of before.

Each of the editing tools on the Picture toolbar lets you change the appearance of an image from within Page view. In all cases, you must select the image first, activating the Picture toolbar, and then you can choose among the toolbar buttons. You can apply only one effect at a time.

Rotate and Flip

You can easily flip and flop your image around and around if you like, by clicking the Rotate Left, Rotate Right, Flip Horizontal, and Flip Vertical buttons on the Picture toolbar. This can be a real time saver; for example, if you insert an image and it was accidentally saved upside down, you can easily make it right in Page view. In the old days, you'd have to get the graphic artist to open the image, resave the file the right way, and get it back to you. Whew! Look at the hassle you just saved yourself.

Contrast and Brightness

You can adjust the contrast and brightness of an image incrementally, one click at a time, by using the More/Less Contrast and Brightness buttons on the Picture toolbar. Remember that your images will be seen by people using a wide variety of browsers and display settings. What looks good to you on your machine might not look good to someone else. If you're trying to improve image quality, be careful when using these buttons; it's easy to make a mistake and create an image that's actually harder to view. You should use these tools for minor adjustments only. Use an image-editing program for any major work that you might need to do to an image.

Cropping Images

Use the Crop tool on the Picture toolbar to crop any selected image in Page view. Cropping the image leaves a portion of the image visible and removes the rest from view, altering the look and dimensions of the image. After you've cropped an image, you'll have the opportunity to either overwrite or rename the image when you save the page. If you want to keep the original image, just rename the cropped version. If you don't need the original image, then overwrite it when you save the page. In either case, the new "cropped" image has a smaller file size than it had prior to cropping.

Select an image, and click the Crop button on the Picture toolbar. A selection border appears around the image, which you can resize to form the border of the area you want to keep. Any portion of the image remaining outside the border will be removed when you crop. Click any of the little cropping squares around the border, and then drag to resize to the area you want to keep. After you've resized the cropping border, you can move it around anywhere within the image by clicking inside the border and dragging it. You can resize and drag the cropping border as much as you like. When you have the portion of the image you want to keep positioned within the border, click the Crop tool again (or press Enter), and the area outside the selection border is cropped and removed.

Set Transparent Color

Okay, so you've been on the edge of your seat, waiting patiently to find out how transparency works. The truth is, it doesn't take Houdini to make a color disappear in an image—it's very easy. You use the Set Transparent Color button on the Picture toolbar. This enables you to make one color in a selected image transparent, allowing the background to show through. Figure 8-12 shows an image before and after the use of the Set Transparent Color button.

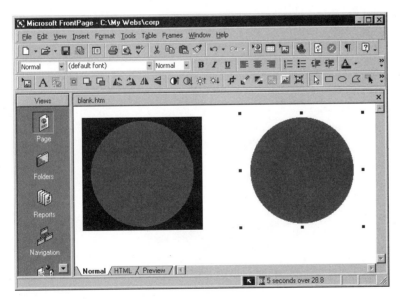

Figure 8-12

An image before and after the use of the Set Transparent Color button. The dark area around the circle has been made transparent, which lets the background show through.

259

Here's how to make a color transparent:

1. Select an image to activate the Picture toolbar.

2. Click the Set Transparent Color button. Once you click this button and move the mouse pointer over the image, the pointer changes to the Set Transparent Color pointer, which looks like a pencil.

3. On the image, click the color you want to make transparent. In the example in Figure 8-12, the dark color around the circle was selected. Voilà—every part of the image that contained that color is now transparent, and the background of the page shows through the image.

Only one color at a time can be transparent in an image. If you select a new transparent color on an image that already has one transparent color set, the first transparent color reverts to its original color.

GIFs are more commonly used for transparency than other file formats, because they contain fewer colors and more solid areas to make transparent. Because JPEG images can contain a wide tonal range, using transparency on a JPEG image would be similar to poking tiny holes sporadically through a photograph with a pin. The image would be transparent only where the holes appear.

TIP

Many graphics packages try to use dithering in a GIF image to give it a more high-resolution appearance. The problem with dithering is that it actually uses many similar colors instead of a single color, which prevents transparency of a single color from working the way you would expect. When creating images that you want to make transparent, make sure that the background of the image is a single, solid color.

Black & White

You can change any color image to a black-and-white (grayscale) image by using the Black & White button on the Picture toolbar. Because grayscale images contain no color, they have a smaller file size, which makes for a quicker download in the browser. When the image is saved, all of the color information is discarded, so if you think you might be changing your mind, keep that backup image that you made close at hand. Of course, we already know that we should always make a backup copy of our images before we edit them, right?

Washout

If you've inserted a background image in the page or in a table, you'll want to make sure it's light enough for text to appear on top of it. The Washout tool "ghosts" the image back, giving you a perfect screened-back background image. Although the Washout tool is great for creating background images, you can also use it to create an interesting effect for any image on your page.

Bevel

If you want your image to have a 3-D button look, select the image and then click the Bevel button on the Picture toolbar. This is a great effect if you're making an image a hyperlink and you want to give it that push-button look. When you use the Bevel tool, FrontPage lightens the image itself alongside the top and left borders and darkens it alongside the right and bottom borders, creating the 3-D effect. This technique doesn't add any width or height to the image.

Resample

If you resize an image up or down by dragging its borders, it may become blurred or out of focus as the browser tries to compensate for the extra height and width. The Resample button can help clean up minor flaws in a resized image, but it's not a miracle worker. If you plan on doing major resizing, do it in your image editing software before you insert the image in FrontPage. When you use the Resample technique, it either resamples down, decreasing the number of pixels and the amount of data in the image, or it resamples up, increasing the pixels and the amount of data in the image. When you resample down, pixels are deleted, and when you resample up, they're added, based on the surrounding pixel colors. Because you're either adding or deleting pixels, resampling changes the file size of the image. Once you've resampled an image and saved it, don't try to return the same image to its original size; if you do, you'll have a mushed pixel mess on your hands. That's another good reason to always have a backup copy of the image around while you're playing with the editing tools.

Image Maps

FrontPage makes use of client-side image maps. Traditionally, for an image map link to work, the client (for example, a browser) would have to communicate with the server to figure out where the link goes when the user clicks a hotspot. However, when you use client-side image maps, the link destination information is stored at the client end, so the image map is no longer server-dependent. This results in less communication between the client and the server, taking pressure off the server and reducing the time it takes to determine the link destination when a user clicks on a hotspot.

By default, FrontPage generates both client-side and server-side image maps, so any browser can use the image maps on the page.

Creating image maps

You can turn part or all of an image into a hotspot that links to other locations. For example, if you own a toy store and advertise your products on the Web, why not use an image of a teddy bear as a link to the section highlighting your stuffed animals? Or, in an intranet site, you can use an image of a dollar bill as a link to the Sales section. In Figure 8-13 below, each area of the puzzle has been made into a hotspot and is defined by the rectangular black border around each piece.

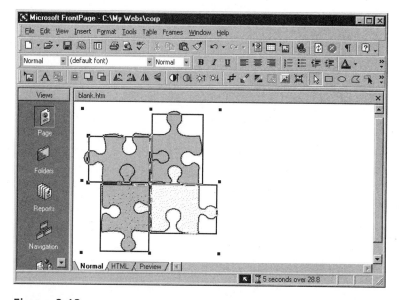

Figure 8-13

An image map in Page view showing hotspots.

You can create an image map in FrontPage in a matter of seconds, using the image map buttons on the Picture toolbar.

1. Select the image that you'll be creating the hotspot on. Notice that the Picture toolbar becomes active and that the Select button is pressed in.

2. Decide which area or areas of the image you want to make "hot." For example, on an image of a house, you might want the user to be able to click on the door and jump to an image of the foyer. If possible, make sure that the entire portion of the image you want to work with is visible on the screen.

3. Click the Rectangular Hotspot, Circular Hotspot, or Polygonal Hotspot button on the toolbar, depending on the area you want to define as a hotspot. The Rectangle and Circle buttons create rectangular and circular hotspots, respectively, and the Polygon button allows you to create a hotspot of any shape. When one of these buttons is selected, the mouse pointer changes to a pencil when it's over an image, indicating that you're ready to draw the hotspot.

4. Carefully draw the hotspot around the portion of the image that you want to be clickable. Here's a rundown on how:

   ● **Rectangular hotspots**. Position the pointer on one corner of where you want the hotspot to appear. Click and drag the pointer to draw and size the hotspot.

   ● **Circular hotspots.** Position the pointer near the center of where you want the hotspot to appear. Click and drag the pointer to draw and size the hotspot.

   ● **Polygonal hotspots.** Position the pointer where you want to begin drawing the hotspot. Click once to insert the first point of the polygon. Move the mouse and click again to draw the first side of the polygon. Continue drawing sides until your hotspot is complete. Finish by connecting to the point where you first clicked.

      Once the hotspot is drawn, you can always move and resize it if it's not quite what you wanted. See the next section, "Moving and Resizing Hotspots," for more information.

5. After you draw the hotspot, the Create Hyperlink dialog box appears. This is where you set the target link for your hotspot. For more information on creating links, see Chapter 7.

Moving and resizing hotspots

Once you draw a hotspot on an image, you have complete control over its size and location. You can drag it anywhere on the image, or you can use the arrow keys to move it and adjust its location. To resize a hotspot, select it and then click and drag a size handle (one of the small squares at the corners of the hotspot). To return a hotspot to its original position, press the Esc key; this action is similar to using the Undo command. Remember to press the Esc key before you release the mouse button.

Editing a hotspot link

To change the target link of a hotspot, double-click the hotspot to display the Edit Hyperlink dialog box. You can also right-click a selected hotspot and choose Hyperlink from the pop-up menu to display the Edit Hyperlink dialog box. A third way is to select the hotspot and then click the Hyperlink button on the Standard toolbar. Change the target link, and then click OK.

Highlighting hotspots

Sometimes it's difficult to see all the hotspots you've created, especially on a complex image. Click the Highlight Hotspot button on the Picture toolbar to see all the hotspots on a selected image. The image is removed and re-placed with a white background, and only the borders of the hotspots are shown. Click on a hotspot, and its borders are filled in black. The Highlight Hotspot button toggles between the two views. Figure 8-14 shows the same puzzle image shown in Figure 8-13 after the Highlight Hotspot button is selected on the Picture toolbar.

Restore

Having all these cool tools at your fingertips could tempt you to use too many of them at once on the same image. If you've become "button happy" and your image shows it, there's a cure: the Restore button. Clicking the Restore button removes all of the image editing you've done since the last save. Pay close attention to that last part: "*since the last save.*" We're always telling you to save, save, save, before lightning strikes and toasts your computer. Well, in this case, it's best to play around with the editing tools, get the image the way you want it, and then save it. If you're worried about losing any infor-mation, it's always a good idea to have a backup copy of the image avail-able, just in case.

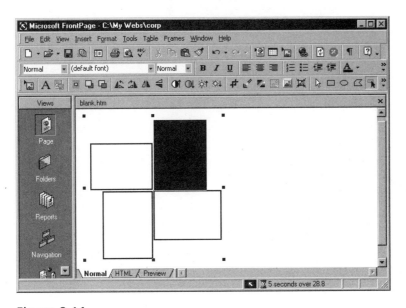

Figure 8-14

An image map in Page view showing highlighted hotspots.

Manipulating Background Images

If your page has a background image, you can apply any of the manipulation effects on the Picture toolbar by clicking the effect of your choice when no other images are selected on the page.

Coming Up

Chapter 9 explores the powerful FrontPage components and forms, which let you add numerous types of functionality to your Webs.

CHAPTER 9

FrontPage Components and Forms

We All Need a Break

Traditional hunters and gatherers knew how to make the most of their time—they conserved their energy by optimizing their food gathering, tool making, and other tasks. They also knew how important it was to rest; many hunting and gathering cultures worked fewer hours than we do today, and they allocated more time for leisure activities.

FrontPage lets you live a life like that again. You'll save so much time by using FrontPage's components and forms to create your Webs that you'll be able to live in a cave and gather roots for dinner if you want to. It might be a little rough, though—there won't be an outlet to plug your television and food processor into, so you won't be able to watch *Melrose Place* and *ER* while you're chopping up those roots. Think you can handle it?

What Are Components?

FrontPage components are drop-in programs that add functionality to a Web. For instance, you can add a Search Component to a page with a few clicks of the mouse, and instantly your page has a full-text search engine for your users. Using the traditional steps, a Web site developer would have to do the following:

1. Create an HTML form that initiates the search.

2. Install a third-party full-text search engine on the Web server.

3. Write a CGI program on the Web server that connects the HTML form to the full-text search engine.

When you use components, you can forget all of this—there's no more need for complicated HTML or CGI programming (or any other type of programming for that matter) to create sophisticated, interactive Webs. Keep in mind that in order for components to work properly, the server hosting the Web must have the FrontPage Server Extensions installed. These extensions must be manually installed on the Web server that will host your Web. For more information on the Personal Web Servers and the FrontPage Server Extensions, consult Chapter 11.

You can insert FrontPage components in a couple of different ways, each one accessed through the Insert menu. Throughout this chapter, as we describe each component, we also describe the method you use to add it to the page. When you select a component, you'll see one or more dialog boxes that let you configure it, and then FrontPage inserts the component on the page where your insertion pointer was positioned. Some components are associated with forms, which are described later in this chapter.

The following sections provide a brief examination of the FrontPage components.

Implementing Search Functionality

To give your users the ability to look for matching words or phrases in the text of a Web's pages or in the text of all the messages in a discussion group, you can insert a Search Component on your page. You can configure the Search Component to check every word used within the Web for a match. (This feature is called *full-text searching.*)

Adding a Search component

The Search Component, as shown in Figure 9-1, creates a form that allows users to enter one or more words they want to locate on the pages of your Web.

FrontPage doesn't actually have to examine each page of the Web; instead, it searches a list of words that's maintained by the FrontPage Server Extensions. FrontPage returns a list of pages that contain the word or words the user is searching for.

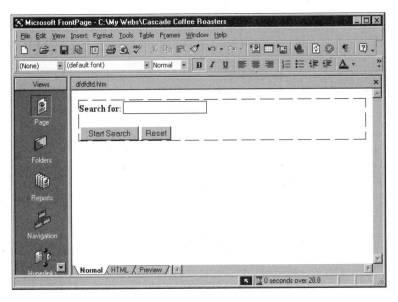

Figure 9-1

Page view showing a search component.

To give users the ability to search for matching words or phrases in your Web, do the following:

1. In Page view, position the insertion pointer at the place on your page where you want the upper left corner of the search form (the label, text box, and buttons created by the Search Component) to appear.

TIP

If you want to exclude certain pages from a search, save them directly in the _private folder under the folder for your Web. (FrontPage typically doesn't search a folder with a name that starts with an underscore.) If you save the page to a different location and then move it to the _private folder, I recommend that you use the Recalculate Hyperlinks command to update the search index.

2. Choose Components from the Insert menu and then Search Form from the pop-up menu. You'll see the Search Form Properties dialog box, as shown in Figure 9-2, which contains two tabs, Search Form Properties and Search Results. Select the Search Form Properties tab.

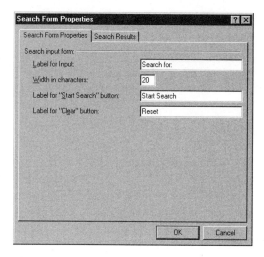

Figure 9-2

The Search Form Properties tab of the Search Form Properties dialog box.

3. In the Label For Input text box, enter the text you want to use for the label of the text box. The default is *Search for:*.

4. In the Width In Characters text box, enter the width (in characters) of the input field. The default here is *20*.

5. In the Label For "Start Search" Button text box, type the text that will appear on the button that starts the search. The default is *Start Search*.

6. In the Label For "Clear" Button text box, type the text that will appear on the button that clears the search. The default is *Reset*.

To configure the results of the Search component, select the Search Results tab on the Search Form Properties dialog box, shown in Figure 9-3.

1. In the Word List To Search text box, enter *All* if the search is intended for an entire Web. If you created a discussion group using the Discussion Web Wizard, you can enter the name of a discussion group folder. This restricts the search to entries in the discussion group.

Figure 9-3

The Search Results Tab of the Search Form Properties dialog box.

2. You can also select check boxes to display the following information in the search results list:

   ● **Display Score.** This indicates the quality of the match, or how closely the results match what you searched for.

   ● **Display File Date.** This indicates the date and time the document containing the match was most recently modified. Only if you select this check box do the Date Format and Time Format options become available. Select the format of your choice.

   ● **Display File Size.** This indicates the size of the document containing the match, in kilobytes. This information can be especially useful for users on slow dial-up connections, who can see how large a document is before they download it.

3. When you finish entering the information in the Search Form Properties dialog box, click OK. FrontPage inserts the search form on your page.

You can easily reconfigure the properties of your Search Component by right-clicking the component in Page view and choosing Search Form Properties from the pop-up menu, or by selecting the component and then pressing Alt+Enter on your keyboard.

Limitations of the Search component

One limitation of the Search Component concerns the updating of the search index. Suppose a page called *test.htm* has the word *Jenny* on it when you save it to your Web. The index maintained by the Search Component records the fact that *test.htm* contains the word *Jenny*. However, suppose that you delete the word *Jenny* from *test.htm*. The search index doesn't get updated automatically, so it will continue to show that *Jenny* is on *test.htm*. Thus, if someone were to use the Search Component to search for *Jenny,* he or she would get a false hit for *test.htm*. The way to fix this problem, and to update your search index so it has the correct information, is to use the Recalculate Hyperlinks command on the Tools menu. For more information on this command, see Chapter 3.

Including a Table of Contents

You can use the Table Of Contents component to create an outline for your Web that has links to each page. You can direct the component to update the outline each time pages are added, deleted, or edited.

Adding a Table Of Contents component

To insert a table of contents (TOC) on your page, do the following:

1. In Page view, position the pointer at the place on your page where you want the TOC to appear.

2. Choose Component from the Insert menu and then Table of Contents from the pop-up menu. You'll see the Table Of Contents Properties dialog box, as shown in Figure 9-4.

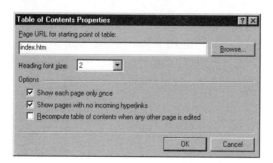

Figure 9-4

The Table Of Contents Properties dialog box.

3. Enter the URL of the page you want the TOC to begin with. The TOC will include all pages that have links that originate from the page you select. If you want a full TOC, specify the home page, often called *default.htm* or *index.htm,* of your Web. If you have a Web open, you can click the Browse button to see a list of pages in the Web. If you do so, select a page in the Current Web dialog box, and then click OK.

4. From the Heading Font Size drop-down list, select a heading size for the first entry in your TOC. Select a number from 1 (the largest size) to 6 (the smallest size), or select None if you want to use the default size.

5. You can select check boxes to have FrontPage do the following:

   ● **Show Each Page Only Once.** Select this check box to allow each page to appear in the TOC only once. If a page in your Web has multiple links that can be traced back to your starting page, it can appear more than once unless you check this option.

   ● **Show Pages With No Incoming Hyperlinks.** Select this check box to include *orphan* pages in your TOC. (Orphans are pages that have no incoming links from other pages in the Web.)

   ● **Recompute Table Of Contents When Any Other Page Is Edited.** Select this check box to automatically recreate the TOC whenever you add, delete, or edit pages in your Web. If your Web is large and if you often edit pages, having this option checked can slow down your work, when you're saving, for example. An alternative is to recreate the TOC manually by opening and saving the page containing the Table Of Contents component.

6. When you finish entering your information in the dialog box, click OK. Your TOC appears on the page in Page view. You can't format the individual entries in the TOC—any formatting changes you apply will be applied to all of the entries. For example, you can't set the heading in italics and the list as normal at the same time.

Figure 9-5, on the next page, shows the Table Of Contents component as it appears on a page in Page view.

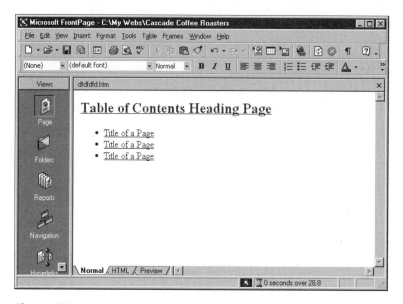

Figure 9-5

Page view showing a Table Of Contents component.

Presenting One Page on Another Page

Using the Include Page component, you can present the entire contents of one page wherever you want on another page. The page you insert must be a page from the current Web. The Include Page component differs from the Scheduled Include Page component (discussed later in this chapter) in that it presents a page on another page *at all times,* and not just at specified times.

Suppose you have a "Site in Summary" section in your company's Web that presents the most important pages in the Web in one place, such as pages for urgent news and company information that your sales force needs to know. This kind of section might be good to include for those viewers who are "on the go" and who need to see only certain pages of your Web. Plenty of businesspeople don't even have the time to look at specific pages of your Web one by one—they may be quickly scanning the Web for information and need to get on with their other daily tasks. Your "Site in Summary" section can be a one-page section in which you use several Include Page components, one for each page you want to pull in from the rest of your Web. The included pages can be presented in full, one after another, and all of the content will be scrollable as a single page.

PART

III

Adding an Include Page component

To insert the contents of one page on another page, do the following:

1. In Page view, position the pointer at the place on the current page where you want the inserted page to appear.

2. Choose Component from the Insert menu and then Include Page from the pop-up menu. You'll see the Include Page Properties dialog box, as shown in Figure 9-6.

Figure 9-6

The Include Page Properties dialog box.

3. In the Page To Include text box, enter the URL of the page you want to have appear. If you have a Web open, you can click the Browse button to see a list of pages in the current Web; if you do so, select a page and then click OK.

4. After you enter the URL, click OK. The contents of that page are inserted on your page. The HTML from the other page isn't inserted, but an Include Page component link is embedded in the page. The embedded page is fully functional to your users, but if you want to make any changes to it from within FrontPage, you need to go to the target page.

Another fun use for the Include Page component is to include the copyright information for your company on every page. If you want to include a special note or disclaimer, you can do that as well. And if you ever need to change the contents of the Include, just open the page it's calling and make any changes you need, and those changes will appear on each page that uses that Include component.

Making Images Appear at a Certain Time

You can use the Scheduled Picture component to make an image available to users during a specified time period. The image is displayed on a page when the time period begins, and it's removed when the time has expired.

For example, suppose your human resources department is trying to increase employee enrollment in the company's 401K plan, and it's running a seven-day special sign-up event on its intranet pages. The pages will feature different "catchy" images each day. To avoid having to update the images manually every day, you can insert several Scheduled Picture components to make those images appear automatically when you want them to.

To be certain that a Scheduled Picture component works on the day that the image is scheduled to appear or disappear, either make a change to your Web or use the Recalculate Hyperlinks command on the same day to "refresh" the links and other information on the pages. These actions act as a reminder to FrontPage to update the information related to the components.

Adding a Scheduled Picture component

To make an image appear during a specified time period, take the following steps:

1. In Page view, position the pointer at the place on your page where you want the image to appear.

2. Choose Component from the Insert menu and then Scheduled Picture from the pop-up menu. You'll see the Scheduled Picture Properties dialog box, as shown in Figure 9-7.

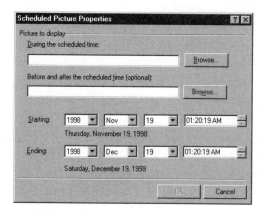

Figure 9-7
The Scheduled Picture Properties dialog box.

3. In the During The Scheduled Time area of the dialog box, enter the name of the image you want to have appear at a specific start and end time. If you want another image to appear as a placeholder during the time before and after the scheduled image, enter the name of that image in the Before And After The Scheduled Time area of the dialog box. You can click the Browse button to see a

list of images available in the currently open Web; if you do so, select an image and then click OK.

4. Enter the Starting date and time and the Ending date and time for the period that you want the scheduled image to appear. (Note that the starting and ending times affect only the scheduled image, not the image that you may have entered in the Before And After The Scheduled Time area of the dialog box.)

5. When you finish entering information in the Scheduled Picture Properties dialog box, click OK.

If you're within the time period you specified for the image to appear, the image will appear on the page. If you've specified that the image appear at a future time (a more likely scenario) and haven't specified a placeholder image, the words *Expired Scheduled Picture* will appear in the component on the screen in Page view (but not in a browser). If you see these words, don't worry—the image will appear at its scheduled time. If you specified that a placeholder image appear when the scheduled image doesn't appear, that image will appear in Page view and in the browser when the scheduled image doesn't appear.

Making Content Appear at a Certain Time

You can use the Scheduled Include Page component to make specific content available to users in the same way that the Scheduled Picture component works with images. In fact, if we use the same 401K scenario discussed in the previous section, you can make an entire page of 401K information appear at a certain time. The Scheduled Include Page component inserts an entire page at a specified time.

Like the Scheduled Picture component, the Scheduled Include Page component works only if a change is made to the Web or the Recalculate Hyperlinks command is executed on the day the content is scheduled to appear.

Adding a Scheduled Include Page component

To make the contents of a page appear during a specified time period, do the following:

1. In Page view, position the pointer at the place on your page where you want the content to appear.

2. Choose Component from the Insert menu and then Scheduled Include Page from the pop-up menu. You'll see the Scheduled Include Page Properties dialog box, as shown in Figure 9-8, on the next page.

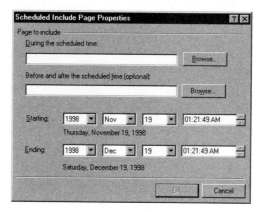

Figure 9-8

The Scheduled Include Page Properties dialog box.

3. Use the During The Scheduled Time text box to enter the URL of the page you want to have appear at a specific start and end time. If you want another image to appear as a placeholder during the time before and after the scheduled page, enter the URL of that page in the Before And After The Scheduled Time area of the dialog box. You can click the Browse button to see a list of pages in your Web, select one, and click OK.

4. Enter the Starting date and time and the Ending date and time for the period that you want the page to appear. Note that the starting and ending times affect only the scheduled page, not the page that you may have entered in the Before And After The Scheduled Time area of the dialog box.

5. When you finish entering your information in the Scheduled Include Page Properties dialog box, click OK.

Confirming User-Entered Information

When you're using your Web to collect information from users, you want to do everything you can to make sure that the information they provide is correct. In particular, you should give them an opportunity to review the text that they've submitted. Not only does this give them a chance to discover any typographical errors, but it also emphasizes that the information they provide is important. Maybe they'll read it a second time to make sure it really says what they want it to say.

PART

III

In FrontPage, you can specify validation rules for a form field; for example, you can specify that numbers be within a certain range or that a text field contain only certain characters. FrontPage automatically generates the JavaScript or VBScript directly on the page so that the browser will enforce those validation rules. For more information on validation rules, see "Validating Form Fields," later in this chapter.

If you've seen Web pages or other forums where information that you've entered is presented to you later for your confirmation, you've seen an example of this process. If you find that some of the information is incorrect, you can usually go back to the original page, change it, and resubmit it, and if all the information is correct, you can click a button to say so. The Confirmation Field component manages this process of presenting the information back to the viewer. (For more information on confirmation pages, see "Creating a Confirmation Page," later in this chapter.)

The Confirmation Field component presents the contents of one form field—a single item such as name, age, or occupation—on a form confirmation page. (We'll discuss forms and form fields later in this chapter.) Each form field requires a separate Confirmation Field component, but several of these components can be combined on a single page. So if a user has entered lots of information in different form fields, you can use a page of Confirmation Field components to replicate that information in one place for the user to confirm.

Confirmation Field components are case-sensitive. That means that *FirstName* isn't the same as *firstname*.

Adding a Confirmation Field component

To present the contents of one form field on a confirmation page, do the following:

1. In Page view, position the pointer at the place on the confirmation page where you want the Confirmation Field component to appear.

2. Choose Component from the Insert menu and then Confirmation Field from the pop-up menu. You'll see the Confirmation Field Properties dialog box, as shown in Figure 9-9, on the next page.

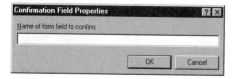

Figure 9-9

The Confirmation Field Properties dialog box.

3. In the Name Of Form Field To Confirm text box, enter the name of the form field whose contents you want to confirm, and then click OK.

When you click OK, the Confirmation Field component appears on your page as a set of brackets surrounding the name of the field you just typed in. In a browser, the user sees the field's contents, not the Confirmation Field component. It's a good idea to provide appropriate text on the page to make sure users know what information is being shown back to them.

Inserting a Configuration Variable

You can use the Substitution component to insert the contents of a configuration variable (also called a *parameter*) on a page. This is useful for many purposes, such as for noting who created or modified a page, or the page's URL. The Substitution component can also be used to present text strings that you might want to modify later, such as a company's fax number.

Adding a Substitution component

Here's how to insert the value of a configuration variable on a page:

1. In Page view, place the pointer on the page where you want to insert the Substitution component.

2. Choose Component from the Insert menu and then Substitution from the pop-up menu. You'll see the Substitution Properties dialog box, shown in Figure 9-10.

Figure 9-10

The Substitution Properties dialog box.

3. From the Substitute With drop-down list, select a configuration

variable, and then click OK. If you've added parameters to your Web, they appear in this drop-down list.

When you click OK, the Substitution component appears on the page in Page view, showing the actual value of the configuration variable.

For more information on adding configuration variables and setting their values, see Chapter 3.

Editing a Component's Properties

If you want to modify a component's properties, you don't have to replace the entire component—you can change its properties instead. To edit a component's properties, simply right-click the component and choose the components properties from the pop-up menu. For example, if you want to change the properties for a Substitution Component, right-click the component in Page view and select Substitution Properties from the pop-up menu. The Properties dialog box for the component appears; you can make your changes here. When you finish, click OK to exit the dialog box and return to your page in Page view.

Insert This...

There are a couple of other interesting elements to be found on the Insert menu. If you're interested in displaying the time and date a page was last modified on a page, you can do that. If you're interested in placing a comment in the HTML for a page, you can do that too. The following sections show you how.

Creating a Timestamp

To insert a *timestamp*, which denotes the date and time the page was last edited or automatically updated, you use the Date and Time component.

Adding a timestamp using the Date And Time component

To insert a timestamp on your page, do the following:

1. In Page view, position the pointer at the place on your page where you want the timestamp to appear. Often, the component is placed following a phrase such as *This page was last modified*.

2. Choose Date And Time from the Insert menu. Figure 9-11, on the next page, shows the resulting Date And Time Properties dialog box.

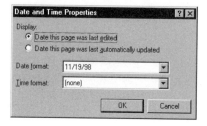

Figure 9-11

The Date And Time Properties dialog box.

3. In the Display section, select the option for the date you want to display: either Date This Page Was Last Edited or Date This Page Was Last Automatically Updated. There's a slight difference in meaning between "edited" and "updated." A page is considered to be *edited* when it is changed and saved to the Web server. A page is considered to be *updated* when it is changed and saved to the Web server or when an included page is changed. You can include pages on other pages using the Include Component discussed earlier in this chapter.

4. From the Date Format and Time Format drop-down lists, select a format for the date and time that you want displayed. The Time Format options containing the letters *TZ* indicate Time Zone. If you don't want to include either the date or the time, select None from the respective drop-down list.

5. When you finish entering information in the Date And Time Properties dialog box, click OK. The timestamp is inserted on your page. You can then format the text used for the timestamp information using the standard tools within Page view.

Figure 9-12 shows an example of the Date And Time component in Page view.

Inserting a Comment

Sometimes you'll be the person adding all of the pages in the Web and creating the structure, but someone else will be actually placing content on the page. If you leave a comment for them on the page, that text will appear only in Page view and HTML view, but not in the browser. Comments are also useful if you want to leave yourself a reminder of an important piece of information about the page. Comments are like sticky notes in HTML.

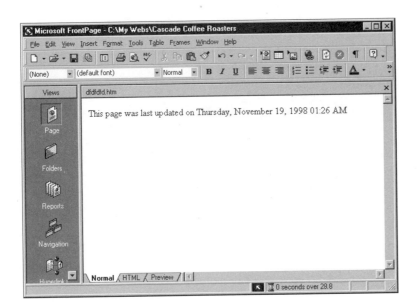

The Date And Time component in Page view.

Adding a comment

To insert a comment on the page, do the following:

1. In Page view, position the insertion pointer at the place on the current page where you want the comment to appear.

2. Choose Comment from the Insert menu. You'll see the Comment dialog box, as shown in Figure 9-13.

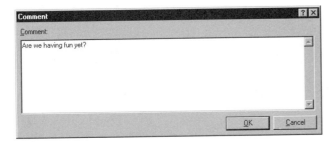

Figure 9-13
The Comment dialog box.

In the Comment dialog box, you can type the message you want to leave on the page. When you're finished entering the comment, click OK.

In Page view, you'll see the text in color, just as you've typed it, with the word "Comment:" preceding it. This text will be visible only in Page view and HTML view, but not in the browser.

Creating and Using Forms

Forms give you an opportunity to make your Web interactive. A *form* is a collection of text and *form fields* that allows users to enter information. FrontPage form fields include one-line text boxes, scrolling text boxes, check boxes, option buttons (called *radio buttons* in FrontPage), and drop-down menus. In addition, you can add command buttons (known as *push buttons* in FrontPage) to your form to perform actions. You can include each of these fields by choosing Form on the Insert menu and choosing the form field of your choice from the pop-up menu. Figure 9-14 shows an example of form fields on a page in Page view.

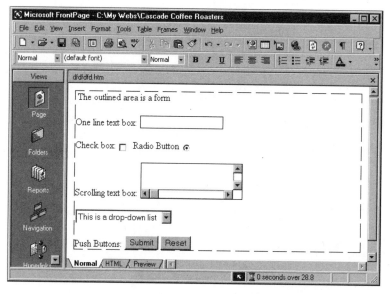

Figure 9-14

Form fields in Page view.

You use a combination of these form fields to collect the information you want from the user. For instance, in an intranet setting, forms can be used to gather and store employee identification information. Or perhaps you want to find out what users think of your Web or the products showcased in your Web. Users provide answers to your questions in the form fields.

You create a form whenever you add a form field to a page. Some templates (such as the User Registration, Feedback Form, and Confirmation Form templates) and some wizards (such as the Form Page Wizard and the Discussion Web Wizard) create pages that already contain forms.

Forms use applications on Web servers called *handlers,* which take the data from the form fields and process it. A handler can also respond to the user when it receives the input, by presenting a confirmation page so that the user can confirm the information submitted. So, in a sense, the handler is a go-between for the form and the Web server. For example, a handler can be a Discussion component, a Registration component, a custom ISAPI DLL, an NSAPI module, or a CGI script. (These handlers are discussed in "Assigning a Form Handler," later in this chapter.)

Creating a Data-Collection Form

Once you know how to create a form, the process will seem fairly simple, but learning it can be a little tricky. We'll step through the process by modifying two pages we created using FrontPage's Feedback Form and Confirmation Page templates. The templates already contain working examples of forms and confirmation pages; we'll create more examples on these pages so you can learn how to build them yourself.

Let's get going with some preliminaries.

Creating a Feedback Form page

We'll begin by creating a Feedback Form page in Page view.

1. Choose New from the File menu and then Page from the pop-up menu. Select Feedback Form from the list of templates and wizards on the General tab in the New dialog box that appears, and then click OK.

2. When the page appears in Page view, save it with the title *Feedback Form* and give it the name within the current Web, *feedback.htm.* We'll refer to this page from now on as the Feedback Form, an example of which is shown in Figure 9-15. Notice that the page name, *feedback.htm,* appears above the comment on the page in Page view.

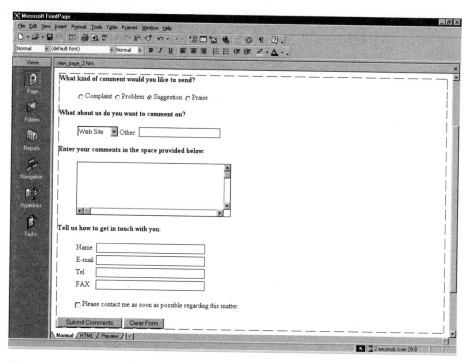

Figure 9-15

Page view showing a feedback form.

The Feedback Form includes several fields. In fact, it includes at least one of each of the five field types, plus two command buttons (push buttons):

- **Option button.** The buttons on the page under the line "What kind of comment would you like to send?" are option buttons (radio buttons). These buttons act as a group; you'll find out more about their group functions shortly. Each of the buttons was added to the form separately, and the text for each was typed next to that button. You use option buttons when you want the user to select a single option from a group of options. For example, you might have a form where you're asking people the color of their eyes. You would list each color along with an option button, and the user would make one selection in the form. Only one radio button within a group can be selected at a time. (You can also use a drop-down list for this purpose.)

- **Drop-down list.** The field below the line "What about us do you want to comment on?" is a drop-down list. You can customize the list choices when you modify the field properties. A drop-down list allows the user to select one or more items (which is why these form fields are often called *drop-down menus*).

- **One-line text box.** The text box next to the drop-down list is a one-line text box. Users can type text in this box. You set the width of this box as part of its properties.

- **Scrolling text box.** The large box under the line "Enter your comments in the space provided below:" is a scrolling text box. This type of text box allows users to type lengthy comments.

- **Check box.** The box near the bottom of the page next to the line "Please contact me as soon as possible regarding this matter" is a check box. When a user clicks a check box, a check mark appears in it. Use check boxes to offer the user a Yes/No choice.

- **Command button.** The two buttons at the bottom of the Feedback Form labeled *Submit Comments* and *Clear Form* are command buttons (push buttons). A user clicks these buttons to perform either of these tasks.

Now we'll replicate some of these fields and the buttons directly below them on the Feedback Form, to show you how to create them.

Creating an option button group

Let's create a group of two option buttons that resembles the group of four on the Feedback Form.

1. Position your insertion pointer to the right of the option button labeled *Praise* below the line "What kind of comment would you like to send?" (The pointer should be blinking beside the *e* in *Praise*.) Press and hold down the Shift key and press Enter.

2. With the pointer on the blank line you just created, just below the Complaint option button, choose Form from the Insert menu, and then click the Radio Button option from the pop-up menu. (Remember, FrontPage uses the term *radio button* rather than option button.)

287

3. Right-click the button you just inserted, and choose Form Field Properties from the pop-up menu. Figure 9-16 shows the resulting Radio Button Properties dialog box.

Figure 9-16

The Radio Button Properties dialog box.

4. Fill in the following information:

- **Group Name.** Enter the word *CommentType*. This is the name of the group of option buttons you'll be creating. You'll use this name later on the confirmation page. If you give the same group name to a series of buttons, a user will be able to select only one of them. Assigning the same group name is what actually creates a group of mutually exclusive option buttons.

- **Value.** Enter the word *Compliment*. The word will appear on the confirmation page if the user selects this option while using the Feedback Form. You'll see how this works shortly.

- **Initial State.** Select the Selected option. When the user sees the Feedback Form, this option will be selected as the default. Only one option button in a group can be initialized as Selected (because only one option in a group can ever be selected). FrontPage doesn't require you to initialize any option button as Selected; this is your choice.

- **Tab Order.** You can specify the tab order of this field by entering a value in the Tab Order text box. Tab Order controls the order in which a user moves from field to field within a form using the Tab key. Only Internet Explorer 4.0 or later supports Tab Order; all other browsers will ignore tab order settings. If you leave the Tab Order box blank, Internet Explorer 4.0 or later will use the default order, which is the order in which the field was placed on the page within its group.

5. Click OK to exit the Radio Button Properties dialog box, and then position your pointer next to the Option button you just inserted and type the word *Compliment.* You've just created an option button that, when selected, indicates that the user is sending a compliment to you.

6. Using the same procedure, create another option button immediately to the right of the Compliment button. (You might want to press the spacebar to create a little space between the buttons.) In the Radio Button Properties dialog box, give the option button the same group name, *CommentType,* but give it the value of *Criticism.* Select the Not Selected option for its initial state. When you finish, click OK to exit the Radio Button Properties dialog box.

7. Type the word *Criticism* following the option button you just inserted. The option button is now complete. Figure 9-17 shows how the option button section of your page should look.

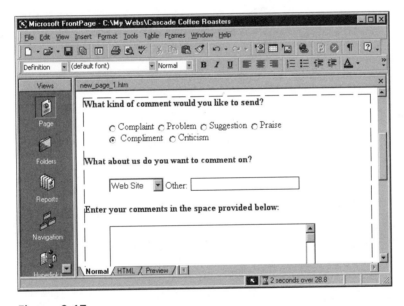

Figure 9-17
A form that has newly created option buttons.

Make sure you save your changes as you go along.

You've just created a two-button group called *CommentType.* If you look at the properties for the buttons directly above (the Complaint, Problem, Suggestion, and Praise buttons), you'll see that their group name is

MessageType. You've just created a similar group. You can create any option button group in the same way.

Creating a drop-down list

Next, we'll create a four-element drop-down list (known as a drop-down menu in FrontPage) directly below the existing one.

1. Position the insertion point to the right of the one-line text box below the sentence "What about us do you want to comment on?" Press and hold the Shift key and press Enter.

2. With the pointer just below the existing drop-down list, choose Form from the Insert menu and then click the Drop-down Menu option from the pop-up menu. A drop-down list appears on the page.

3. Right-click the new drop-down list and choose Form Field Properties from the pop-up menu. You'll see the Drop-Down Menu Properties dialog box, as shown in Figure 9-18.

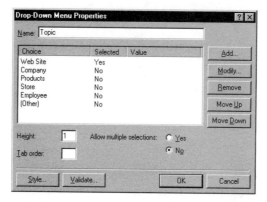

Figure 9-18

The Drop-Down Menu Properties dialog box.

4. Enter the name *Topic* in the Name text box. You'll use this name later on when you configure the confirmation page.

5. Click the Add button to add an element to the box. You'll see the Add Choice dialog box, shown in Figure 9-19 below.

6. In the Choice text box, enter the word *Site*. By default, the value that is submitted to the form handler for this menu choice is the same as the name of the menu choice. If you want to specify a different value to associate with this choice, click Specify Value

and enter the new value. In the Initial State section, select the Selected option. This sets the Site element as the item displayed in the drop-down list when the user first sees it in a browser.

Click OK when you finish entering information in the Add Choice dialog box.

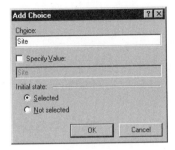

Figure 9-19
The Add Choice dialog box.

7. Add three more elements, named Technical Support, Prices, and Other, using the same procedure. For each one, select the Not Selected option in the Initial State section of the Add Choice dialog box. The width of the drop-down list will automatically expand to accommodate the widest element you add. Figure 9-20 shows the Drop-Down Menu Properties dialog box after all the elements have been added.

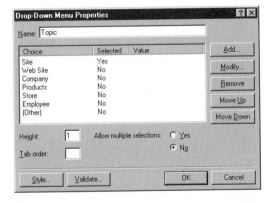

Figure 9-20
The Drop-Down Menu Properties dialog box showing new choices.

8. You can click the following buttons in the Drop-Down Menu Properties dialog box to perform some additional functions:

- **Modify.** To modify any element in the list, select the element and click Modify. You'll see the Modify Choice dialog box for that element, which has the same options as the Add Choice dialog box explained previously.

- **Remove.** To remove any element from the list, select the element and then click Remove.

- **Move Up.** To move an element up in the list, select the element and then click Move Up. (The elements will appear in the drop-down list in the order that they appear in this list.)

- **Move Down.** To move an element down in the list, select the element and then click Move Down.

In addition, you can enter the height of the list in the Height text box. Keep the height at 1 for now. The height of the list determines how the list is displayed. In most browsers, if Height is set to 1, the drop-down list displays only one element and you can click the down arrow button to view the rest of the elements. If Height is set to a value greater than 1, the list typically behaves like a scrollable text box, in which the number of elements displayed at any one time equals the Height.

You can specify the tab order of this field by entering a value in the Tab Order text box. The way Tab Order works was explained previously in the "Creating an Option Button Group" section.

Finally, for the Allow Multiple Selections option buttons, select the No option to disallow multiple selections. Clicking Yes allows the user to select more than one element at a time from the list. This is useful in many situations, such as when you offer the user choices for receiving information about multiple products that you can display in a drop-down list.

9. When you finish entering the information, click OK. Figure 9-21 shows how the drop-down list section of your page should look.

You've created a four-element drop-down list. You can create a drop-down list that has as many items as you like, in the same fashion.

PART
III

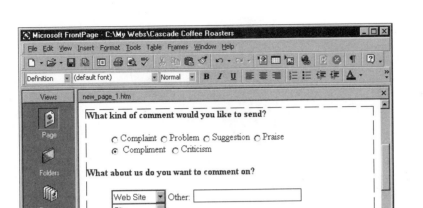

Figure 9-21

A form in Page view containing a newly created drop-down menu.

Creating a one-line text box

Next, we'll create a one-line text box that appears next to the drop-down list, for users to enter an element if they selected "Other" from the drop-down list.

1. Position the insertion pointer to the right of the drop-down list you just created. Press the spacebar to create a little space between the drop-down list and the text box. Type *OTHER:*, and then press the spacebar one more time.

2. Choose Form from the Insert menu and then One Line Text Box from the pop-up menu. A one-line text box appears.

3. Right-click the new one-line text box and choose Form Field Properties from the pop-up menu. You'll see the Text Box Properties dialog box, as shown in Figure 9-22, on the next page.

4. In the Name text box, enter *IfOther.* You'll use this name later on when configuring the confirmation page.

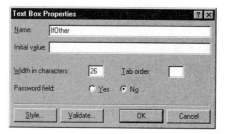

Figure 9-22

The Text Box Properties dialog box.

5. Don't enter anything in the Initial Value text box. In this instance, because the user will enter additional elements in the text box, there's no need to add an initial value. If you do enter an initial value, it appears in the text box when the user first views the form. However, the user can change the text.

6. Type *20* in the Width In Characters text box if the current value is different. This sets the initial width of the text box to a rather wide 20 characters, giving it a user-friendly look. If you want to reset the size later, you can click and drag the text box's size handles in Page view.

7. Select No in the Password Field section to specify that the text box won't be used as a password field in this instance.

8. You can click the Validate button if you want to set restrictions on the information that a user can enter in the one-line text box. For instance, you can set a maximum amount of characters that the user can enter in the text box or restrict the entries to text or numbers only.

9. Click OK after you finish entering information in the Text Box Properties dialog box. Figure 9-23 shows how the drop-down lists and the one-line text boxes should look on your page.

You've just created a one-line text box in which a user can enter additional comments.

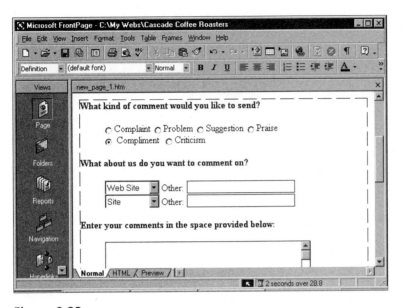

Figure 9-23

A form showing a newly created one-line text box.

Creating a scrolling text box

Next, we'll create a scrolling text box directly below the existing one on the Feedback Form.

1. Position the insertion point to the right of the existing scrolling text box, below the line "Enter your comments in the space provided below:" and then press Enter twice.

2. Choose Form from the Insert menu and then Scrolling Text Box from the pop-up menu. A scrolling text box appears on the page.

3. Right-click the new scrolling text box and choose Form Field Properties from the pop-up menu. You'll see the Scrolling Text Box Properties dialog box, as shown in Figure 9-24, on the next page.

4. In the Name text box, enter *UserComments*. You'll use this name later on when configuring the confirmation page.

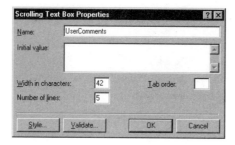

Figure 9-24

The Scrolling Text Box Properties dialog box.

5. Don't enter anything in the Initial Value text box. In this instance, because the user will enter additional elements in the scrolling text box, there's no need to add an initial value.

6. Type *40* in the Width In Characters text box. This sets the initial width of the text box to a wide 40 characters, giving it a user-friendly look. If you want to reset the size later, you can click and drag the text box's size handles while in Page view.

7. Type *5* in the Number Of Lines text box. This sets the height of the scrolling text box in number of lines, and 5 is a good number to start with. Because the text box is scrollable, a user can enter more than five lines of text, and it's often unnecessary to set the initial height to more than five lines.

8. Click the Style button if you want to specify a format for the text inside the text box.

9. Click the Validate button if you want to set restrictions on the information that a user can enter in the scrolling text box. For instance, you can set a maximum amount of characters that the user can enter in the text box, or you can restrict the entries to text or numbers only.

10. You can specify the tab order of this field by entering a value in the Tab Order text box. The way Tab Order works was explained previously in the "Creating an Option Button Group" section.

11. Click OK after you finish entering information in the Scrolling Text Box Properties dialog box. Figure 9-25 shows how the scrolling text box should look on your page.

PART
III

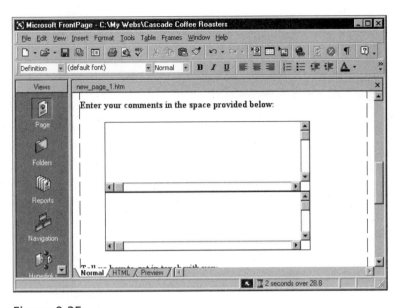

Figure 9-25

A form that contains a newly created scrolling text box.

Creating a check box

Next, we'll create a check box below the existing check box at the bottom of the Feedback Form. The check box will allow the user to indicate that he or she wants more information sent by way of e-mail.

1. Position the pointer at the end of the line that reads "Please contact me as soon as possible regarding this matter." Press and hold the Shift key and press Enter.

2. With the pointer below the check box, choose Form from the Insert menu and then Check Box from the pop-up menu. A new check box appears on the page.

3. Right-click the new check box and choose Form Field Properties from the pop-up menu. You'll see the Check Box Properties dialog box, as shown in Figure 9-26, on the next page.

4. In the Name text box, enter *RequestInfo*. You'll use this name later on when configuring the confirmation page.

9

Figure 9-26

The Check Box Properties dialog box.

5. In the Value text box, enter the same value, *RequestInfo*. You'll see this value later when you're reviewing the information the user has sent to you with the Feedback Form. When you see this value, you'll know that the user wants more information sent.

6. In the Initial State section, select the Not Checked option, if it isn't already selected. The check box won't be checked when the user first sees it in a browser. In instances like this, it's wise to leave check boxes clear so that you'll know for certain whether a user actually wants information sent.

7. You can specify the tab order of this field by entering a value in the Tab Order text box. The way Tab Order works was explained previously in the "Creating an Option Button Group" section.

8. Click OK after you finish entering information in the Check Box Properties dialog box.

9. Position the pointer to the right of the check box you just inserted and press the spacebar to create a little space between the check box and the text label you're about to add. Type the following sentence: *Please send me more information via e-mail.* Figure 9-27 shows how the check box should look.

You've just created a simple check box and labeled it to allow users to indicate they want more information from you. You can create all your check boxes in FrontPage in the same way.

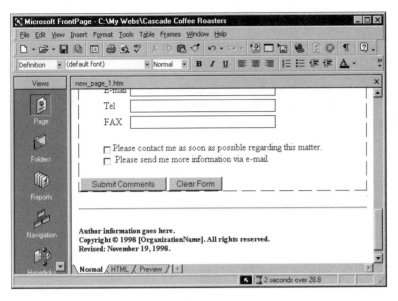

Figure 9-27

A form showing a newly created check box.

Creating a command button

Next, we'll create a command button for users to click when they finish entering information on the form and are ready to send it to you.

1. Position the pointer after the command button labeled *Clear Form* at the bottom of the screen, and then press Enter.

2. Choose Form from the Insert menu and then Push Button from the pop-up menu. A command button appears on the page.

3. Right-click the new push button and choose Form Field Properties from the pop-up menu. You'll see the Push Button Properties dialog box, as shown in Figure 9-28, on the next page.

4. In the Name text box, leave the name as B1. If you supply your own handler by using a CGI script or other script, you can enter a name here and process the form based on the name. But for the purposes of this exercise, don't enter a name now.

299

Figure 9-28

The Push Button Properties dialog box.

5. In the Value/Label text box, enter the text that will appear on the push button: *Submit Now.*

6. In the Button Type section, select the Submit option. This allows the button to submit all information that a user has entered in the form to the handler on the Web server. Selecting the Reset option changes the button to one that resets the form to its initial state when a user clicks the button in a browser. You'll select Normal when you want to assign a script to the button.

7. Click OK after you finish entering information in the Push Button Properties dialog box. Figure 9-29 shows a sample of how the push button should look on your page.

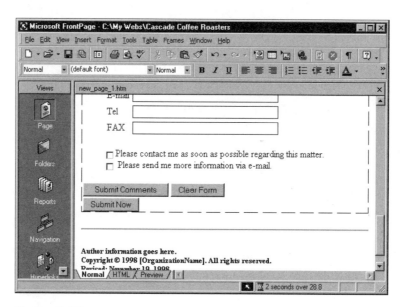

Figure 9-29

A form that contains a newly created push button.

Using alternative command buttons

FrontPage provides several additional styles of command buttons that you can use on your pages, so you're not limited to the style of the standard command button. These buttons don't give you the same options as standard command buttons; for example, you can't set them to reset or submit information. You can, however, assign your own scripts to these buttons. Here's how to add them to your page:

1. Position the pointer where you want the button to appear.

2. Choose Form from the Insert menu and then Picture from the submenu. The Picture dialog box appears.

3. Select an image from the current Web open in FrontPage, from a file on your local machine, or from a file on the World Wide Web. For more information about the Picture dialog box, see Chapter 8.

4. After selecting an image, click OK. The image appears on the page.

You can right-click the Image and choose Form Field Properties from the pop-up menu to display the Form Field tab of the Picture Properties dialog box, as shown in Figure 9-30.

Figure 9-30

The Form Field tab of the Picture Properties dialog box.

In the Picture Properties dialog box, you can adjust the image properties by selecting the other three tabs. For more information on the Picture Properties dialog box, see Chapter 8.

301

Validating Form Fields

FrontPage allows you to confirm that certain information you receive from users in form fields is the type of information you want or that it's in the correct format. For instance, you can require that a text box contain a minimum or maximum number of characters, or that a selection be made from a drop-down list or group of option buttons. This process is called *form field validation*.

To specify validation rules for a form field, right-click the field and choose Form Field Validation from the pop-up menu. You'll see a dialog box specific to the form field you're validating, such as the Text Box Validation dialog box shown in Figure 9-31.

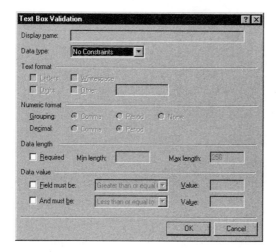

Figure 9-31

The Text Box Validation dialog box.

This is one of the most complicated Validation dialog boxes. It allows you to set validation rules for the type of data a user enters in the text box, as well as for the format of text or numeric characters, minimum and maximum data length, and values for the data. When you finish specifying the rules you want for the form field, click OK to exit the Validation dialog box.

You can also reach the various Validation dialog boxes by clicking the Validate button in the Form Field Properties dialog box for the following form fields: text box, scrolling text box, option button, and drop-down list.

If you set up validation rules for a field, it's a good idea to explicitly tell users on the page (next to the form field, if possible) what you expect from them—for example, that a text field requires a value. If users submit information that doesn't fit the rules you've specified for a particular form field, they will receive a validation error message in the browser notifying them that they must enter the correct type of information in the form.

NOTE

When a user receives a validation error message, the information from the form *has not yet been submitted* to the Web; only when a user submits all information according to any specified validation rules does the information get sent to the Web.

A neat technique you can use for drop-down list validation is to specify that the first item be something like "Pick One," to remind users that they really do need to make a selection. Form validation can then require the user to make a selection. To specify this, in the Drop-Down Menu Properties dialog box, make "Pick One" the first item in the drop-down list and make it selected by default. Then, in the Drop-Down Menu Validation dialog box, select the Disallow First Item check box in the Drop-Down Menu Validation dialog box. The user will see a validation error message if he or she tries to submit the information when the first item in the drop-down list is still selected.

An alternative technique is to have the Web display an error message if the user doesn't pick a valid option from the drop-down list.

Creating a Confirmation Page

A confirmation page displays information to a user confirming some action. For example, the user can receive confirmation that the information submitted in a form was received by the server. Users do make mistakes; the confirmation page can help them catch many mistakes and allow them to make corrections and resubmit the form. Also, a confirmation page can add a professional touch to your Web.

Note that once a user submits a form to a Web, the information submitted is stored at the Web (or wherever the site creator specifies) and can't be changed. Confirmation pages simply allow users to confirm that the information is what they want to submit. It's a good idea to advise users to review all information on a form before they submit it. You can take some steps to ensure that information is submitted correctly; see "Validating Form Fields" earlier in this chapter for more details.

A confirmation page is just a standard page that can be specified in the Form Properties dialog box for a form. (You'll learn more about this in "Specifying Form Settings," later in this chapter.) A confirmation page

typically uses Confirmation Field components to present information back
to the user for review.

Let's step through the process of creating a confirmation page. For this
example, we'll use the form fields we created earlier in this chapter. First
we'll start the easy way—by using a template to create a confirmation page.

1. In Page view, choose New from the File menu and then Page from
    the Pop-up menu. Select Confirmation Form from the list of tem-
    plates and wizards on the General tab of the New dialog box, and
    then click OK.

2. When the page appears, save it with the title *Confirmation Form*
    and give it the name within the current Web, *confirmation.htm*.
    We'll refer to this page from now on as the Confirmation Form,
    as shown in Figure 9-32.

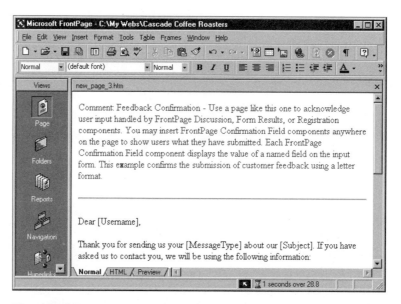

Figure 9-32

A page showing the Confirmation Form template.

You'll see that the Confirmation Form is a template that's ready for you
to customize. It's designed to be used with the Feedback Form template, and

it includes many of the form field names used in that template. These names appear in brackets; they're actually individual Confirmation Field components.

If you move the mouse pointer over one of these components, such as the component labeled *[UserName]*, you'll see that the pointer changes to the Properties pointer, which looks like a hand holding a piece of paper. The value of the UserName field will replace the string *[UserName]* when the Confirmation Form appears to a user in a browser; whatever name the user entered will appear there. All Confirmation Field components on the Confirmation Form work in the same manner.

The Confirmation Form includes a comment at the top giving you some ideas on how to use this form. The comment is for production purposes only and won't appear in a browser. Also included on the form are some introductory and concluding sentences that you can use; you can change any of this information if you want.

Inserting a Confirmation Field component

When you know what information you want to present to the user for confirmation, you're ready to insert Confirmation Field Components on the page. Using the fields you created earlier, here's how you can do it:

1. First, you delete the component labeled *[MessageType]*. Position your cursor immediately to the right of the [MessageType] Confirmation Field component and press the Backspace key. (This is an easy way to delete any component on a page.)

2. Next, you insert a Confirmation Field Component for the form field called *[CommentType]*. Choose Component from the Insert menu and then Confirmation Field from the drop-down menu. The Confirmation Field Properties dialog box appears, as shown in Figure 9-33.

Figure 9-33

The Confirmation Field Properties dialog box.

305

3. Enter the name of the form field for which you want information presented; in this case, enter *CommentType*. Then click OK.

TIP

For option buttons only, the name you enter is the group name.

You'll see that the Confirmation Field Component that has the label *[CommentType]* has been inserted in the middle of the sentence. This example only shows how you can replace a component, but of course you can create original sentences and insert components in the same fashion for presenting form field information on a Confirmation Form. Figure 9-34 shows how the Confirmation Form should look after the component has been added.

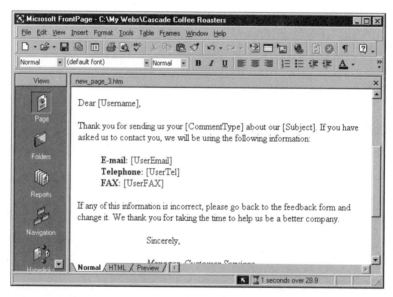

Figure 9-34

A page showing a confirmation form that contains a new confirmation field called Comment Type.

4. Using the same procedure, you can create original sentences or replace existing components for the other form fields you created earlier. Among these fields are the drop-down list named *Topic,* a one-line text box named *IfOther,* a scrolling text box named *UserComments,* and a check box named *RequestInfo.*

It's a good idea to include a link at the end of the Confirmation Form that returns the user to the Feedback Form if he or she needs to resubmit information.

Our form field and confirmation field examples end here. Read on to learn how to process the information in a form.

Specifying Form Settings

Here's where it all comes together. You create forms by assembling a collection of form fields on one page, and you can present the information back to the user for confirmation on another page using a Confirmation Form. But in order for the two pages to work together, you must specify their relationship in the Forms Properties dialog box. You also specify the type of form handler you want to use on the Web server for processing the information a user enters in a form.

FrontPage includes two forms in addition to the traditional data-collection forms: the discussion form and the registration form. Their handlers are specified in the Forms Properties dialog box. If you create a Web using the Discussion Web Wizard, you're actually creating a form for users to "fill out" as the Web is in use. When a user submits a message to the discussion group, the Discussion Component handler saves the information on the server so that others in the forum can access it. You'll learn more about the discussion and registration form handlers later in this chapter.

Assigning a Form Handler

A *handler* is an application on a Web server that communicates between the server and the user in relation to a form. Handlers can send messages to the user (through Confirmation Forms or e-mail, for example), and they can process the information in a form that a user submits to the Web server. You assign and configure a form's handler in the Form Properties dialog box.

You can easily open the Form Properties dialog box for the form that requires a handler by right-clicking anywhere on the form and then choosing Form Properties from the pop-up menu. You'll see the Form Properties dialog box, as shown in Figure 9-35, on the next page.

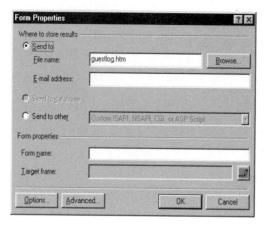

Figure 9-35

The Form Properties dialog box.

What to do with form results?

There are three options in this section of the Form Properties dialog box.

- **Send To.** This is the default handler for a form.

  - *File Name.* The results of the form can be saved to a text file on your server. The default location and name is *_private/feedback.txt*. Remember that the *_private* folder is invisible to a search of your Web. You can select the Browse button and choose any other page in the current Web, or you can type in a relative URL.

  - *E-mail Address.* This is a cool feature that lets you send an additional results file to an e-mail address. You can choose from various e-mail options in the Options For Saving Results To Database dialog box, described below.

- **Send To Database.** By selecting this option, you can configure the form to send its information to a database. You can set the options for saving results to a database by selecting the Options button. In the resulting Options For Saving Results To Database dialog box, shown in Figure 9-36, you can configure the database for use with the form.

  For more information on creating and configuring databases in FrontPage, see Chapter 10.

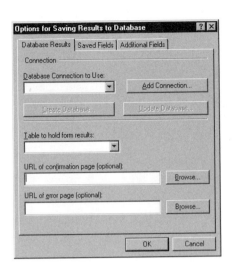

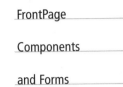

Figure 9-36
The Options For Saving Results To Database dialog box.

- **Send To Other.** You have three "other" choices to use as a form handler, a Custom handler or one of two FrontPage handlers. Select the Send To Other option button and choose an option from the drop-down list.

  - *Custom ISAPI, NSAPI, Or CGI Script.* In terms of forms, these are software components on a Web server that process the information that users submit. These software components can be written to add functionality to your Web beyond what FrontPage's components can offer. For example, a company might want a handler that allows a user special access to certain areas of the Web.

  - *Discussion Form Handler.* This is a component that allows users to participate in an online discussion. FrontPage allows basic discussion-group administration abilities. The Discussion Component gathers information from a form, formats it into an HTML page, stores the page on the Web server, and adds the page to a Table of Contents and a text index. It can also gather other information from the form and store it on the Web server. Note that it's much easier to use the

Discussion Web Wizard than to configure settings here. The Discussion Web Wizard does all of this for you.

- *Registration Form Handler.* A component that allows users to register for a service offered in your Web. It adds the user to the service's authentication database and then collects other information from the form and stores it on the Web server in the file and format you specify.

- **Form Name.** If you're using a custom form handler, you might want to type a form name here and refer to it from the custom handler.

- **Target Frame.** Here you can select a frame to display the results of a form. You can type the name of the frame or use the Target Frame button to locate a frame.

- **Options.** If you select the first Send To option and choose either File Name or E-mail Address and then click Options, you'll see the Options For Saving Results Of Form dialog box (see Figure 9-37), which has four tabs: File Results, E-mail Results, Confirmation Page, and Saved Fields.

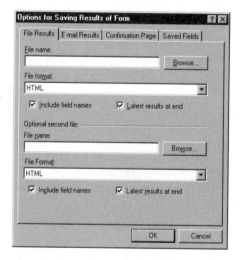

Figure 9-37

The Options For Saving Results Of Form dialog box.

File Results Tab   If you've configured the results to be sent to a file, you can do a little fine-tuning here on the File Results tab.

- **File Name.** This is the same as the File Name field in the Form Properties dialog box. Enter the name and location of the file you want the results saved to. The location can be either within the current Web or outside it. If it's in the current Web, you might enter _private/feedback.txt. The results will be saved to the file called FEEDBACK.TXT in the _private folder in your Web. If a results file doesn't exist when the first results are saved, FrontPage creates the file. If a results file exists, the information is appended to the file.

- **File Format.** Select the file format of the results file from the drop-down list in the File Format section. You have numerous choices:

    - **HTML.** Formats the file in HTML using normal text with line endings.

    - **HTML Definition List.** Formats the file using a definition list to format name-value pairs.

    - **HTML Bulleted List.** Formats the file using a bulleted list for name-value pairs.

    - **Formatted Text Within HTML.** Formats the file in HTML using formatted text with line endings.

    - **Formatted Text.** Formats the file in an easy-to-read text format.

    - **Text Database Using Comma as a Separator.** Formats the file in a text format and uses commas to separate elements. If the Include Field Names check box is checked, names are listed on the first line, enclosed in quotes, and separated by commas. Values are listed on the second line, enclosed in quotes, and separated by commas. Use this format if you want to manipulate the information in a database or similar application.

    - **Text Database Using Tab as a Separator.** Formats the file in the same way as above, but uses tabs instead of commas to separate elements.

    - **Text Database Using Space as a Separator.** Formats the file in the same way as above, but uses spaces instead of commas to separate elements.

- **Include Field Names.** Select the Include Field Names check box to save the field names, along with the field values, in the results file. If you don't check this box, only the values of the fields are saved.

CHAPTER 9

- **Latest Results At End.** This option can be deselected only if you choose HTML as a file format, in which case the latest information will be saved to the bottom of the file. This is the only option for all other file formats, so it will be unavailable if you choose one of those other formats.

- **Optional Second File.** If you want to use the results of the form for different things, such as spreadsheets or databases, you can select a second file to save them to and configure the format differently. So in essence, you get the same results saved in two different formats—cool, huh?

E-mail Results Tab If you want results of a form to be sent by e-mail to someone—a very cool feature, by the way—you can configure the specifics here. See Figure 9-38.

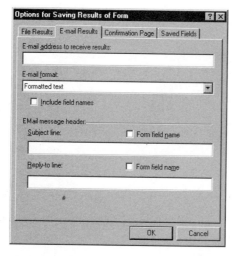

Figure 9-38

The E-mail Results tab of the Options For Saving Results Of Form dialog box.

- **E-mail Address To Receive Results.** In the text box, type in the full e-mail address that will receive the form results, for example, *jodi@mycoolweb.com*.

- **E-mail Format.** If you want the form results to be readable by most e-mail programs, such as Microsoft Outlook, stick with the default format, Formatted Text. The other options available are described above in the section, "File Formats."

PART
III

- **Include Field Names.** If you would like the form field names included along with the form information, select this check box.

- **E-mail Message Header.** If you would like to customize the Subject Line and the Reply To line of the e-mail response, fill in that information here. The default subject line is Form Results. If you want to place the results of a form field in the Subject line of the e-mail, then select the Form Field Name check box. Then type the form field name in the Subject line box. The Reply To line is a good place to enter the form field that lists the user's e-mail address; that way, you can quickly see who filled out the form.

Confirmation Page Tab. If you want the results of a form to be delivered to a confirmation page, make your selections as shown in Figure 9-39.

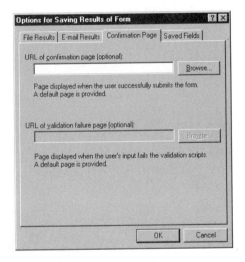

Figure 9-39

The Confirmation Page tab of the Options For Saving Results Of Form dialog box.

- **URL Of Confirmation Page.** If you've created a confirmation page for users to confirm the information they've entered, type its URL in the URL Of Confirmation Page text box. This page will be displayed by the browser whenever the form is successfully submitted to the Web server.

    If you don't specify a confirmation page here, the Save Results component will create and maintain one automatically.

If the URL Of Validation Failure Page text box is unavailable, you haven't specified any validation for your form fields.

● **URL Of Validation Failure Page.** You can also specify a validation failure page in the URL Of Validation Failure Page text box.
A field validation failure page is displayed when a submitted form
contains data that violates any defined form field validation. If a
validation failure occurs, a failure message is generated and displayed in either a VBScript or JavaScript message box. If you don't
specify a field validation failure page here, FrontPage will create
and maintain one automatically.

Saved Fields Tab. Here, as shown in Figure 9-40, you can specify which fields
the form will save, and in which order, as well as some other interesting information available from the server, such as the user name or browser type.

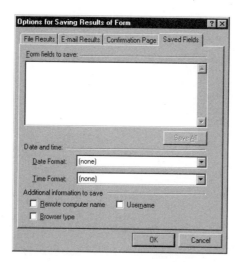

Figure 9-40

The Saved Fields tab of the Options For Saving Results Of Form dialog box.

● **Form Fields To Save.** Here you can write in the name of the form
fields that you want saved, along with the form results, one field
per line. The fields will be saved in the order they appear in the
list. If you leave the list empty, the form will save all fields, in the
order they appear on the form, and list them in the results file.

- **Date And Time.** You can define the date and time format that will be saved with the form results by making a selection from the appropriate drop-down list box.

- **Additional Information To Save.** You can choose between these additional bits of information; each checked item will be listed after the form fields in the results file. Remote Computer Name will list the name of the computer that accessed the form. User Name will list the name of the user who accessed the page. (These will work only on an intranet.) And Browser Type will tell you the name of the browser that accessed the page.

When you've finished configuring the options for saving the results of your forms, click OK to go back to the Forms Properties dialog box. Notice that some of the fields might have changed, based on information you supplied in the Options For Saving Results Of Form dialog box.

Configuring a Discussion Component

You can create a discussion Web using the Discussion Web Wizard, described in Chapter 4. You can configure the settings of a Discussion component in the Options For Discussion Form Handler dialog box, which you can reach in the following way:

1. Open the Form Properties dialog box for the discussion form.

2. Select the Options button. The Options For Discussion Form Handler dialog box appears, as shown in Figure 9-41, with three tabs.

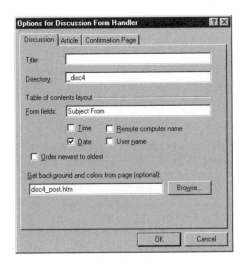

Figure 9-41

The Discussion tab of the Options For Discussion Form Handler dialog box.

315

On the Discussion tab, you can enter the following information:

- **Title.** Name the discussion group in the Title text box. The name will appear on pages containing articles.

- **Directory.** Enter the name of the discussion folder in the Directory text box. If you used the Discussion Web Wizard to create your discussion Web, the folder you specified in the wizard will appear as the default. The folder name must be eight characters or fewer, one of which is the beginning underscore (_).

- **Table Of Contents Layout.** In the Form Fields text box in the Table Of Contents Layout section, enter the names of the form field(s) you want displayed in the Table of Contents in the discussion group. If you enter multiple names, you must separate them with blank spaces.

  Select the appropriate check boxes if you want to display the time and/or date the article was submitted, the remote computer name the article came from, or the user name of the article's author.

- **Order Newest To Oldest.** To place the most recently submitted articles first in the Table of Contents, select this check box.

- **Get Background And Colors From Page.** If you want to use the background and colors from another page in your Web, you can do so by specifying the page in this text box.

You specify the layout of each article in the discussion group on the Article tab, shown here in Figure 9-42.

- **URL Of Header To Include.** To use a page as a header of each article, you can specify the page in the URL Of Header To Include text box.

- **URL Of Footer To Include.** To use a page as a footer of each article, you can specify the page in the URL Of Footer To Include text box.

- **Date And Time.** You can define the date and time format by selecting the appropriate options from the drop-down lists in the Date And Time section.

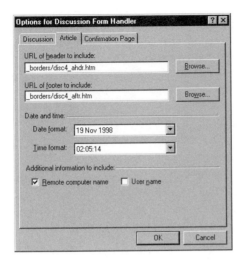

Figure 9-42

The Articles tab of the Options For Discussion Form Handler dialog box.

● **Additional Information To Include.** In this section, select the appropriate check boxes if you want to include the remote computer name the article came from or the user name of the article's author. These options will work only on an intranet.

On the Confirmation Page tab, shown in Figure 9-43, on the next page, you can specify an optional configuration page and an optional validation failure page.

● **URL Of Confirmation Page.** If you've created a confirmation page for users to confirm the information they've entered, type its URL in the URL Of Confirmation Page text box. This page will be displayed by the browser whenever the form is submitted to the Web server. If you don't specify a confirmation page here, the Discussion component will create and maintain one automatically.

● **URL Of Validation Failure Page.** You can also specify a validation failure page in the URL Of Validation Failure Page text box. A field validation failure page displays information pertaining to fields that contain invalid data on a form. If you don't specify a field validation failure page here, FrontPage will create and maintain one automatically.

317

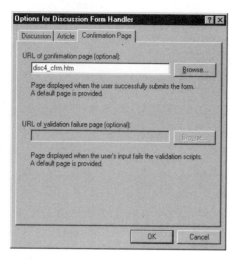

Figure 9-43

The Confirmation Page tab of the Options For Discussion Form Handler dialog box.

After you finish entering all the information you need to configure the Discussion Form handler, click OK to close the Options For Discussion Form Handler dialog box.

Configuring a Custom ISAPI, NSAPI, or CGI Handler

You can also configure settings for a custom ISAPI, NSAPI, or CGI handler if you decide to use one in your Web.

You configure the custom handler in the Options For Custom Form Handler dialog box, which you can reach in the following way:

1. Open the Form Properties dialog box for the form.

2. Select Custom ISAPI, NSAPI, Or CGI Script from the drop-down list in the Send To Other section, and then click the Options button.

    The Options For Custom Form Handler dialog box appears, as shown in Figure 9-44.

    To configure the custom form handler, do the following:

- **Action.** In the Action field, enter the *absolute URL* of the form handler.

- **Method.** Use the Method drop-down list to select a method for submitting information to the handler—Post or Get. The Post method passes the name-value form field pair directly to the form handler as input, and the Get method encodes the form's name-value pair and assigns the information to a server variable, QUERY_STRING.

PART

III

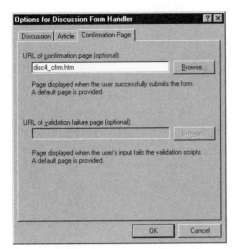

Figure 9-44

The Options For Custom Form Handler dialog box.

● **Encoding Type.** In the Encoding Type text box, enter the standard used to encode the form data that's passed to the handler. The default encoding method is *application/x-www-form-urlencoded;* leave this field blank to use the default.

Coming Up

You've now explored the big, amazing world of FrontPage components and forms. In the next chapter, you'll be introduced to some of FrontPage's more advanced features.

319

PART IV

Finishing Touches

CHAPTER 10

Advanced Features

Getting Interactive

By now, you pretty much know your way around FrontPage. You know how to build a Web, manage it, and work with it page by page. Maybe you're saying to yourself, "Geez, there has to be more than this. What about all of those cool features I keep hearing about? I want my Dynamic HTML!" Well, this is your lucky day. FrontPage directly supports many advanced features—such as ActiveX controls, Java applets, JavaScript, Visual Basic, VBScript, Netscape plug-ins, and yes, even Dynamic HTML. We'll even show you how to use cascading style sheets (CSS) and the style sheet templates included with FrontPage.

TIP When you add a control, script, or applet to your pages in Page view, FrontPage typically inserts an icon representing that feature. You can double-click or right-click the icon and choose Properties from the pop-up menu to reach the Properties dialog box. With an icon selected, you can reach the Properties dialog box quickly by pressing Alt+Enter.

There are plenty of books specifically dedicated to many of these new features. You can hardly walk into the computer section of your favorite bookstore without bumping into a couple of dozen books on Java alone. So, for the purpose of this chapter, we'll only discuss how FrontPage uses these features and how you get them on your page and in your Web.

Most of the advanced features included in FrontPage live on the Insert menu. To select one, choose Advanced from the Insert menu and then choose the feature of your choice. Each of the advanced features is described in the following sections, starting with HTML.

Inserting HTML

Because HTML is a rapidly evolving language, new tags will be introduced that FrontPage might not support directly. Therefore, FrontPage allows you to insert any HTML directly, including new HTML. Be aware, however, that FrontPage won't check to see whether the text you insert is valid HTML. To insert HTML, choose Advanced from the Insert menu and then choose HTML from the submenu. This brings up the HTML Markup dialog box, as shown in Figure 10-1.

Figure 10-1
The HTML Markup dialog box.

Enter your HTML, and then click OK to return to Page view. You can always edit the HTML that FrontPage creates by using the HTML View tab; to learn how, see Chapter 7.

Design-Time Controls

Design-time controls, or DTCs, are elements that are created separately from FrontPage. For example, you can have a DTC write the results of a form into a table on your page. DTCs are similar to FrontPage components in that they add custom functionality to your site at design time, without requiring you

PART

IV

to author any additional HTML to support them.

DTCs usually create their own HTML or use an Active Server Page (ASP), all of which is built into the DTCs and transparent to you.

If you want any DTCs on your page to be visible in Page view, choose Advanced from the Insert menu and then choose Show Design-Time Controls from the pop-up menu.

Each DTC has its own set of properties specific to the control. Right-click the control and select Design Time Control Properties from the pop-up menu to view the properties of the DTC.

Inserting a Java Applet

Java applets are created in a programming language called *Java,* and they're very much like ActiveX controls in that they add dynamic functionality to your Web page. Selecting Advanced from the Insert menu and then choosing Java Applet from the pop-up menu displays the Java Applet Properties dialog box, as shown in Figure 10-2.

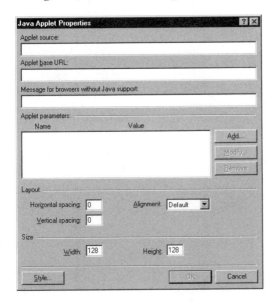

Figure 10-2

The Java Applet Properties dialog box.

- **Applet Source.** Source files for Java applets typically have the file extension CLASS. Enter the name of the Java applet source file in the Applet Source text box. Keep in mind that Java is case-sensitive, so using the correct uppercase and lowercase letters is important.

- **Applet Base URL.** In this text box, enter the URL of the folder that contains the Java applet source file.

- **Message For Browsers Without Java Support.** For browsers that don't support Java applets, use this text box to enter text or HTML that will be displayed in place of the applet. For example, typing *BamBam* causes that word to appear in the browser in place of the applet. You can type HTML to add font, size, and other attributes to the text. You can also type HTML in this text box to show an image in place of the applet, for example *<img src="images/BamBam.gif">*. In this case, *BamBam.gif* is in the Images folder of the page's Web.

- **Applet Parameters.** In this section, specify parameter names and values for the applet. You must use the documentation that came with the Java applet to determine the names and values for the applet.

    The text box lists the names and values of any parameters that have been added. You can use the Add, Modify, and Remove buttons to configure this list.

- **Layout.** In this section, specify the spacing and alignment of the applet on the page.

    - **Horizontal Spacing.** Sets a specified horizontal spacing (in pixels) from the applet to the nearest object or text on the current line, on both sides of the applet.

    - **Vertical Spacing.** Sets a specified vertical spacing (in pixels) from the applet to the nearest object or text on the line above and/or below the applet.

    - **Alignment.** Specifies a type of alignment between the Java applet and the text around it.

- **Size.** In this section, adjust the width and height (in pixels) of the Java applet.

TIP You can adjust the size of a Java applet on a page by selecting it and then dragging its border controls with the mouse.

Figure 10-3, on the next page, shows how the Java applet appears in Page view.

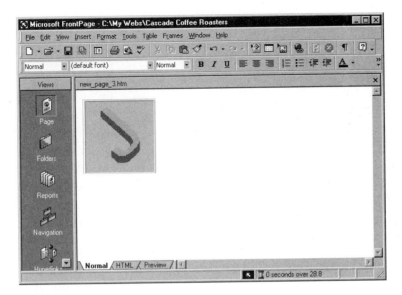

Figure 10-3
A page showing an inserted Java applet.

Inserting a Plug-In

Plug-ins are hardware or software components that allow you to add a specific application to your page. You can use a plug-in, for example, to add audio or video to your site. Plug-ins were originally created for Netscape users, although they are now supported by Microsoft Internet Explorer as well. Choose Advanced from the Insert menu and then choose Plug-in from the submenu to display the Plug-In Properties dialog box, as shown in Figure 10-4.

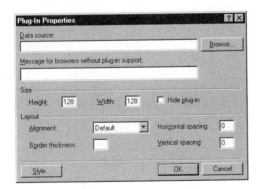

Figure 10-4
The Plug-In Properties dialog box.

CHAPTER
10

- **Data Source.** In this text box, specify the file location or URL of the plug-in, or click the Browse button to select the plug-in.

- **Message For Browsers Without Plug-In Support.** For browsers that don't support plug-ins, use this text box to enter HTML that determines what those browsers will display in place of the plug-in. For example, typing *Dino* causes that word to appear in the browser in place of the plug-in. You can type HTML to add font, size, and other attributes to the text. You can also type HTML in this text box to show an image in place of the plug-in, for example *<img src="images/Dino.gif">*. In this case, *Dino.gif* is in the Images folder of the page's Web.

- **Size.** In this section, you can adjust the size of the plug-in by entering the height and width in pixels.

TIP

You can adjust the size of a plug-in on a page by selecting it and then dragging its border controls with the mouse.

- **Hide Plug-In.** Select this check box if you don't want the plug-in to appear on the page.

- **Layout.** In the Layout section, specify the position of the plug-in on the page.

  - **Alignment.** Specifies a type of alignment between the plug-in and the text around it.

  - **Border Thickness.** Sets a black border around the plug-in. The width of the border is measured in pixels.

  - **Horizontal Spacing.** Sets a specified horizontal spacing (in pixels) from the plug-in to the nearest object or text on the current line, on both sides of the plug-in.

  - **Vertical Spacing.** Sets a specified vertical spacing (in pixels) from the plug-in to the nearest object or text, on the line above and/or below the plug-in.

Inserting an ActiveX Control

ActiveX controls are software components that add functionality to your page—functionality that you can't create by using standard HTML. Examples of ActiveX controls include a label control that can display text at different sizes and angles, a timer control that can generate timed events, a stock ticker control that can display stock information, and an animation control that can display animations. You can create ActiveX controls by using a variety of programming languages, including Visual C++ and Visual Basic. Be aware that some browsers don't recognize ActiveX controls on a Web page. For more information on ActiveX and ActiveX controls, as well as information on how to download free ActiveX controls, check out Microsoft's ActiveX site at **www.microsoft.com/activex/** on the World Wide Web.

To insert an ActiveX control in a page in your site, choose Advanced from the Insert menu and then choose ActiveX Control from the pop-up menu. You'll see the Insert ActiveX Control dialog box, shown in Figure 10-5, listing any ActiveX Controls currently on your computer. Select the control of your choice, and click OK; the control is inserted in your page.

Figure 10-5
The Insert ActiveX Control dialog box.

Each of the ActiveX Controls has an associated properties dialog box, and the dialog boxes can vary depending on the control you're using. To see the properties dialog box for any ActiveX Control on your page, right-click the control and choose ActiveX Control Properties from the pop-up menu. An example of an ActiveX Control Properties dialog box is shown in Figure 10-6, on the next page.

CHAPTER 10

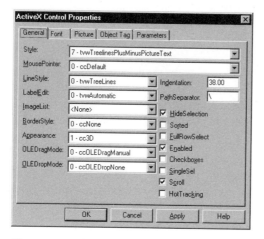

Figure 10-6

The Properties dialog box for an ActiveX Control lists the current properties for the control. You can edit these options as needed.

Macros

FrontPage gives you a few more ways to add advanced elements to your page—by using *macros*. Macros contain code that automatically performs a sequence of tasks, or actions, when it's played back or run.

Adding a Macro

If you've created a macro, or you already have some on your computer, you can use the Macro command to add them to your page. To insert a macro, choose Macro from the Tools menu and then choose Macros from the pop-up menu. You'll see the Macro dialog box, as shown in Figure 10-7.

The Macro dialog box lists all of the currently installed macros on that computer. You can run, edit, create, or delete any macro in the list. If you have macros in any open projects (for example, in Microsoft Visual Basic Editor), you can select them from the macros in the drop-down list by choosing All Open Projects. Alternatively, you can select macros that are already in FrontPage, by selecting Microsoft FrontPage from the Macros In drop-down list.

Adding VBScript or JavaScript

Using a scripting language such as VBScript or JavaScript in a Web page gives you a lot more capabilities. With the support of a script-enabled browser,

PART
IV

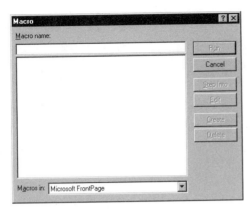

Figure 10-7

The Macro dialog box.

you can use VBScript or JavaScript to read and modify form elements, perform event handling, interact with the browser, and manipulate objects. Writing VBScript or JavaScript is beyond the scope of this book, but this section gives you an introduction.

VBScript is a scripting language developed by Microsoft, based on Visual Basic for Applications. JavaScript is a scripting language developed by Netscape, based on the C programming language. Scripts are included in the HTML and can be understood by a browser that supports that particular scripting language.

Visual Basic Editor

Using the Visual Basic Editor, you can create and edit Visual Basic scripts. Choosing Macro from the Tools menu and then Visual Basic Editor from the pop-up menu brings up the Microsoft Visual Basic dialog box, as shown in Figure 10-8, on the next page.

Script Editor

If you're interested in creating and editing custom scripts, you can use the Microsoft Development Environment, right from FrontPage.

Choose Macro from the Tools menu and then Microsoft Script Editor from the pop-up menu to open the Microsoft Development Environment application, as shown in Figure 10-9, on the next page.

CHAPTER 10

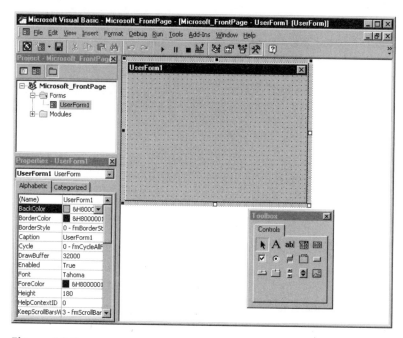

Figure 10-8

The Microsoft Visual Basic editor.

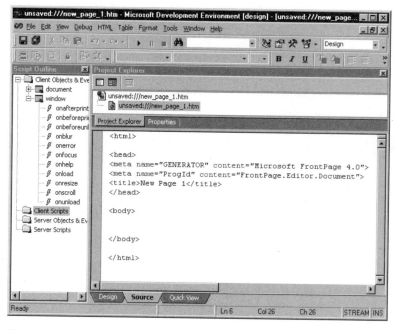

Figure 10-9

The Microsoft Development Environment.

Cascading Style Sheets (CSS)

One of the hardest things about working in HTML has been the inability to customize the text. In the past, if you wanted to display text in a certain *point size* (the term used to define the size of a letter), or adjust the *leading* (the space between lines) of a paragraph, you were plain out of luck. With the advent of *cascading style sheets* (CSS), you now have that power.

When you create a cascading style sheet in FrontPage, you're actually creating HTML code behind the scenes. You can include this code on a page in your site, or you can create a single style sheet as a separate page and link to it from any or all of the pages in your site. You can define attributes of a *style*—its font, color, size, leading, indents, and so on—and you can combine many different styles in a *sheet*, creating a *style sheet*. The term *cascading* means that you can use multiple styles to control different elements on a single page; the browser will apply styles in a cascading order to resolve conflicts and to define which styles take precedence. Cascading style sheets work in these different ways:

- **External Style Sheet.** This is probably the most powerful CSS option. You create one style sheet and link as many pages to it as you like. If you need to make a change, you need to do it in only one place. An external, or linked, style sheet is a separate file that has a .css extension.

- **Embedded Style Sheet.** With this method, the style sheet is placed in the HTML of the page, but the styles apply to that page only.

If a page in your site is linked to an external style sheet and you create an embedded style sheet, the embedded styles will add to or override the attributes defined in the external style sheet.

We'll walk through these style sheet methods, one at a time.

External Style Sheets

When you create a linked style sheet in FrontPage, it can be used on any of the pages in the current Web. As I mentioned earlier, this is the most powerful CSS option. You can either create the style sheet yourself or use one of the FrontPage style sheet templates, which are described later in this section. If you want to create the style sheet yourself, you can easily find information on the correct style sheet syntax by using your favorite Web search engine. Try the keywords "cascading style sheet syntax," and you should find more than enough information.

CHAPTER 10

NOTE Writing style sheets is beyond the scope of this book, but this is the basic methodology. Style definitions can be any HTML tag ("H2," for example), and they're followed by a list of properties, which are contained within braces, with each property separated by a semicolon from the one that follows it. A basic example would look like this: H2 {font-size: 14 pt; line-height: 16 pt; font-style: italic; font-family: Arial; color: blue; text-align: center}. In this example, whenever you use the Heading 2 style in FrontPage, on a page using this style sheet, the text of the heading will be blue, Arial, italic, and centered, and the font size of the text will be 14 points, while the leading, or the space between the lines of text, will be 16 points.

Linking to a style sheet

If you want a single page or all the pages on your site to use a style sheet that's already a part of your site, you'll have to link the page to the style sheet. Here's how:

1. Open the page that you want to link to the style sheet.

2. Choose Style Sheet Links from the Format menu. This brings up the Link Style Sheet dialog box, as shown in Figure 10-10.

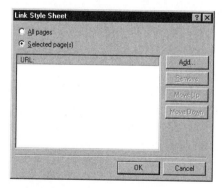

Figure 10-10
The Link Style Sheet dialog box.

3. Select All Pages, to link a style sheet to all the pages in your site, or Selected Page(s), to choose which style sheet will link to the current page. Use the Add button to add style sheet pages to the list.

4. After you've finished selecting pages, click OK. FrontPage creates the appropriate HTML to link the style sheet to the page or pages you selected.

Embedded Style Sheets

This procedure describes how to create an embedded style sheet on a page:

1. Open, in Page view, the page in which you want to embed the style sheet.

2. Choose Style from the Format menu to display the Style dialog box, as shown in Figure 10-11.

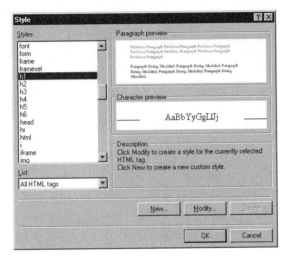

Figure 10-11
The Style dialog box.

3. In the Styles section of the Style dialog box, select the style that you want to manipulate. Choose either All HTML Tags or User Defined Styles from the List drop-down menu. The example shown in Figure 10-11 shows the H1, or Heading 1, tag selected for modification.

NOTE

Clicking the Style button in any properties dialog box that contains one applies an embedded style sheet for that element on the page.

4. If you want to create a new style, click the New button in the Style dialog box to display the New Style dialog box. If you want to modify an existing style, click the Modify button to display the Modify Style dialog box. These two dialog boxes work in the same

335

way. In this example, we'll use the Modify Style dialog box, shown in Figure 10-12, to modify the H1 tag.

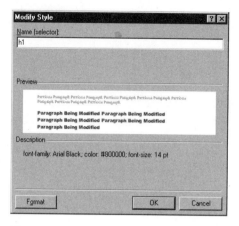

Figure 10-12

The Modify Style dialog box.

5. Use the name *H1*, which is entered for you, or enter a new name.

6. Clicking the Format button offers you four choices: Font, Paragraph, Border, and Numbering. Each of the four choices has its own dialog box.

7. Make your modifications using the Format options; when you click OK in each formatting dialog box, the description in the Modify Style dialog box is updated to reflect your changes. The Preview window is also updated, so you can see what you're getting before you finish.

8. When you're finished making modifications to the style, click OK.

To use your new style, select some text on the page, and choose the Heading 1 style from the Style drop-down menu.

Figure 10-13 shows our new Heading 1 style applied to some text on a page. As you can see, you have many possibilities when you use this method of creating style sheets. Notice that Heading 1 is selected in the Style drop-down menu.

If you're curious about how these style sheets affect the HTML for your page, Figure 10-14 lets you in on the secret.

PART

IV

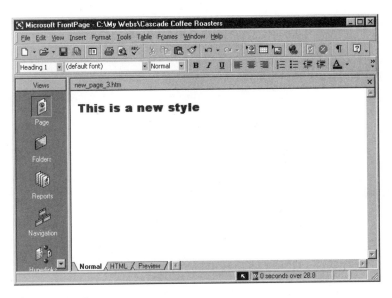

Figure 10-13

Our new Heading 1 style applied to some text.

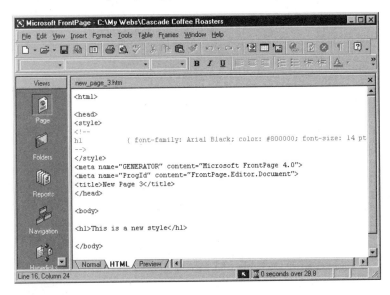

Figure 10-14

Our new Heading 1 style as it appears in HTML view. The style sheet information is located between the <style> tags in HTML.

337

Style Sheet Templates

Ok, so you've just learned a couple of ways to add style sheets to your FrontPage Webs. But let's say that you're just not interested in doing all that work yourself. You want someone else to do it for you. FrontPage is one step ahead of you on this one—when you use the style sheet templates, all that work *is* done for you.

Choose New from the File menu and then choose Page from the submenu. You'll see the New dialog box; selecting the Style Sheets tab results in the dialog box shown in Figure 10-15.

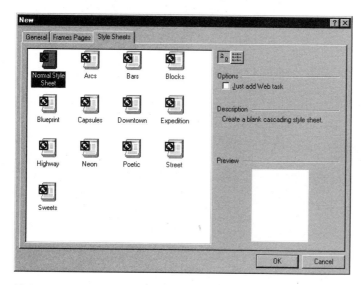

Figure 10-15

The Style Sheets tab of the New dialog box.

The style sheet templates are based on the FrontPage themes. Selecting a style sheet template opens that file in Page view. Figure 10-16 shows the Expedition style sheet in Page view.

As you can see, a style sheet can be a pretty complicated thing to write yourself. Aren't you glad that FrontPage did it for you? I thought so. Just in case you're not happy with that, if it was just too easy, don't worry. FrontPage treats this file pretty much like any HTML file—you can edit the page just like any other page. It would be a good idea though, to have at least a basic understanding of HTML and style sheet syntax.

Style sheets use a .css extension, as opposed to the .htm extension used for HTML pages. So when you save the style sheet page, make sure that you give it that extension. It's also a good practice to give the style sheet a name that you can easily recognize, just so it's easy to spot when you go to link to it.

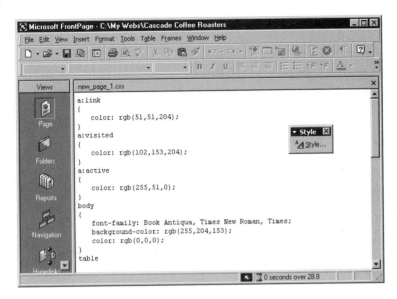

Figure 10-16
A style sheet in Page view.

Applying a Style to Text

Now that you know how to create different types of style sheets and get them linked or embedded on your page, you need to apply the styles in the style sheet to some text on the page. You can do this in your choice of two different ways:

● Highlight the text in Page view and choose the appropriate style from the Style drop-down menu

● In HTML view, add the tag yourself.

If you're using an external style sheet, it's a good idea to print the .css file; that way, you have all of the names and definitions as a handy reference.

Dynamic HTML—What the Heck Is It?

So, do you want to add a little action to your page, well, do ya? If you're using a browser that supports Dynamic HTML, then you're ready to power up, leave the kiddies behind, and join the big boys. Dynamic HTML harnesses the power of the latest and most powerful browsers. You can make text fly right off of your page or apply cool transition effects between pages. The power is in your hands, so grab hold and take advantage: step into the world of Dynamic HTML.

CHAPTER 10

NOTE Be aware that these features work only in a browser that supports Dynamic HTML, like Internet Explorer version 4 or later.

Animations

If you want to make words and letters dance on the page, apply one of the many animation options built into FrontPage.

Select the text that you want to animate and choose Dynamic HTML Effects from the Format menu to display the DHTML Effects toolbar. You can also activate the toolbar by choosing Toolbars from the View menu and then choosing DHTML Effects from the pop-up menu.

When the user visits a page that contains an animation effect, the animation plays and the text ends up where you placed it on the page in Page view. FrontPage comes with 14 different predefined animation effects, as follows:

Fly From Bottom	Fly From Top-Right
Fly From Left	Fly Top Right By Word
Fly From Right	Fly Bottom Right By Word
Fly From Top	Drop In By Word
Fly From Bottom-Left	Spiral
Fly From Bottom-Right	Zoom In
Fly From Top-Left	Zoom Out

To apply an animation effect to your text, select an Event from the DHTML toolbar, such as Mouse Over, then select an Effect, and finally select the settings. The animation plays when the page is viewed in a browser that supports DHTML. If you want to remove an animation effect, select the text and then click the Remove Effect button on the DHTML toolbar.

Page Transitions

You can add a little magic to your page, and you don't even need a top hat or a fuzzy rabbit. If you want to add that something extra to set a page apart from the rest, try one of the transition effects included with FrontPage. For example, you can have the page fade through as the user visits or leaves a page, or you can have the page dissolve away. A transition effect can be seen when users first visit or when they leave, and you can apply the effect either to a page in the site or to the site itself.

You implement transition effects in the Page Transitions dialog box, shown in Figure 10-17. To view the dialog box, choose Page Transition from the Format menu.

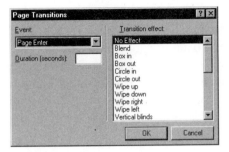

Figure 10-17

The Page Transitions dialog box.

To set a Page Transition, first pick an event, then select an effect, and finally choose the duration, in seconds, that the effect will take to complete. It's a good idea to keep the duration setting low—you don't want the transition to get in the way of an enjoyable user experience.

Collapsible Outlines

If you have information styled in a list, you can add a little action to show and hide the contents of the list. When users come to the page, they'll see the first item in the list; as they move the mouse over the list item, the next item in the list appears, and so on, throughout the list.

Select the Collapsible Outlines check box in the List Properties dialog box to add the Collapsible Outline feature to the selected list on the current page. If you want the list to be collapsed when it first appears, select the Initially Collapsed check box in the List Properties dialog box.

Form Field Extensions

If you've created a form, FrontPage automatically sets a certain tab order for each field in the form, based on when the field was placed on the page. If you want to define your own custom tab order, enter a number between 1 and 999 in the Tab Order field of the Form Field Properties dialog box.

When users are viewing your form, they can tab through the fields in the order you define; number 1 first, number 2 second, and so on. This is a great help for users who have disabilities and for anyone who has trouble using a mouse. If your site is being viewed in a browser that doesn't support tab order, the default order is used.

CHAPTER 10

Database Integration

If you want to be able to access data in a database and display results on a Web page, this section helps you get started. Using the Database Results Wizard, you can create an area on your page that displays information obtained from a database connection. The results are used with a custom form handler—in this case an Active Server Page (ASP)—to generate the information for display in a browser.

Active Server Pages

An *ASP* is basically the same as any other HTML page, except that it contains server-side scripting embedded within the HTML, and it has an .asp extension. Any Web servers that are compatible with ASP can read and then execute the server-side scripts in the HTML.

Database Results Wizard

To start the wizard, choose Database from the Insert menu and then choose Results from the pop-up menu. Figure 10-18 shows the first screen of the wizard.

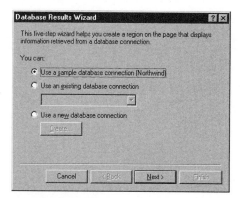

Figure 10-18
The first screen of the Database Results Wizard.

The first screen of the Database Results Wizard gives you three options for the type of connection you want to create. They are as follows:

● **Use A Sample Database Connection (Northwind).** If you're new to databases or just curious and want to experiment, you can use the sample database included with FrontPage.

- **Use An Existing Database Connection.** Use the drop-down menu to choose from any databases available in the current site.

- **Use A New Database Connection.** If you want to create a new database connection, select this check box and click the Create button. You're presented with the Database tab of the Web Settings dialog box. For more information, see "Creating a New Database Connection," later in this chapter.

For now, we're going to use the sample database that comes with FrontPage.

Select the first option, Use A Sample Database Connection (Northwind), and then click the Next button to display the second screen of the Database Results Wizard, as shown in Figure 10-19. Remember, you can always use the Back button to move back through the wizard.

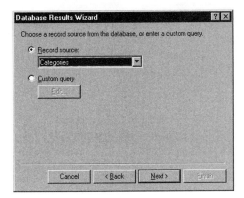

Figure 10-19

The second screen of the Database Results Wizard.

Here you can either select a Record Source or create a Custom Query. The available record sources are displayed in the drop-down menu. If you want to create a custom query in a program like Microsoft Access, select the Custom Query check box and then click Edit. The Custom Query dialog box is displayed, as shown in Figure 10-20, giving you options to insert a parameter yourself or paste one in from the clipboard. You can also verify that any of the listed queries are connected to the database properly.

Once you've made your selections in the Custom Query dialog box, click OK to return to the Database Results Wizard. Click the Next button on the Database Results Wizard dialog box to move to the next screen, as shown in Figure 10-21, on the next page.

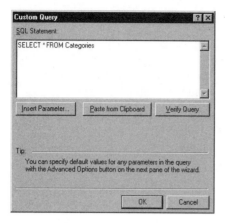

Figure 10-20

The Custom Query dialog box.

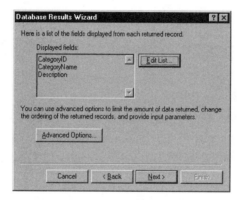

Figure 10-21

The third screen of the Database Results Wizard.

This screen shows you a list of the fields that will be displayed in the browser. If you want to make changes to the list, click the Edit button. You can then make changes based on the fields available for the current database.

If you want to change the way the information is returned, modify the ordering of the records, or add input parameters, click the Advanced Options button.

When you're finished making your selections, click the Next button to move to the fourth screen of the Database Results Wizard, shown in Figure 10-22. This screen gives you the opportunity to make changes in the formatting of the database results—the way they'll be presented in the browser.

Select the options you want, and then click the Next button to move to the final screen of the Database Results Wizard, as shown in Figure 10-23.

PART
IV

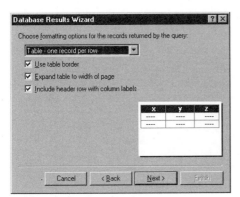

Figure 10-22
The fourth screen of the Database Results Wizard.

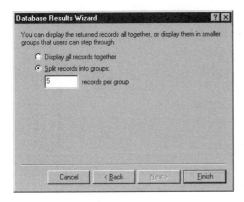

Figure 10-23
The final screen of the Database Results Wizard.

In the last screen of the Database Results Wizard, you can modify the display of the returned records. You can choose between displaying all of the records together or splitting the records into groups.

Make your selections as needed. When you're done making changes, click the Finish button. FrontPage creates the database results, using the formatting you chose in the third screen of the Wizard, and presents the database on the current page in Page view. Figure 10-24, on the next page, shows what your page should look like.

NOTE

The page in which you're inserting the database results must be an ASP page. If it's not already an ASP page, FrontPage warns you to change the page's extension when you click the Finish Button on the final screen of the Database Results Wizard.

CHAPTER 10

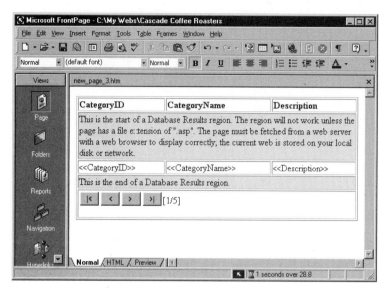

Figure 10-24

A database as it appears in Page View after the Database Results Wizard has been run.

Once the database results table is on your page, you can make changes to it if you like.

Modify the database

You can open the Database Results Wizard to modify the settings you've already entered by right-clicking the Database Results Wizard component and then choosing Database Results Properties from the pop-up menu. If you want to quickly enter a new column value name or choose from an existing one, right-click the Database Results Wizard element and choose Database Column Value Properties from the pop-up menu.

The ability to access information in a database from a Web page is a powerful feature. This section has given you a brief introduction to the feature, which you can explore further on your own.

Creating a new database connection

If you want to create a new database connection or modify an existing connection, you can do this from the Web Settings dialog box.

Choose Web Settings from the Tools menu, and you'll see the Web Settings dialog box; select the Database tab, as shown in Figure 10-25. You can also access this dialog box by selecting Use A New Database Connection from the first screen in the Database Results Wizard.

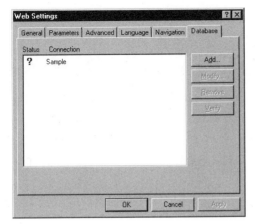

Figure 10-25

The Database tab of the Web Settings dialog box.

Any databases currently in the Web are listed, along with their status. You can modify any current database by making a selection from the list and clicking the Modify button. You can also remove or verify any database in the list by clicking the appropriate button.

Click the Add button to display the New Database Connection dialog box, as shown in Figure 10-26.

Figure 10-26

The New Database Connection dialog box.

In this dialog box, you can choose a name for the new database in the Name text box. In the Location Of Database section, select the method by which you'll be creating the new connection.

If you want to create user names and passwords or set query timeouts, click the Advanced button.

CHAPTER 10

Accessibility

When you create this great site, you want it to be available to the greatest number of people possible, no matter how they use the Web. Sometimes, as we're clicking away on this button and that one, enjoying all of the cool colors and graphics, the fancy layouts, and the sophisticated interactive elements popular today, we tend to forget about the person who can't see or hear, or who has trouble using the mouse or keyboard, not to mention the person who has a slow connection.

There are a few things you can do to improve the accessibility of your site, without giving up the flash. These are not so much advanced features of FrontPage as they are advanced ways to *think* about the creation of your site.

- Always use the Alternative Text option on the Image Properties dialog box, and make the text short and functional. Do this for *every* graphic on your site, whether it's navigational or decorative.

- If you're using thumbnail images and linking to a larger version of the picture, add descriptive text to the page along with the larger graphic. That way, people using a reader device can get a complete description of the image when they follow the thumbnail link.

- If you use image maps as the only way to navigate through your site, people who can't see or who have graphics turned off can't navigate the site, even if you use alternative text. You can easily place a text-only version of your navigation at the bottom of every page so that your site is navigable by everyone.

- If it's at all possible, create a separate text-only version of your site and give users a choice. If that's impossible, consider making text-only versions of selected pages in your site and placing a text-only link from the graphic page to the text-only page. For instance, if you have an online catalog, you can easily generate a text-only descriptive page for your products.

There are many more ways to make your site accessible to everyone. You can find more information by doing a search on the Web. Try the keywords, "accessibility HTML web site development", and you'll get plenty of hits. For a nice page that contains many helpful links, try the URL http://www.ability.org/design.html.

Other Advanced Features

FrontPage includes other advanced features that you should know about, but they're too technical to discuss at length in this book. For more information on these features, see the FrontPage Web at **www.microsoft.com/frontpage/**.

The following are two examples of the many FrontPage-related topics on the FrontPage Web site:

● The FrontPage Software Developer's Kit (SDK), which you can download from the Microsoft Web site, allows you to create custom wizards and custom FrontPage components, add custom menu commands, and create custom "Designer HTML" fragments that you can add to pages by using the drag-and-drop method.

● FrontPage supports integration with Microsoft Visual SourceSafe (VSS), in order to provide multi-user revision control on changes made to the Web.

Coming Up

Next, we'll round out our tour of FrontPage by looking at FrontPage's server related offerings, including the FrontPage Server Extensions.

CHAPTER 10

CHAPTER

11

Web Servers

FrontPage and Servers

All the wonderful Webs you'll design and create with FrontPage will more than likely be stored on a Web server. A Web server is software or a computer that stores Web sites, scripts, databases, and other related files and makes Web pages accessible from a browser. Because the term can refer either to software or to a computer, you must look at the context to determine which. The Web server market is becoming large and competitive, with versions of Web servers that meet various needs and run on different platforms.

This chapter discusses how FrontPage interacts with the numerous Web servers; it doesn't discuss the pros and cons of the servers themselves. For information on the advantages and disadvantages of major Web servers, look in Internet-related periodicals and on the server manufacturers' World Wide Web sites.

Once you make a choice of a Web server to use with FrontPage (perhaps you already have a server up and running), chances are that FrontPage will interact with it smoothly. FrontPage supports the most popular shareware and commercial Web servers in use today, by means of software programs and scripts known as the *FrontPage Server Extensions*, which are discussed later in this chapter. (You'll also find a list of the Web servers that FrontPage supports later in the chapter.) The Server Extensions act as the go-betweens for the FrontPage client and the Web server, helping both parties communicate behind the scenes.

The FrontPage Server Extensions

Suppose for a second that you're stranded in the Ukraine, but you speak only a wee bit of Ukrainian. Can you survive? Probably. Can you communicate? Sure, maybe a smidge. But can you communicate *well?* Probably not. You need a translator, or one of those English-to-Ukrainian pocket dictionaries, to make sure your messages come across the way you want them to.

The FrontPage Server Extensions perform this kind of translation duty between your FrontPage Web and a Web server. Each set of Server Extensions is software that lives on the Web server and gets involved whenever communication takes place between your Web and the server. Because these extensions are available for a variety of Web servers, FrontPage can communicate with many different Web servers.

The FrontPage Server Extensions are a good bargain for a number of reasons:

● They're free.

● They make uploading a Web to a Web server fast and easy with FrontPage.

● They allow you to set author and end user permissions for your Webs.

● They ensure that FrontPage components work the way they're intended to. For example, if you use a Search Component in your FrontPage Web, the Server Extensions ensure that the component performs as it's supposed to. Without the Server Extensions installed, the FrontPage component won't work.

Web Servers and Platforms

As of this writing, FrontPage Server Extensions are available for the following Web servers:

Commercial Web servers:

● Microsoft Internet Information Server 3.0 & 4.0 (for Windows NT Server)

● Microsoft Peer Web Services (for Windows NT Workstation)

● Netscape Enterprise Server (for Windows NT and UNIX)

- Netscape FastTrack Server (for Windows, Windows NT, and UNIX)
- Netscape Commerce Server (for Windows NT and UNIX)
- Netscape Communications Server (for Windows NT and UNIX)
- O'Reilly WebSite and WebSite Professional 2.0 (for Windows 95 and Windows NT)

Noncommercial Web servers:

- NCSA (for UNIX)
- Apache (for UNIX)
- Stronghold (for UNIX)

Platforms:

- Microsoft Windows 95 & 98
- Microsoft Windows NT Workstation and Windows NT Server
- UNIX (Solaris, SunOS, HP/UX, IRIX, BSDi, Linux, and Digital UNIX)

Where to get 'em

The FrontPage Server Extensions for all Windows 95 & 98-based and Windows NT-based Web servers (including those from Microsoft, Netscape, and O'Reilly) are included with FrontPage 2000. You can download the FrontPage Server Extensions for UNIX–based Web servers from **http://officeupdate. microsoft.com/frontpage/wpp/default.htm**.

Extracting the Server Extensions

Server Extensions are typically in the form of a self-extracting, or .exe file. Follow the specific instructions accompanying the Server Extensions to extract them on your Web server. Normally, you just double-click the .exe file to begin the process.

The normal FrontPage Server Extensions setup process emphasizes ease of installation and is oriented toward a low-security intranet environment. However, Internet Service Providers wanting to host the FrontPage Server Extensions or customers who want a higher-security installation should visit the Web Presence Providers section of the FrontPage Web site at **http:// officeupdate.microsoft.com/frontpage/wpp/default.htm**. There you can download the documentation and software provided for Web Presence Providers.

Internet Service Providers

You can always forego the potential headaches of running your own Web server and let someone else take the aspirin for a change. Internet Service Providers (ISPs), also called Web hosts, are companies that house your site on their server and provide you with a variety of services. Often they charge a very low fee, when compared to the cost of hospitalizing those who suffer nervous breakdowns when their Web servers go on the fritz three times in the same week.

Most ISPs charge periodic fees (often monthly, biannually, or annually) to house your site; these fees generally include a maximum megabyte allotment on the server, as well as at least one e-mail account. Most ISPs also offer some help in getting set up, and they usually have CGI scripts and other goodies available to subscribers.

The advantages of using the services of an ISP include faster user access to your site and not having to worry about maintaining an in-house Web server. ISPs often have the fastest connections available on the Internet. In addition, when you use an ISP you avoid the expense and hassle of having to install a *firewall server* to protect your company's computing resources if your site is on the World Wide Web.

The disadvantages of using an ISP are relatively few; among them is the fact that you're not the one in control. Nearly all business owners dream of having business go so well that their sites must expand to meet the growing consumer need for information. If these dreams come true for you, it might be easier (and ultimately less expensive) to manage a large site in house instead of over a distance.

There are hundreds of ISPs nationwide that have the FrontPage Server Extensions installed and that are specifically set up to host FrontPage sites. You can find a complete list at http://microsoft.saltmine.com/frontpage/wpp/list.

If your Web is already hosted by an ISP that doesn't support FrontPage and you'd like to turn the site into a FrontPage site, refer the ISP to the FrontPage Web Presence Providers (WPP) information in the FrontPage Web. In the meantime, you can still post your FrontPage site to your ISP as long as the ISP provides you with FTP access for posting your Web content. Whether or not your ISP supports FrontPage, you can use the Publish command to post your Web content easily. When you use this command, if FrontPage doesn't detect the FrontPage Server Extensions on your ISP's Web server, it automatically launches the Web Publishing Wizard if it is installed. The wizard allows you to post your site to Web servers that don't have the FrontPage Server Extensions installed.

For more information on the Web Publishing Wizard, see its online help. For more information on the Publish Web command, see Chapter 3. For more information on FrontPage and ISPs, see the FrontPage Web site at www.microsoft.com/frontpage/.

Index

J

K

L

M

N

R

W. Brett **P**olonsky has more than 10 years of experience in award-winning graphic design and art direction. Self-taught in computers, he learned on early Macintosh computers and PageMaker 1.0 and has climbed the ladder to high-end Web development, incorporating site planning, structure, UI, and design. He has consulted as a Web producer at Microsoft, helping to create one of their largest Intranet sites. He has also written exams for the Microsoft Certification & Skills Assessment group, and has recently added the title of Instructor to his ever-growing resume, teaching a class called Seniors and the Internet at a local technical college. He lives in his apartment near Seattle, Washington, where he eats way too many tacos, and he plans on buying a plant one of these days.

Brett's other business interests include Polonsky Design, a firm specializing in graphic design for print and online. He is also the founder and president of Skywards Consulting, Inc., a Web presence development company dedicated to designing and implementing Web solutions for corporate clients. Brett is also co-founder of Sandstone 3, a firm that specializes in corporate seminars relating to the Internet. You can reach Brett via email at brett@polonskydesign.com, or on the Internet at one of these sites:

www.polonskydesign.com
www.skywards.com
www.sandstone3.com

The manuscript for this book was prepared and submitted to Microsoft Press in electronic form. Text files were prepared using Microsoft Word 97. Pages were composed by Helios Productions using Adobe PageMaker 6.52 for Windows, with text in Garamond and display type in Frutiger. Composed pages were delivered to the printer as electronic prepress files.

Cover Graphic Designer
Patrick Lanfear

Interior Graphic Designer
Kim Eggleston

Principal Compositor
Sybil Ihrig, Helios Productions

Technical Editor
Douglas Giles

Copy Editor /Principal Proofreader
Gail Taylor / Rebecca Taff

Indexer
Maro Riofrancos

Microsoft Press offers *comprehensive* learning solutions to help new users, power users, and professionals get the most from *Microsoft technology.*

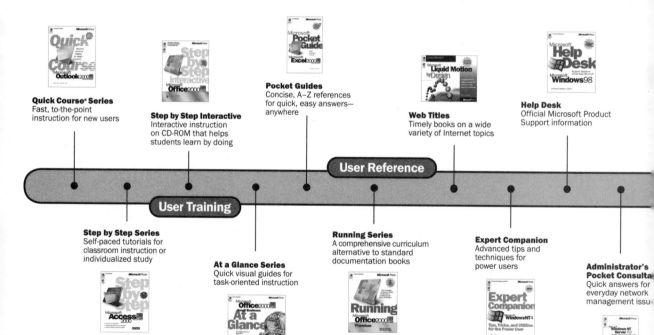

Quick Course® Series
Fast, to-the-point instruction for new users

Step by Step Interactive
Interactive instruction on CD-ROM that helps students learn by doing

Pocket Guides
Concise, A–Z references for quick, easy answers—anywhere

Web Titles
Timely books on a wide variety of Internet topics

Help Desk
Official Microsoft Product Support information

User Reference

User Training

Step by Step Series
Self-paced tutorials for classroom instruction or individualized study

At a Glance Series
Quick visual guides for task-oriented instruction

Running Series
A comprehensive curriculum alternative to standard documentation books

Expert Companion
Advanced tips and techniques for power users

Administrator's Pocket Consulta
Quick answers for everyday network management issu

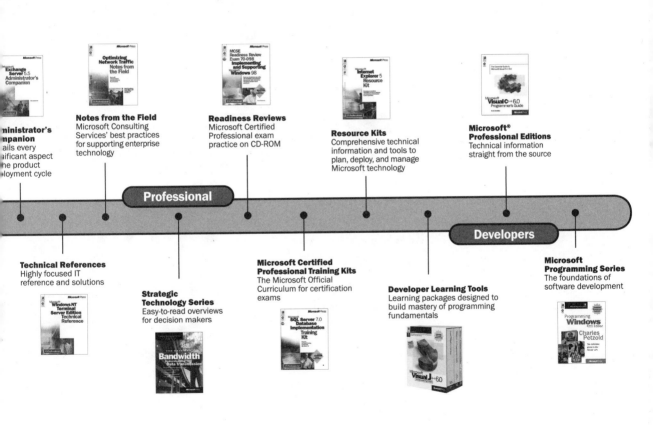

Register Today!

Return this
Official Microsoft® FrontPage® 2000 Book
registration card today

Microsoft®Press

mspress.microsoft.com

OWNER REGISTRATION CARD   **1-57231-992-5**

Official Microsoft® FrontPage® 2000 Book

FIRST NAME   MIDDLE INITIAL   LAST NAME

INSTITUTION OR COMPANY NAME

ADDRESS

CITY   STATE   ZIP

(   )

E-MAIL ADDRESS   PHONE NUMBER

U.S. and Canada addresses only. Fill in information above and mail postage-free.
Please mail only the bottom half of this page.

For information about Microsoft Press® products, visit our Web site at **mspress.microsoft.com**